Psychoanalysis and Maternal Absence

Experience of maternal absence manifests in a variety of ways and this book explores a selection of its emotional, psychical, and somatic consequences as they relate to an individual's relationship with their body, psychic-emotional internal life, and intimate relationships.

This book is not about mothers, but how individuals handle the trauma of mothers they have not had. Spanning backgrounds such as the collective child-rearing method of the kibbutz in Israel through to the possible difficulties of children who are parented by single parents, born out of sperm or egg donation, and adults who have suffered chronic sexual abuse, Shapira-Berman observes the precarious position of the analyst and the tension between the acts of witnessing and participating in client interventions. Espousing the values of authenticity and creativity, this text concludes with a reconfiguration of the roles of faith and trust within psychoanalysis and offers hope to those on their therapeutic journeys.

This book will be a valuable resource for psychotherapists, as well as for various undergraduate and postgraduate studies in object relations, childhood trauma, sexual trauma, and clinical therapy.

Ofrit Shapira-Berman, PhD, is a psychoanalyst and a professor at the Hebrew University, Jerusalem, and a member of the Tel -Aviv Institute for Contemporary Psychoanalysis. She maintains a private practice in Tel Aviv.

"Ofrit Shapira-Berman's book brings together two fundamental subjects that preoccupy psychoanalysis: Motherhood and faith; or, taken from the other side of it, motherly-absence and trauma. With a unique and lively voice, and with a wealth of experience and knowledge in trauma, Berman portrays the phenomena of the absent mother from an intriguing variety of perspectives – sociological, psychosomatic, and literary – all met by a bold, fresh and original psychoanalytic eye. The reader is not only moved by the stories and enriched by their insights, she is also gaining hope and trust in the ability to understand and repair deep wounds. The clinical evidence and the theoretical elaborations reflect deep faith in psychoanalysis; in the profound reparatory power embedded in being with someone who is willing to be present."

Merav Roth, *Head of the Psychoanalytic Psychotherapy Program, Sackler School of Medicine, Tel Aviv University, Israel*

"This is a beautifully written exploration of the nature of maternal care and its effects on the very experience of being human. The book offers insightful clinical discussions of some of the most fundamental qualities of human life: the complementarity of the roles of faith and trust, and of witnessing and participating; the place of dreaming in the communication of psyche and soma; and ways analysis may provide a form of experiencing in which formerly unlived aspects of the self are reappropriated. This is a remarkable book not to be missed. I cannot recommend it more highly."

Thomas Ogden, *Personal and Supervising Analyst, Psychoanalytic Institute of Northern California, USA*

Psychoanalysis and Maternal Absence

From the Traumatic to Faith and Trust

Ofrit Shapira-Berman

LONDON AND NEW YORK

Cover image: dra_schwartz / Getty Images

First published 2022
by Routledge
2 Park Square, Milton Park, Abingdon, Oxon OX14 4RN

and by Routledge
605 Third Avenue, New York, NY 10158

Routledge is an imprint of the Taylor & Francis Group, an informa business

© 2022 Ofrit Shapira-Berman

The right of Ofrit Shapira-Berman to be identified as author of this work
has been asserted in accordance with sections 77 and 78 of the Copyright,
Designs and Patents Act 1988.

All rights reserved. No part of this book may be reprinted or reproduced or
utilised in any form or by any electronic, mechanical, or other means, now
known or hereafter invented, including photocopying and recording, or in
any information storage or retrieval system, without permission in writing
from the publishers.

Trademark notice: Product or corporate names may be trademarks or
registered trademarks, and are used only for identification and explanation
without intent to infringe.

British Library Cataloguing-in-Publication Data
A catalogue record for this book is available from the British Library

Library of Congress Cataloging-in-Publication Data
A catalog record has been requested for this book

ISBN: 978-1-032-06645-5 (hbk)
ISBN: 978-1-032-06647-9 (pbk)
ISBN: 978-1-003-20319-3 (ebk)

DOI: 10.4324/9781003203193

Typeset in Times New Roman
by Deanta Global Publishing Services, Chennai, India

With Love and Gratitude

To my parents – for being my family, the landscape from which I have grown

To Inon, and Gali, Yair, Ori, Yahel, and Itamar – for teaching me everything I have ever wanted to know about love and commitment.

To Merav Roth – whose significance in my life is beyond words.

To Thomas H. Ogden – whose friendship and wisdom I treasure.

To my patients – who have trusted their hearts in my hands. I value this profoundly.

Contents

	Introduction	1
1	A "mother-of-one's-own": An analytic perspective of object-relationships of adult patients raised in the kibbutz	5
2	"Love thy work": From having no mother to being everybody's mother – re-examining the professional choice of women psychotherapists who grew up in the kibbutz	31
3	That which was "not": Some thoughts regarding Oedipus's modern conflicts	53
4	The "choice" between illusory life and acceptance of the death of one's love object	72
5	Psychosomatic symptoms as physical dreams: Emotional experiences given expression through the body	91
6	When hunger strikes: Re-thinking Kafka's "A Hunger Artist" in light of Winnicott's theory of the psyche-soma	114
7	What do faith and trust have to do with psychoanalysis?	128
	Index	151

Introduction

Each one of us is weaved out of endless threads. We are all influenced, consciously and unconsciously by culture, social norms, gender, family histories, the era in which we were born and raised, etc. Personally, ever since I can remember myself, I have always been preoccupied with mothers and babies, and specifically with maternal absence.

I cannot think of a more difficult role than that of being a mother. Perhaps only second to being a baby. Yet, this book is written from the perspective of the "child," regardless of her/his current age. If I was to write a book about mothers, I would without a doubt have written about how difficult it is to be a mother, and to mother another individual. As a socially constructed ethos, mothers and women are being held responsible for children's well-being and as such, are often held responsible and guilty for everything that goes wrong. It is not easy to distinguish the sociological constructs from the psychological and the biological, when it comes to "mothers" and "motherhood" and even in the psychoanalytic jargon, we do not speak of the "good enough parent," but of the "good enough mother."

Mothers are worshipped and judged, almost equally. They are often valued based on their devotion and ability to intuitively understand their children, and they are harshly criticized and held guilty when they fail to supply their children's needs. They are expected to hold and to let go, in accordance with what the child needs, putting their own needs, desires, pains, and fears aside. They need to be an object and a subject, at the same time, serving the needs of their children and their spouses, regardless of their own struggles. Although contemporary social constructs allow a wider definition of what is a "family" (at least in Western secular societies), influenced by various factors, such as women's participation in the labor force, and the LGBT community, still women are the main caretakers of young children, both within and outside the home (mothers and educators, in accordance).

A mother is not merely a role. It is, so I believe, the most fundamental and crucial psychic construct, often undefinable. The mother-construct goes back to our most primary experiences – sensual, physical, emotional. For many it is the colors, smells and textures of all that was (and is) good. For some, it is the void of that which was not. Mother is the most basic language we talk, although some

DOI: 10.4324/9781003203193-1

2 Introduction

feel they have learned it with a person to whom they have no biological ties. Some regain their mother tongue in therapy (or analysis), some curve it out of art, literature, or religion. Mother is often the most concrete, physical experience we have had, but it is also an abstract, an idea, an ethos, a myth.

Every human has a mother, and most probably none of us has only "one." There is always the mother who was there, and the mother who was not. The fortunate have experienced good enough maternal care, enough to help them through life. Alas, some children have experienced maternal absence to an extent that has caused them substantial pain.

Maternal absence may be the result of various variables that impact the mother's inability to be fully present. It can also be a "subjective experience" of the child and the child's unconscious fantasies regarding the mother. Other social variables may be socially contexted (war, famine, personal illnesses, severe losses etc.).

This book focuses on the subjective experience of maternal absence and its innumerous manifestations in the adult's life. If one's mother is the landscape of one's life, inscribed into one's psyche are all the ways by which she was present and all the forms of her absence. The mother's presence and absences will express themselves in the individual's soma and somatization, in the linguistic constructs (the "how" of the language, not only the "what"), in the career one chooses, in one's ability to form an intimate relationship, to parent a child, as well as in one's ability, or inability, to mourn what is lost and accept reality, as partial and as painful as it is. The mother's quality of presence and extent of absence impact the ability of her child to feel safe and to be protected from physical, sexual, and emotional abuse by others. In many ways it determines the amount of trust we will have in others and the faith we have in ourselves.

This book focuses on one's experience of maternal absence and is written from the vantage view of the child-as-an-adult. In no way is it aimed to blame mothers for their children's pain. Parents do the best they can. When a child grows up, she, or he, has the choice of entering psychoanalytic therapy, in the attempt and hope, of finding her/his way of becoming an adult more fully alive. As analysts we know that what is inscribed in the patient's psyche will express itself within the therapeutic relationship, which I have come to experience as perhaps one of the most intimate and significant ones, both as a patient and as an analyst.

Out of the many people who have trusted me with their pains, I have chosen merely a few to write about, all of whom represent issues that are close to my heart.

The first two chapters are a discussion of the various implications of growing up in the unique communal child-rearing system of the kibbutz. Working analytically with many patients who have been raised in a kibbutz, I have become very interested in the long-term effects of such a childhood. In these two chapters, I discuss the implications on object–relations ("A mother of one's own") and on the career choice of becoming a psychotherapist ("Love thy work: from having no mother to being everybody's mother"). Given that children in the kibbutz were not raised by their parents, it is most interesting to look at the ways it has influenced their lives, both in terms of "love" and "work."

In the third chapter – "That which was 'not': some thoughts regarding Oedipus's modern conflicts" – looking into a relatively new sociological phenomenon of single mothers to fatherless babies, born via sperm donation, I debate the necessity of re-conceiving the Oedipus complex. Does the "third" need to be a man? Or is it a psychic-emotional and mental configuration within the mother? What role does psychoanalysis have, if any, in the treatment of single parents to mother-/fatherless children? Should psychoanalysis even take a stance on this complicated and sensitive issue?

Moving from the baby's (as adult patient) experience of parental absence, the next chapters deal with other experiences of absence, and their possible implications on our emotional and psychic well-being.

The fourth chapter – "The "choice" between illusory life and acceptance of the death of one's love object" – is a discussion of a unique psychic choice to live a life following an actual traumatic maternal loss. The clinical material presented in this chapter concerns an analysis of a young woman whose mother had died when she was seven years old. For her, "maternal absence" is not only a metaphor or a description of psychic-emotional unavailability. Even though there are significant differences between the actual loss of one's mother and her psychic-emotional absence, there are also significant implications and consequences that bind the two together. By discussing this clinical case, I wish to highlight a specific defensive psychic "choice," that of creating an illusory life, in which the subject and her/his lost (love) object keep on "living together." For these people. the "real" (un-illusory) life means the desertion of the love object. By creating the 'illusory' life, these individuals deny not only the object loss, but also their sense of guilt for being alive.

The fifth and sixth chapters focus on the relationships between "psyche" and "soma" and on somatization as another result of one's experience of the infant–mother relationship.

In the fifth chapter – "Psychosomatic symptoms as physical dreams: emotional experiences given expression through the body" – I will offer my perspective of psychosomatic symptoms as an experiential phenomenon that functions as a "physical dream," through the reflection on how some patients may employ symptoms, in the service of conducting unconscious psychological work. With the aid of the analyst, the patient may restart her/his interrupted "physical" dreaming and/or (re)form an "undreamt" dream (Ogden, 2004a, 2004b). The psychesomatic symptom is understood to be a vehicle through which the patient's psyche transfers and transforms "physical" into "psychical" and verse versa.

The sixth chapter, "When hunger strikes: re-thinking Kafka's "A Hunger Artist" in light of Winnicott's theory of the psyche–soma" is a psychoanalytic reading of Kafka's short story "A Hunger Artist." Eating disorders, especially anorexia nervosa is often related to sexual trauma, but I take it to a somewhat different direction, that of the patient's experience of the absent of the good enough

4 Introduction

mother, s/he needed. Generally speaking, I think that the absence of the mother is one of the most fundamental experiences, lying at the core of various traumas, including sexual trauma. Yet, this chapter focuses not on specific trauma, but on the trauma of the absence of that precious gaze each one of us needs. The first gaze is that of the mother, but the *need to be seen* continues through life, wearing many costumes – sometimes disguised. Kafka's "A Hunger Artist" is, in my eyes, not only a wonderful story but also a very complex one, calling for our attention to the ecological system within which we live – from the intrapsychic to the interpersonal, from the most intimate relationships, between one and one's own body, to the social constructs, played out by the "audience" cheering for the hunger artist's hunger strikes. "A Hunger Artist" is analyzed and discussed in light of Winnicott's theory, both in regard to the psyche and soma, and to one's ability to establish a "true self."

The seventh chapter – "What do faith and trust have to do with psychoanalysis?" – goes back to "the beginning," in an attempt to reconsider the roles "faith" and "trust" have in the psychoanalytic process and relationship. In a world torn apart by religious wars, in which many people have lost faith in their ability to thrive, I feel there is much importance in the reconsideration of the two concepts, of "faith" and "trust." The debate of the role faith should (not) have in psychoanalysis, has started with Freud's ambition to position psychoanalysis within the realm of science. This chapter offers a different perspective of "faith" as in inborn potentiality and quality, unlike "trust" that is perceived as object-related and experience based. I cannot think of any analytic encounter that "faith" does not play a crucial part in, as in any other kind of change.

Chapter 1

A "mother-of-one's-own"

An analytic perspective of object-relationships
of adult patients raised in the kibbutz[1]

Introduction

Winnicott (1960) famously wrote, "There is no such thing as a baby." That is to say that babies and mothers should be perceived as a unit, especially at the beginning of life, as you cannot expect babies to thrive without their mothers. I think of Winnicott's statement as the first half of a paradox. The second half is: Anyone can see that there are a mother and an infant who are separate beings. Without the second half of the paradox, the mother and the infant are one, and no development can occur (Ogden, 1994, p. 4). Winnicott elaborated on the issue of the crucial significance of the infant receiving maternal care in numerous articles. One of Winnicott's (1963a) most significant contributions to traditional psychoanalysis is his emphasis on the "external factor," i.e., the significance of the actual external environment (the mother) who is responsible for making active adaptation to the baby's needs (1963, p. 340). This "external factor" is so significant to the infant's well-being that early traumatic separations can lead to physical illness. Moreover, this awareness of total dependency and vulnerability on the baby's part may be experienced as so threatening and potentially annihilating that the baby may feel the need to defend him- or herself by experiencing (unconscious) "death wishes" that may serve the baby's need to feel in control.

Although Winnicott alternates between the concepts of "mother" (1958 [1965, p. 37]) and "maternal figure" (1965, pp. 9, 34), he does seem to suggest that these concepts are not the same (1958 [1965, p. 34]) in terms of their significance to the baby's psychic welfare. In his paper "The Theory of Parent–Infant Relationship," Winnicott clearly states:

> The mental health of the individual, in the sense of freedom from psychosis or liability to psychosis (schizophrenia), is laid down by this maternal care, which when it goes well is scarcely noticed, and is a continuation of the psychological provision that characterizes the *prenatal state*.
>
> (1960, p. 49, italics added)

DOI: 10.4324/9781003203193-2

6 A "mother-of-one's-own"

This seems to be a significant recognition and suggestion of the possible differences between "maternal care" and the care of a "maternal figure"; by referring to the prenatal state, there can be no mistaking the significance and particularity that Winnicott attributes to the biological mother. Referring to a "biological" quality of mothering does raise questions, but taking into account Winnicott's theory of the psyche-soma (1949/1975), we should be willing to examine that there is, indeed, a significant impact of the biological mother's soma on the development of the baby's psyche.

Following Winnicott's (1949/1975) and Bion's (1962a) ideas, I am suggesting that the interactions between "psyche" and "soma" are not merely intra-psychic (i.e., the baby's psyche and soma) but also interpersonal (i.e., for example – the baby's psyche and mother's soma). As exciting and essential as this line of inquiry may be, I will focus on the long-term effects seen in adults who, as babies, did not have a "mother of their own," not taking up the question of biological as compared with non-biological mothering[2].

Winnicott (1963b) offers an explanation for the reluctance of "traditional" psychoanalysis to examine and write about the environmental factor, but suggests that psychoanalysis was by then already established enough to be able "to afford to examine the external factor both bad and good" (p. 340). This issue of the measure of "realness" (or accuracy) of the infant's perception of his environment in an earlier paper (1960). In this paper, Winnicott addresses the similarities and differences between the patient's infancy and his or her experience in analysis. He stresses that

> The paradox is that what is good and bad in the infant's environment is not, in fact, a projection, but despite this, it is necessary if the individual infant is to develop healthily, that everything shall seem to him to be a projection.
>
> (p. 567)

Here, Winnicott tackles another matter relevant to my thesis that the infant's mother holds significance, emphasizing that this mother, who performs the needed childcare, is not merely a projective "makeup" on behalf of the baby. This could also be read as Winnicott making the point that the infant's mother is unlike other maternal figures as far as the baby may be concerned. Yet, this is not to say that other care-givers should not support parents, but it is to say that there are "things" which the infant's biological mother can provide her baby that no other figure can. The fact that the mother has carried her baby physically during forty weeks of pregnancy cannot be devoid of meaning, psychically and physically, both for the mother and infant. By suggesting that the "mother" is not merely a projection of the infant that can be received and contained by "any figure," I understand Winnicott to suggest that each mother has her unique way of taking care of her infant and that uniqueness holds significance to the infant's emotional and psychic well-being. By addressing the mother's preparation for her baby's psychic holding during the last stages of her pregnancy, Winnicott (1963b, p. 340) makes a subtle, albeit significant, reference to the biological mothering as being of crucial importance to the mother–infant relations.

I aim to address and re-evaluate some of the possible consequences of the unique mode of child-rearing that was the norm in Israeli kibbutzim at that time. I am suggesting that what the kibbutz infant and child were missing was "a mother of one's own." These infants and children were subjected to multiple care-givers while the mothers (and fathers) had little or no influence on their children's daily lives, and no "active adaptation" was allowed. Having said that, and in consistency with our psychoanalytic perspective regarding the complex interactions of nature and nurture, the influences of any particular upbringing are never identical, as Winnicott says it so well:

> Infants come into *being* different according to whether the conditions are favorable or unfavorable. At the same time, conditions do not determine the infant's potential. This is inherited, and it is legitimate to study this inherited potential of the individual as a separate issue, *always provided that it is accepted that the inherited potential of an infant cannot become an infant unless linked to maternal care.*
> (Winnicott, 1960, p. 589, italics in original)

This is, in my eyes, a focal point in Winnicott's theory of maternal care and the development of a healthy baby, as well as a focal point of my proposed thesis regarding the possible effects of growing up in a kibbutz. Babies raised by their own mothers experience a variety of difficulties in integrating their fantasies (internal reality) with their mothers' external reality. The infant–mother unit is naturally exposed to various internal and external effects, influencing or influenced by both the infant and the mother. Following Fairbairn's (1944, p. 110) conception of the impact of the infant's inevitable traumatic experience deriving from his or her encounter with the limits of the mother's capacity to love the child and to accept the baby's love, Ogden (2010) further elaborates on the question that follows from this notion. He quotes Fairbairn (1940/1952, p. 13):

> Does "failure on the part of the mother to convince the child that she really loves him as a person" reflect the mother's failure to be convincing, or does it reflect the child's failure/inability to be convinced, i.e., the child's inability to love?

Ogden (2010) indicates that his response to this question, "leans in the direction of the former interpretation, but by no means, rules out the other" (p. 103). Ogden elaborates on this idea and states that

> every infant or child accurately perceives the limits of the mother's ability to love him; and, at the same time, every infant or child misinterprets inevitable privations as the mother's lack of love for him. From this vantage point,

8 A "mother-of-one's-own"

Fairbairn's conception of early psychic development should be considered a trauma theory. To some degree, each baby is traumatized by his realistic perception that he is fully dependent on a mother whose capacity to love him has passed a breaking point.

(p. 103)

Following Fairbairn's concept of the limits of the mother's love and Ogden's elaboration of this, I would like to suggest that what is valid for babies who are raised by their "own mothers" has to be even more true for kibbutz babies who were deprived of having a "mother of their own." By this, I refer to the unique, particular way of child-rearing in the kibbutz system, as will be described later.

I have come to understand that although each infant raised in the kibbutz system had a different mother, the lives of these individuals – on reaching adulthood – evidenced similar pathology in their capacity to form mature object-relationships. I do not think there is disagreement among analysts concerning the idea that experiences in infancy and early childhood influence one's subsequent life in fundamental and life-long ways. However, there is a dispute concerning measuring the mother's degree of influence in terms of the quality and quantity of time she spends with her infant/child. I propose that these disputes are not only psychological but political as well. Positioning the infant's own mother as the care-giver (for whom there is no other equivalent care-taker of the infant) may add further complexity to the decisions many women make regarding how to combine and prioritize motherhood and career. The idea that there may not be a genuine, good-enough substitute for the mother is something that I (as both a mother and someone who highly values her career) feel is vital to re-evaluate. How significant is the mother's care, specifically in the early stages of the infant's life? I chose to re-examine this turbulent issue by studying adult patients raised in the Israeli kibbutz's unique system. Although they represent, in my eyes, an *extreme* case, I do think an in-depth re-examination of their upbringing and possible consequences can benefit us. My aim is in no way to blame mothers or to disapprove of mothers pursuing a career. Neither am I proposing that mothers (and parents generally) should not use the support of nannies, kindergartens, or any other child-rearing support systems. Instead, I aim to better understand how psychoanalysis can help patients with this type of kibbutz upbringing; a lack of consistently involved early maternal care, and multiple care-takers during daytime and none during the night had negative consequences.

I would like to consider Fairbairn's concept of the "tantalizing object" (1944, p. 112) regarding the kibbutz's mothers because of the unique way they were present in their infants' lives – the average kibbutz mother was not absent from her infant's life. Still, neither was she able to actively adapt to the infant's needs. The kibbutz infants and children were not "neglected" in how we have come to perceive and understand "neglect." It can be said that they were provided with quite generous care, addressing all their basic needs. And yet, given the unique circumstances of their upbringing – mainly the fact that they spent 21 hours a day without their parents – they were most certainly deprived of what Winnicott (1949/1975) considers crucial: active adaptation on behalf of the infant's mother. Fairbairn's (1944, p. 112) term "tantalizing" object refers to the infant's splitting of the "unsatisfactory" (internal) mother-object. The infant internalizes (unconsciously identifies with) the unsatisfactory mother and then splits this object into (1) the tantalizing (internal) object, and (2) the rejecting (internal) object. Winnicott (1974) refers to what he describes as the "tantalizing mother" in his paper "Fear of Breakdown":

> It is wrong to think of psychotic illness as a breakdown. It is a defense organization relative to a primitive agony. It is usually successful (except when the facilitating environment has been not deficient but tantalizing, perhaps the worst thing that can happen to a human baby).
>
> (p. 104)

Since parents in the kibbutz had little "say" regarding their children's upbringing and were physically separated from them, they were at a severe disadvantage in terms of being able to "hold" and/or "contain" their children's emotional distress (Ogden, 2004). In the absence of maternal consistent "holding"–"containing"– "dreaming" of the infant's experiences, it can be reasonably assumed that this vacuum would be filled with internalizations of "bad objects" as a way of compensating and comforting oneself (Fairbairn, 1944). The infant/child may rely heavily on his or her internal object-relations with these internalizations of bad-tantalizing (i.e., seducing–rejecting) internal objects. One of the splits the kibbutz infant experienced was between the loving object and the "authoritative" one. Parents in the kibbutz had no authority over the rearing of their infant (it was the kibbutz's management who had the final say on everything). Since their actual–physical participation in their children's life was minimal (amounting to three hours a day), the care-taker who was there to "handle" and "hold" the infant and child was not the parent who loved her or him. This split is often evident in the analytic experience (transference and countertransference) with adult patients who grew up in the kibbutz, as I will illustrate and, I propose, is closely related to the actual lack of "unity" between such infants and their mothers. Of mother–infant unity, Winnicott (1960, p. 587) writes, "The infant and the maternal care together form a unit," which, from his perspective, is the most crucial component of the infant's healthy development.

Infants' development in terms of "unity" and "otherness"

Development requires not only the experience of "unity," but that of "otherness" as well (Ogden, 1985). As analysts, we often hold our patient's mothers in mind. What I mean is that we unfold the mother, "dream" her, and in a way "carry" her, for the patient until the patient can carry (hold) her for him- or herself, internally in a way that informs, not suffocates, who the patient is. The patient's relationship with the unconscious internal object mother plays a significant role in the qualities of internal and external object-relationships, including transferences in the analytic relationship.

Winnicott seems to be the analyst who has contributed most to an analytic understanding of the unique relationship between infant and mother (1945, 1960, 1963a, 1963b) and the manifestations of the early mother–infant relationship in the analytic relationship. Ogden (1985) in discussing various aspects of Winnicott's work says:

> When the infant is in the womb, the mother's role is to provide an environment that will buy the infant time that he needs to mature before he will have to face the inevitable task of physical separation at birth. In precisely the same way, the mother's role in the first months of life before the infant enters into the period of the transitional phenomena is to provide an environment in which the phenomena of psychological separateness can occur while the infant develops as a result of the interplay of biological maturation and experience.
>
> (Ogden, 1985, p. 348)

Winnicott has indeed asked us to take into account those patients who come to see us, not knowing how to make use of us or therapy (1969). Still, it has occurred that possibly even he could not have imagined a motherless baby, a baby for whom there is no mother in the mind. The idea of a motherless baby is shocking. It would lead most analysts to reflexively respond, "If there is no mother in the baby, the infant will die or become severely ill mentally and/or physically." There seems to be an analytic assumption that within the patient's psyche-soma, there is always some shred of experience with a good mothering figure. It is also widely accepted that the presence of a nurturing relationship with the mother or mother-substitute is required for the baby's development into a lively human being. It is also thought that even in less fortunate cases, there may be threads, or fragments, of motherly experiences, whether it be a quality of, or a short-lived experience with, the baby's mother or other "maternal figure." Throughout my work, I have come to doubt the validity of these two assumptions: the idea that there is for every baby some good mothering experience, and that "maternal figures" may adequately substitute for the baby having "one's own mother." I believe that we misread Winnicott if we come away from his work with the idea that his conception of "good enough" mothering refers to a "good enough" relationship with *any* care-taker/care-giver, not necessarily the baby's own mother and I am taking into account that this may be a radical departure from conventional analytic thought.

Bowlby (1940) has studied hundreds of infants and children, trying to identify and understand the possible variables that influence their well-being throughout life, especially in terms of their ability to form healthy and satisfying intimate relationships. Bowlby concentrated his "attention on the emotional atmosphere of the home and the *child's personal environment*" (p. 156). Bowlby mainly focused on two aspects of the infant's early environment:

> 1) Specific events, such as the death of the mother and prolonged separation of the child from his mother; and 2) The general color of the mother's emotional attitude to her child. Under this heading are to be counted her handling of feeding.
>
> (p. 157)

Of the sixteen cases Bowlby presents in this paper, almost all are prolonged breaks: "gross breaches of the mother–child relations had occurred during the first three years" (pp. 160–161). But Bowlby also claims that "minor breaks are likely to have a damaging effect on the child's development" (p. 162). Bowlby (1958) is certain that "recognizing the child's first object-relations as the foundation stone of his personality" and adds that "we are all agreed on the empirical fact that within 12 months the infant has developed a strong libidinal tie to the mother figure"[3] (p. 350). In this paper, Bowlby cites Alice Balint's (1949, p. 253) conclusion that "We come nearest to it with the conception of egoism. It is in fact an archaic, egoistic way of loving, *originally directed exclusively at the mother*" (quoted by Bowlby, 1958, p. 355, italics added).

Many of Bowlby's conclusions regarding the grief and anxious reactions of infants and young children in response to separation from their mothers (1960a, 1960b) are well known. Bion (1962a) also discusses the mother's crucial role in her infant's psychic health and the mother–infant interdependence in his conceptualization of the container–contained. In "Elements of Psycho-Analysis" (1962b), Bion refers specifically to the baby's projections of fear of dying onto his or her mother (p. 27). This fear needs to be "detoxified" by the mother, that is, modified in such a way "that the infant may take it back into his own personality in a tolerated form" (p. 27).

All of the writers whose work I have just discussed agree that the mother *or mother figure* has a crucially important role in facilitating her baby's psychic and emotional health. In the absence of such maternal attentive care, the baby may become grief-stricken, anxious, full of crippling dread, psycho-somatically symptomatic, or unwell in numerous other ways. In contrast, carefully reading Winnicott, I find that when he writes about healthy early infantile experience, he is, in fact, not referring to good enough care-taking by *any* maternal figure; instead, he believes that maternal provision by the *baby's own mother* is significant to the healthy psychological development of the baby, noting that the mother's "primary maternal preoccupation" begins already in the last trimester of her pregnancy, evolving over the early weeks after birth. This, he believes, is necessary for the mother to be able to put "herself in the place of the infant" in an undifferentiated way (1965).

One of the points I would like to make is that for Winnicott, in these instances, "mother" means the baby's own mother. I suggest that we do not pay enough

12 A "mother-of-one's-own"

attention to the need to be taken care of by "his or her own mother," care that may be different than that he or she receives from other types of care-giver.[4] The infant's major care-giver bears significance to today's cultural norms in Western societies, as many women take an active role in providing for the family financially or pursuing a professional career. This puts most young parents in need of hiring someone else to take care of their young children or putting them in childcare only a matter of weeks after birth. There is an essential difference between this and how children were raised in the kibbutzim in Israel.

Nevertheless, the apparent similarities of the two methods of childcare (kibbutz child-rearing versus substitute maternal figures in current Western culture) make it necessary to study the differences in the emotional development of infants raised under each of these two sets of circumstances. Perhaps there is an inherent conflict, to some extent, between a woman's need to fulfill her own ambitions and her need/desire to satisfy the baby's need for his or her mother. I am not suggesting that women should put aside their other needs and ambitions. Rather, I am referring to the fact that for many women, the balance between caring for their infant and pursuing career results in a painfully difficult and guilt-inducing emotional struggle. Mothers' guilt is an issue this chapter (or book) cannot address adequately, as it is a complex psychological state, rooted not only in the mother's psyche but also in the social constructions of motherhood (Chodorow, 2000).

Nevertheless, my focal point is to stress the significance mothers and maternal care have on babies' welfare *in the early stages of their life*. As controversial as this may be for some of the readers, psychoanalysis has *always* taken the vantage point of the baby. This is not to say that mothers' subjectivity has no importance to the baby. It certainly does. But mothers' and fathers' subjectivity should not blind us from seeing the possible consequences and significance of maternal care of their babies at the beginning of life.

Considering the different effects on the infant of child-rearing provided by the mother, and child-rearing provided by substitute maternal figures, it must be borne in mind that throughout history care-takers other than the actual mother have provided much of the care of infants and children. Nachman's (1991) and Ainsworth's (1963, 1968) findings indicate that most infants establish a stronger emotional bond with their mothers than with their care-takers, and that the baby establishes her/his emotional ties with earlier and with greater emotional consistency. Building upon these studies of the differences in the psychological effects on infants raised by their mothers as opposed to infants raised predominantly by other maternal figures, I want to look at the "experiment" in child-rearing conducted by all Israeli kibbutzim, from the early 1920s until the 1970s and 1980s.

The kibbutz as a "utopian" society

The kibbutz was based on an ideology of egalitarianism and on the "universalistic ideals of returning to nature and creating a new human being" (Beit-Hallahmi & Rabin, 1977, p. 533). To create this "new human being," a society of equals was established in which uniformity was held as an ideal. One of the principal forms of egalitarianism involved developing a unique system of child-rearing. Bringing together ideology and the objective circumstances created childcare facilities that were founded on two principles. The first was "that communal child-rearing would work against individualism and identification with the family unit" (Beit-Hallahmi & Rabin, 1977, p. 533). The second was "that experts in child-rearing could inculcate the ideology of the kibbutz with greater ability and objectivity than the parents" (p. 533). A popular saying and guiding principle during this era of the kibbutz movement were: "Almost every person can become a parent, but not every person can become an effective socializer" (pp. 533–534).

During that era, children raised in the kibbutzim were brought up in a special "home," called a "children's home," and were separated from their parents soon after birth. Every parent of a child born in a kibbutz was obliged to place their child, from the first days of the infant's life, in the "children's home."

Within this system, parents were secondary to the educators and care-givers chosen by the kibbutz committee. Parents were thus no longer the authoritative figures in their children's lives, at least not formally.

I cannot go into all of the details of this child-rearing arrangement (for a useful review, see Rabin, 1965; Spiro, 1958). Nevertheless, it is possible to review the most significant features of the kibbutz child-rearing practices: The children's care-takers were women from the kibbutz community (not the actual mothers of the children), who worked in shifts, replacing each other throughout the day. At night, two women were responsible for taking care of all the children in the kibbutz (about 200), who were grouped according to age in different communal homes situated throughout the kibbutz grounds. The two women guarding the children at night were called "night-keepers"; they did not sleep in the "homes," and were connected to the homes via a wireless connection system. The children (even the infants) were alone throughout the night. They were instructed to call[5] the "night-keepers" when in need. Parents and their children spent time together for three hours each afternoon and all daily care-taking activities were carried out by the formal care-takers; including, for the infants, bottle-feeding, diaper-changing, and meal-preparation; and, for older children, help with schoolwork and overseeing social interactions. Parents had almost no say regarding the way their children were raised. The kibbutz management dictated every aspect of the upbringing of the children.

The effects of the communal sleeping arrangements on object-relations

Given that the kibbutz community was such a unique and extraordinary social experiment, it naturally drew the attention of academic researchers regarding the possible developmental, psychological, and emotional short- and long-term effects on the lives of the children raised in the communal (collective) system. Sagi, who conducted a series of studies on the kibbutz experience (1982, 1985, 1986, 1994), is one of the chief contributors to the knowledge concerning the kibbutz method of child-rearing. The 1990s offered a historic opportunity to compare the communal child-rearing system to the new one, in which the kibbutz's children were allowed to sleep in their parents' homes, a change that swept most of the kibbutzim. During the 1980s, the kibbutzim underwent major changes, particularly in the methods of child-rearing. Many kibbutzim transformed these methods, allowing children from their birth until adolescence to spend the nights at their parents' homes. This was a major shift in the ideology of the kibbutz movement, initiated by the second generation of parents who were raised in the kibbutz. This paper cannot elaborate on this issue, or examine the various factors contributing to this change. It is most likely that this change was influenced by global changes in Israeli society and the personal experiences of the second generation, raised as children in the kibbutz, maturing into parenthood, demanding that the "system" change. Over the past two or three decades, the kibbutzim have deepened the changes, and the traditional kibbutz I am describing here no longer exists. Sagi's research was able to study the effects of the communal system, before and immediately after the initial changes. In his 1994 study, Sagi (Sagi et al.) found that more than 50% of the infants who spent the night in the kibbutzim's communal sleeping arrangement developed an "insecure attachment pattern" (Ainsworth et al., 1980), while only a fifth of the kibbutz's infants who spent the nights at their parents' homes developed this form of attachment. It is important to note that other than their sleeping arrangement, all other childcare features of this group of infants were identical, including the amount of time each day the two groups of infants spent in the kibbutz daycare. Sagi et al. note that

> It may seem surprising that the communal sleeping arrangement should alter attachment security so profoundly, whereas the long separations accompanying illness and hospitalization do not (van IJzendoorn et al., 1992). We suggest, however, that because the nightly separation in the communal sleeping arrangement recurs as an integral part of the childcare environment and is normative for all children in the community even sensitive parents may not think it is necessary to either compensate for their absence during the night or to communicate the exceptional nature of the experience to the children.
>
> (p. 1001)

The insecure attachment pattern of the communal system's kibbutz children was identified in other studies (Oppenheim et al., 1988; Sagi et al., 1982; Sagi et al., 1985).

Van IJzendoorn, Sagi, and Lambermon (1992) have examined the child's attachment to multiple care-givers, comparing data regarding infant attachment in dual-earner Dutch families to a sample of communal-sleeping kibbutz children. In their study, they discuss Bowlby's "law of continuity," which suggests that "the more stable and predictable the regime, the more secure a child's attachment tends to be; the more discontinuous and unpredictable the regime, the more anxious his attachment" (Bowlby, 1973, p. 261). This should be added to Bowlby's "law of accumulated separations" (1973, p. 255), in which he states that "effects of separations from mother during the early years are cumulative and ... the safest dose is, therefore, a zero dose" (p. 255). In the van IJzendoorn et al. study, data was gathered from Dutch and Israeli samples. The Dutch sample consisted of eighty infants, their mothers, fathers, and professional care-givers. It was compared with the Israeli sample, which included eighty-six kibbutz infants alongside their mothers, fathers, and care-takers. The results indicated that although infants were found to be indeed attached to their non-parental care-giver and that the quality of this attachment is influenced by the infant's attachment to the mother, the Israeli children's attachment was significantly less secure than that of the Dutch children.

The communal sleeping arrangement reinforced an accumulation of separations, not only during daytime (which may be equivalent to separations endured by children who spend their daytime in daycare facilities) but with even more significant impact when coupled with spending the nights separated from the mother. Based on these studies, it is indeed possible that the non-maternal care-taker could provide, for some children, the secure attachment needed for his healthy development. In other words, not all kibbutz children who were separated from their mothers suffered insecure attachment, and the reasons for that are probably varied. Sagi et al. do not give much insight into this, and we can hypothesize that environment is not the only factor influencing a child's development. No psychoanalytic theorists claim this (neither Winnicott, Fairbairn, Ogden, nor any other psychoanalytic theorists). Psychoanalytically, even those who emphasize the environmental or "external" actual factor refer to it as an additional factor, never exclusive. Attachment theory stresses the significance of sensitive and responsive caregiving of attachment figures, particularly when children experience distress or emotional needs (Ainsworth et al., 1980), which are often experienced by children during nighttime. Therefore, it is safe enough to hypothesize that, in the case of kibbutz communal-system-raised children, the nighttime separation from the mother (and father) had a fundamental impact on the kibbutz children's well-being.

Possible effects of the disruptions to the mother-infant unit

Mary Ainsworth is one of the most significant contributors to our understanding of infant–mother attachment. Grossmann et al. (2013) write:

> it often goes unrecognized that Mary Ainsworth's evaluation of maternal care as adapted to an individual infant's characteristics was revolutionary. The phylogenetic program is sufficiently open to allow all babies to become attached to care-givers, even if the quality of care they receive is insensitive or even abusive. Infants' attachment to the care-giver under these circumstances, however, is likely to be insecure.
>
> (p. 444)

The Grossmann et al. study, as have many others, found that parental sensitivity has to do with parents' capacity to respond to their children with "prompt and appropriate behaviors" as well as by interpreting and giving "words to their children's feelings and experiences" (ibid.). Grossmann suggests that the parents "serve as translators between child and environment, and between the child and her peers or other adults" (ibid.). Furthermore,

> over and above responding to an infant's or child's needs for protection and affection, sensitivity, as conceptualized in Mary Ainsworth's scales, also involves respect for the child as a valuable person with autonomous feelings, needs, wishes, goals, and a mind of her own.
>
> (Ibid.)

Once again, what is conceptualized as crucial to the infant's and child's well-being (*secure attachment* in Ainsworth's terms) is maternal (or parental) sensitivity to their subjectivity and autonomous self. Kibbutz mothers may have been as varied as mothers elsewhere, but the system was not. The kibbutz system did not facilitate, favor, or enhance variation or differences among its members (children and adults alike). On the contrary, "equality" and "sameness" were considered to be the ethical way and choice. This influenced all aspects of life, including motherhood, mothering, and babyhood. Mothers were expected to cancel and disguise any personal preferences, which was made clear by their minimal ability to decide on any of the variables of child-rearing; all were subject to decisions made by the "education committee" or the kibbutz "general Assembly."

Under such circumstances, when the collective external system has such immense power over the individual, mothers had to shape themselves to conform to the community expectations. It is reasonable to hypothesize that few mothers and infants can benefit from such a dismissal of personal uniqueness and that this dismissal of individual difference gives rise to a particular form of mother–infant tie.

The kibbutz mother, unlike Green's "dead mother" (1999), was not absent entirely, nor was she necessarily depressed (although one wonders about the effects of this method of child-rearing on the mothers themselves, in that they, too, had to endure the painful early separation from their babies). The maternal care characteristic of the communal-collective upbringing is reminiscent of Fairbairn's (1944) "tantalizing mother" whose inconsistent presence is the fundamental feature of her maternal care. In such cases, it could be argued; the infant internalizes an inconsistent emotional presence, which could be quite emotionally disturbing for some infants (Fairbairn, 1944, p. 81). The shifts between glee, hope, and despair may contribute to rifts in the infant's trust and faith: Unlike the satisfying object, the unsatisfying object has, so to speak, two facets. On the one hand, it frustrates, and, on the other hand, it tempts and allures. Indeed, its essential "badness" consists precisely in the fact that it combines allurement with frustration. Further, it retains both these qualities after internalization (p. 82).

The infant, growing up in the communal-collective system had to find a way to integrate (1) the care-taker (day), (2) his or her own (biological) mother (and father), with whom the child spent only three hours each afternoon, and (3) the inconsistent, sporadic presence of the "night-keepers." Given a higher vulnerability of some infants, this complicated situation precluded their internalization of a more integrated internal-object mother. Instead, it gave rise to the internalization of a tantalizing object relationship with the mother as the never-fully available "exciting object" in Fairbairn's terms (1944).

We now accept the idea that babies are both different and alike and that each baby has his or her own constitution (i.e., "temperament," see Kagan, 1997), which may take an endless variety of forms, Kagan's studies of infants' inherent temperament emphasize the significant, if hard to trace, the contribution of non-environmental factors. Kagan (1997) states that "the environment acts on that temperament to produce personality" and "that once personality develops as an adult, it's difficult, if not impossible, to distinguish environmental influence from biological bias" (p. 149). I think there is no way, or reason, to dispute Kagan's claim. Yet, as psychoanalysts, our role is not to distinguish between "environment" and "inheritance," but rather to listen carefully and attempt to articulate and understand our patient's subjectivity, the subjectivity that is woven from threads of the individual's emotional experiences.

The communal-collective method of child-rearing is at odds with much of what is held by psychoanalysis to be optimal in meeting children's emotional needs (as described by Winnicott (1966), Fairbairn (1944), Anna Freud (1966), Selma Fraiberg (1950), and many others) and would lead one to expect that such methods of child-rearing would result in severe impairment to the children's earliest sense of well-being, as well as impairment in their subsequent psychological and emotional development. *The focal point I would like to emphasize is the illustration of the possible long-term effects of growing up in the kibbutzim of that time, specifically the effects that the multiple care-takers and the minimal involvement of the baby's parents had on the emotional development and well-being of the child.* Based on my analytic work with several patients (two of whom I will describe) who were raised in the kibbutz's communal system, I will illustrate some of the short- and long-term effects. I will focus on child-rearing practices (separation from mother, inconsistent care-takers) on childbearing, adult object-relatedness, capacity for intimacy, and transference–countertransference in the analytic setting.

Clinical illustrations

I. Rachel – "It's a matter of 'day' and 'night'"

Rachel was born and raised in the communal system, in a kibbutz in the mid-1970s, the second of five children. She was thirty when we started working together in analysis, married for almost five years at the time, and the mother of a

18 A "mother-of-one's-own"

son aged eighteen months. She came to see me, complaining about her husband's emotional absence, which filled the sessions for many months. At the start of our work together, she struck me as a high-functioning woman who was very intelligent and vibrant (a partner in a successful, high-profile law firm), with a good sense of humor and what seemed to be a good capacity for intimacy. Yet, when Rachel began using the couch, a significant change occurred in the analysis. While in the initial face-to-face meetings, she expressed herself with vitality, she became much stiffer and withdrawn when using the couch. As with other patients, the couch seemed to bring up a much earlier set of object-relationships, but, with Rachel, my experience was that there was "no object" in the transference. A split between a "no-object" and a "never-enough-object" became apparent.

On the one hand, Rachel did not seem to expect anything of me and expressed gratitude for whatever I gave her; on the other hand, she seemed never to have enough of me. In the transference–countertransference, this experience led me to say to her:

> You constantly feel that I am not here, that you are entirely on your own. This makes it very difficult for you to accept my presence, as well as my human limitations. I think you cannot figure out "what to do with me," because you have no idea that I am here, with you.

Regardless of her high level of professional functioning, Rachel regressed in the analysis and could hardly bear the space between sessions. She experienced the breaks as a total cessation of any emotional tie between us, both internally and externally. She seemed to be unreachable during these states of intrapsychic and interpersonal "breakdown" and described feeling alone in the world. It was not, for her, a "feeling" of breaking down the connection with herself or with me; it was an experience of the actual breaking of all internal and interpersonal ties, i.e., a total breakdown. This led me to accept various communications between the sessions (such as emails and text messages) to which I would always respond, in order not to leave her in a void. It soon became evident that she could not endure the profound sense of aloneness when not with me in sessions, regardless of her four-times-a-week analysis.

It was often striking to experience the shifts in Rachel's moods: She'd range from feeling utterly alone and helpless to being vitally alive. We later came to understand this "split" as representing the two fundamentally different states of mind of her childhood. Whereas she recalled herself as a lively, playful, and friendly girl during the daytime, she was different at night. The "nights" of her childhood were represented not only by the gaps between the sessions but also by how she would lie on the couch in tormented silence for whole sessions, some-times for an entire week. During these long, horrible, silences, I would try my best to talk with her about what I felt was going on. For example, over time, I would say things like, "I feel you are very far away, in a world of your own, to which I am not allowed to enter," or, "I want you to know that I am out here, waiting for

A "mother-of-one's-own" 19

you. I will be waiting here until you feel safe enough to come out and talk with me about how you feel," and, "I think you are feeling utterly alone, and probably extremely frightened. If you feel that you can come out and talk with me, I am here, and I want to know what you are feeling." To this and similar comments I made, Rachel would respond with a sound that I heard like a wounded animal, letting me know that she was alive, somewhere beneath the "rubble." Once in a while, after a few sessions of silence, she would gradually come out and tell me about "the hell I have been in" – elaborating only a little, saying: "I have been out half the night, just driving around aimlessly. There is no one there for me, or with me, at these 'places.' I am all alone." When I referred to the "No Entry" sign I felt she was putting up, she would say, "It's a place no one can be with me, but you are here when I go in, and you are here when I come out, and this is more than anyone else has ever done with me." I could not always tell whether Rachel was trying to comfort herself or me, but I accepted this for long periods. It was clear to me that her trust was fragile, at best.

Rachel often remarked:

> I know that probably no one would believe how miserable I am. I know that I have everything I have ever dreamed of. Don't I? I have a husband, a home, a baby. I am doing fine financially. But I just don't want to live. I wish it were over already.

One of the specific childhood traumas Rachel talked about, at length, was an accident she was involved in as a young girl of nine. She was wounded and required hospitalization of about two weeks. During this time, her parents visited her only occasionally, as the hospital was not very accessible to them. The painful memories included all the things that should have happened, but did *not* happen – after she came back to the kibbutz (I am aware that this is paradoxical as we are accustomed to think of memories as concerning things that *did* happen). Rachel recalls that the accident and her hospitalization were never discussed. She suffered dreadful nightmares throughout the next years that were never treated in any way. Much of her bewilderment, pain, and anger was directed at her mother, who worked in the kibbutz's laundry room. Rachel, who would stay awake through much of the night, would keep her bedside lamp on, burning her pillowcases. She could not understand how her mother, who washed the laundry of the kibbutz, did not notice that *her* pillowcases were burned.

This resembled Rachel's experience of not being seen by others as a child – a feeling she has had throughout her life – as well as the split between her high-functioning days as a child and her terrifying nights. I said to her that it seemed to me that this "split" between her "well-functioning self" and her "ill self" was first and foremost an internal split, also apparent in her attitude toward the analysis. Often, she was a hard-working analysand, compliant with "the rules" of analytic treatment (observing boundaries, for example). The limits I have imposed (the duration of the sessions, my holiday breaks), were perceived as a form of impersonal care and desertion of her: analysis was all about "handling." Rachel often questioned my devotion to her by asking, "if I were sick, would you visit me? If I was to mourn somebody's loss (i.e., death of someone close to her), would you ever consider coming and visit me? Do you ever leave this office of yours?" Her anger toward the setting was complicated. It reflected a combination of hate and respect, trust and mistrust, which manifested itself in her insistence on paying me on time: She felt distraught when she happened to forget to pay on the exact date. Rachel was very demanding and often angry with me. Yet, it was almost unbearable for her to feel that she had deprived me of something or had harmed me, probably because she felt utterly dependent on me and did not want to risk falling out of favor. Overtly expressing her anger was too "dangerous" for her. I talked with her about her difficulty in accepting me as a person who is both there for her and limited, given that her early experience was with an absent object (mother) whom she could not perceive as "present" and "limited" at the same time. It took many years of working together to begin to experience my presence as trustworthy and me as someone who was not going to disappear suddenly.

Rachel's combination of dependency, hate, fear, primitive guilt, and persecutory anxiety contributed to how she handled relations with all people in positions of authority. She hated and feared them and did her best to be liked by them. She tried to hide both her compliance and her largely unconscious urge to rebel, speak her mind, and challenge their authority; she was often unable to understand what caused people to be angry with her (the prospect of which terrified her). Aggression, when directed at her, was traumatic, threatening her to the point of near breakdown. She experienced these feelings, though to a slighter extent, when she felt (rightly or wrongly) that I was "not there," for example, in a moment of inauthenticity or momentary emotional withdrawal on my part. This a quality that I repeatedly encountered with all of my kibbutz-raised patients. They have all manifested this anxiety concerning people in authority, which I came to understand as a representation of the split they endured as children in the communal system, between "love" (their parents) (albeit limited!) and "authority" (the "system").

I conveyed to Rachel my sense of this psychic splitting between love and authority by saying, "I think that once I say 'no' to something, or am responsible for setting the rules, you can no longer experience me as someone who cares deeply for you. I can be one or the other." Children raised by their parents have more opportunities to integrate "love" and "authority." Children who were raised in the communal system needed to endure a systemic split between these two parental qualities, a split that, for many, became the basis for fear of authority figures throughout childhood and continuing in their adult lives.

In the countertransference, I felt Rachel as very strong, fragile, alive, and dead. She often felt entirely on her own, terrified that there was no one "out there" to catch her when she fell. This was manifested in her deep mistrust of me (and others) and her death wishes. Death was a place of serene no-pain, utter aloneness, and unity. I often talked with her about the miserable combination of the "system" she grew up in with her parents, and her mother, whom she continually experienced as being absent. The continuing absence of Rachel's mother was a recurrent theme, apparent mostly in her accounts of the minimal current contact they had with one another. Rachel would tell me, repeatedly with bitterness in her voice, about her attempts to connect with her mother, and about their "empty, shallow phone conversations."

> My mother never calls me. She texts me maybe every other week only to remind me that I have to come to dinner on Friday, but – other than that – it's a big nothing. I have no parents; I am the only one responsible for my life.

I kept replying, "*These* are the parents you have, as partial and limited as they are, these *are* your parents." Such verbal exchanges, repeated repeatedly, constituted an essential aspect of working through the splitting Rachel relied upon so heavily.

So much of Rachel's analysis was dedicated to the working through these traumatic early object-relations, in which hope, aliveness, dread, and despair were entangled. Over the years, Rachel was able to connect her difficulties with her early experiences in the kibbutz setting; she recalled many memories of how she was treated by her care-takers, the "night-keepers," and her parents. She recalled traumatic experiences of being handled, without much "care" or compassion by various care-takers, and being terrified at nights. She recalled being sick, waiting, often for hours, for the night-keeper to come and tend to her. She talked about staying awake through endless nights, feeling that she was alone, looking into the darkness, hoping someone would come to check on her. As her analysis progressed and her terror was relived out in the transference–countertransference, happier memories emerged, of daytime activities, in which she thrived.

II. Rona – A falling star

Rona, a young woman of twenty-eight, began therapy with me following a long string of therapies beginning when she was four or five. She was the third child in a family of six children. Her parents were born and raised in two different kibbutzim. They met when they were twenty, married a year later, and moved together to the kibbutz where Rona's father had been raised. Rona was born two months premature and was in a neonatal ICU until her "due date," when she was released from the hospital and taken to the kibbutz. In those days, parents were not allowed to be with their hospitalized babies, yet her parents traveled a few times weekly to visit her. Upon coming home to the kibbutz, Rona was placed, like any other baby, in the communal baby's unit.

At the age of five, her first therapy was initiated in response to severe anxiety that made it almost impossible for her to sleep. She would stay awake at night, sitting on her bed, looking into the dark, terrified by the belief that a comet would hit her. As a child, Rona was well aware that there were children who ran away

22   A "mother-of-one's-own"

from the "children's home," looking for their parents; she was puzzled by the fact that she had never done so. Rona told me,

> These "run-away children" were firmly scolded by the care-takers in the morning. I was so afraid that I "preferred" to stay put, wide awake, and terrified. I didn't dare leave my bed. I was so fearful of even going to the bathroom because it was always so dark. Besides, I knew for sure that if I did run away to my parents, they would take me right back to the children's home. They were always so afraid of the kibbutz. They would have never dared to do anything that would make anyone angry at them. So, I just stayed put.

Rona's inability to escape her terror – both as a child and during her analysis – was reflected physically and emotionally. On the couch, for example, she never moved. She never cried aloud (until her fifth year of analysis), seldom used a tissue, never used the bathroom. The minute I ended the session, she would jump from the couch. It seemed that Rona suffered from such a terrible fear of being abandoned, when dependent upon someone else, that she could not "use" me as a good object. This, in turn, served to intensify her profound sense of loneliness. At first there were only tears, streaming silently down her face; later on came her words: "How can I know that you will not leave me? You don't owe me anything, do you?" This feeling lasted for years, and it may have been our most significant achievement when, after years of analysis, she could finally tell me, "Perhaps you don't owe me anything, but maybe you will stay anyway."

Throughout her therapy, Rona was continuously preoccupied with "What is it that connects us?" and with "What would have happened if I had fallen on another analyst?" Although, in part, she said this as an expression of her mistrust of me that echoed a childhood feeling of hers that she just happened to "fall" on her mother as a mere coincidence, a mother with whom her connection was not inevitable or inviolate. I said to her, "I think you feel that what is going on between us is mere happenstance, not an authentic, unique connection that could *only* happen between the two of us, unlike any other pair in the universe." Rona agreed with this but more significant was that I sensed she relaxed. In time, she was able to convey the feeling that she was more secure in our unique, one-of-a-kind relationship. Her mistrust manifested by her use of the term "all on" was a trace of her "falling, prematurely, out of the womb." This experience was manifested and reenacted in the way she kept sabotaging many of her handful of friendships. Now and then, she would come in and tell me. "I fell out of touch with … I just don't have any desire to see her or talk with her. It's not that anything has happened. I just don't have the energy for it." I suggested to Rona that "these two emotional experiences, that of 'falling out' and that of 'nothing happened' are very significant." I did not add that perhaps it was the "nothing happened" that traumatized Rona who had experienced, both as a premature baby and as a very lonely and terrified young child, that "nothing happened" when it was essential that something happen in response to her need to be held and contained.

A "mother-of-one's-own" 23

It took many years of therapy and analysis for Rona to establish a relatively secure attachment to me. Throughout most of those years, I had to endure endless "on-the-spot" decisions to end the therapy, telling me how unrelated she felt to me, or how "nothing matters" in life. Other than these occurrences, I often felt as if the setting was transparent, or "dead" to Rona. She never "argued" or "broke" the analytic frame. She regularly came to her sessions, insisting on paying at the end of each session in cash. Her rare, although extremely meaningful, references to me or the "setting" were along the lines of "this is not a real relationship, this is professional, you are my *metapelet*.[6] It's nothing personal."

More than anything else, the "nothing personal" had a lifeless quality to it. Rona seemed angry at me for being "just her *metapelet*," she just seemed defeated by it. In a way, I think that Rona was killing all three of us – herself, me, and the analytic relationship. We were all transparent (invisible); it was as if no one knew or cared much about our existence. She often felt "dead" and rarely expressed distress about this way of being. She once said to me, "If I'd been more alive, I would have killed myself." I found this sad statement incredibly meaningful. Psychic death, for Rona, was a way of defending herself from actual physical death. More than death, it was life that scared her the most: "I am not fit for this world, for this life. I am here only because I am too scared to kill myself. I just don't have what it takes to live." I was pained to hear this, partly because I felt I understood and sympathized with what she said. I said to her:

> Life scares you so much that the only way you feel you can survive it is by killing all your feelings and wishes and desires. If there is nothing that you want from me, I cannot hurt you in any way. But should you want something of me or life, then you will be in great danger of being disappointed and deserted.

Rona's only response to this was silent crying, which I only knew because she reached out for a tissue and blew her nose. To Rona, when our connection seemed to disappear within her, these incidents felt "like death." I told her that I thought this experience of deadness was a sort of reminiscence of her early experience of "not mattering to anyone," which felt deadening and murderous when she was a fragile infant.

Rona's accumulated loneliness was also manifested in her self-image: She saw herself as a "grotesquely ugly person," and swore to me that she was "an ugly child." Once, when she once brought a picture of herself as a little girl, I was amazed to see how cute and lovely she was. It took years of therapy for Rona to start caring about her physical being compassionately, for example, to enjoy playing with makeup and dressing up. But her turbulent relations with her physical being continued throughout her therapy, prohibiting her from having any kind of romantic ties, or becoming a mother. Though her capacity for intimacy improved significantly, having an intimate relationship with another person (i.e., a romantic relationship) was beyond her ability.

24 A "mother-of-one's-own"

To some extent, she was able to mourn this absence and to accept that she, perhaps, was "too-wounded to fall in love with anyone, not to mention to get married or have a child. It makes me very sad, but this is who I am." The conventional "happy ending" of this story was incomplete, but this did not mean that Rona could not come to life in ways that had once seemed impossible.

Rona's experiences of being utterly alone, of not mattering to anyone in the world, of being "ugly," were all representations of her early experiences in life in which she was not being taken care of by one specific maternal figure, her own mother, with whom she spent only three hours each day. To reiterate, the caretakers who took care of all her physical and developmental needs were not her parents, that is, were *not* people who loved her as her parents. Throughout most of the day and night, she was deprived of the intimacy, enthusiasm, and sense of wonder shared by babies and their mothers. We understood Rona's extreme childhood anxiety of "being hit by a comet" – transformed into other manifestations of anxiety in adulthood – as representing her extreme vulnerability, which was enhanced by her profound sense of loneliness. Rona's experience was of being continually exposed to a disaster, threatening her at any given moment, relived during the night when she experienced her most significant loneliness. She had little trust in the adults' ability to protect her from these (or other) disasters. She was taken care of by so many people, and yet by no one in particular. This led to a paradoxical state-of-mind where she felt like the center of the universe (on a collision course with a comet) and felt utterly helpless and defenseless, at the same time. It is a matter of perception and speculation to determine the extent to which Rona's difficulties, both in her childhood and in her adult life, result from her characterological makeup, mother's scarce presence, or are they the result of her exposure to multiple care-takers.

Although each child is different, Rona's experience is not unlike the experience of many children raised in the communal kibbutz system.

The three-hour parental limit, always from 4:00 p.m. to 7:00 p.m. included time spent not only with the child's parents, but also with other children who were involved in all sorts of afternoon playtime activities. Additionally, the child's parents, as I have mentioned before, had little or no say concerning their child's daily activities (which were decided upon by the kibbutz system). Both during the day and the night, the child was expected to share everything with other children and to accommodate to a set of uniform, systemic rules and routines, meaning that he or she was supposed to adapt to the external world, and almost never the other way around. This type of child-rearing stands in vast contrast to the child-rearing ideas of Winnicott (1958, 1960, 1963a), who stresses the importance of the good-enough mother–child relationship: For Winnicott, it is the mother's role to adapt the surroundings to the baby's needs – particularly during the first weeks of life – in order to allow the infant, the matrix for the undisrupted "going-on-being" that he considered vital to the individual's becoming an alive subject.

Discussion

Some significant themes emerge from these two clinical illustrations. The first, and perhaps most striking, are these patients' profound loneliness: Both perceived themselves as being utterly alone in the world, regardless of their marital status or the number of friendships they had. These patients often spoke of feeling like "strangers" and "guests" in the world, an experience that was repeatedly acted out in the transference–countertransference. From the time of their birth, these women grew up without maternal care-taking, which caused them to question the authenticity of their relationship with me as their analyst. Both expressed mistrust of me: Although generally "friendly" and "polite," their anger emerged in rather subtle ways. Despite my stable and consistent presence, I often felt that these patients could not and would not entrust themselves. Yet, at the same time, they were able to share their belief in the deep "truth" of their profound mistrust. I was treated as if I were a stranger who could abandon them at any moment. Their sense of my inconsistency was also evident in the constrained way in which they spoke in sessions: Even when speaking about the most painful things, both hardly shed a tear and certainly did not cry or weep. When I was experienced as an adult in a care-taking role, I often felt that I could not be trusted, but that trust was possible when I was seen as a peer. Both often insisted, "you are not a mother-figure. I don't want you to 'play mother to me.' I need us to be 'equals.'" It was evident that to these two patients, the concept of "mother," "mothering," and "mother-figure" was saturated with intense negativity, which made it remarkably difficult for them to differentiate me-in-the-present from their experiences-in-the-past.

Another striking similarity between these two analyses was the way Rachel and Rona perceived their parents. They used almost identical terms in describing them. Both viewed and treated their parents as "children," too immature to take on any responsibility. The mothers were described as either "weak" or "anxious" and "unemotional." Whereas they often described their parents as having "good intentions," they questioned their parents' abilities. A recurrent theme was the "unemotional" quality of their relationships with their mothers. This was very apparent in their sense of self, especially in how they referred to the "child/ish" aspect of themselves.

Additionally, there was a pervasive splitting: They referred to "other children" in a very loving way, yet described themselves as "ugly" and "unworthy" children. Both Rachel and Rona felt that being a child was a most unwanted and even dangerous state, meaning that one was all alone in the world. Again, this was manifested in the transference as profound mistrust of me and my capacity to fulfill my responsibility.

Their mistrust was different from other patients who mistrusted my ability to help them. Rachel's and Rona's suspicion were not primarily directed at my professionalism; instead, it focused more on my "humanism," doubting my essential sense of responsibility and genuine care for them. This was often expressed in the

26 A "mother-of-one's-own"

heart-wrenching question: "What is it that you owe me?" And in their answer to this question: "You owe me nothing. No one owes me anything." This, as I understood it, was not merely a protest, or declaration of (pseudo)-independence, it was an expression of what was perhaps their most primary terror in life – complete and utter isolation and helplessness. Only rarely did either of these two patients express resentment regarding payment, and, when they did, it often felt as if they were so used to having to "pay" for being taken care of that their protest was not heartfelt. These patients exhibited ambivalence in relation to the analytic setting, which was sometimes stormy – as if in protest – and at other times very quiet – in a submissive position. What continued to reoccur, in times of distress, was the ambivalence, the caution, and mistrust of my "realness." It has often felt that my existence was so questionable and so conditional that, not only might I disappear, but I could also be eliminated in the blink of an eye.

Finally, regarding transference and countertransference, much of the negative transference was directed at me as "The System." "The System" had a constant presence in these analyses, and it represented whatever they perceived and felt to be impersonal, uniform, unattended to, and unattuned. Simultaneously, "The System" was a "given," not-to-be-argued-with, a "negative," and a "thing" you cannot expect to be anything other than what it is. This was, naturally, coupled with Rachel's and Rona's intense needs to be recognized as "unique" by their mothers, which was, in my opinion, their most fundamental longing, the need to have "a mother of one's own," someone they could identify as being "theirs." Interestingly, I seldom experienced any form of "sibling rivalry" in my work with these patients.

On the contrary, "siblings," including their own and children and other patients of mine, were – more often than not – experienced by them as allies. Jealousy was rarely expressed. It was adults, and specifically adults who held power or authority, who most bothered them. The most intense feeling experienced by Rachel and Rona was the extreme fear of encountering anger from a person who held power over them. The possibility that an adult man or woman would become angry with them was often experienced as the most dreadful experience, eliciting severe depression that bordered, at times, on the wish to be dead.

Despite the negativity toward the so-called "System," it seemed to have a gravitational pull greater than that of parents. Of course, we can (and rightfully so) presume that "The System" and "The Parents" were fused to a certain degree, mutually influencing one another. A lot of work was directed at differentiating "The System" from "the parents," a differentiation that was intended to enable the formation of a new concept, that of "*my* parents." This proved a critical differentiation that facilitated a unique experience as an adult. It differentiated between "the" system and "a" system (whether it was the kibbutz system vs. other systems or "parents" vs. "parental").

As difficult as it may be to accept one's parents truly, this is even harder for adults who feel they were deprived of essential parenting. Recognizing and accepting our past as part of who we are is an achievement that, I believe, is dependent, to a great extent, on the transference–countertransference experience the analyst can establish with each patient. This may be extremely difficult for patients, such as Rachel and Rona, who were raised in the kibbutz and whose early object–relations centered around non-parental figures. It is particularly challenging for those who were raised by multiple care-takers (as in the kibbutz, orphanage institutions, or boarding schools). It seems reasonable to assume that a child raised by multiple adults will develop a sense of not-belonging anywhere or to anyone, in particular. Thus, the analyst must develop a way of talking with each patient – that is, be with him or her in a way that considers one's unique experience and differs from how this analyst talks to other patients (Ogden, 2016).

It took Rachel and Rona several years of analysis to sort through their feelings toward their "missing mother" and to acknowledge that regardless of what they believed and declared, they had been waiting and longing their whole lives for their parents (especially their mothers) to show up and take up their responsibilities.

Rachel and Rona are merely representatives of a group of my patients over the years. They grew up with the experience of being "motherless" babies while being raised on a kibbutz. Throughout the years, I have treated several adults who were brought up in the kibbutz method of child-rearing and found their impaired capacity for genuine and profound object-relatedness to be different in certain respects, but strikingly similar in others. Although mothers are as various as their babies, the match between them may be more crucial than any single, individual feature of either one. The kibbutz communal-collective system was aimed precisely at diminishing the mothers' responsiveness to individual differences in their children, putting uniformity above almost all other values. Under the sway of the dictates of the system-wide upbringing of this sort, many mothers felt the need to disavow their emotional needs and those of their infants to adapt to the system's norms and expectations.

I need to note that the kibbutz should not be demonized for its communal child-rearing methods, but neither should the possible harmful impacts be ignored. The kibbutz methods bear significance, not only on the first and second generation of people who grew up with this type of childcare; the impact on the children of those raised in these collectives must also be explored, as evidence emerges of inter-generational transmission of troubled object-relations (Koren-Karie & Aviezer, 2017). Kibbutz infants were raised in such a unique environment. There was a "System" with powerfully enforced norms, expectations, regulations, and rules that have governed every aspect of the infant' s/child's life. This can allow us an extraordinary opportunity to gain a greater understanding of the possible long-term effects of a uniform environment on the individual psyche.

Notes

1 This text was published in *Contemporary Psychoanalysis* (2018), 54(3), 431–464.
2 I am very cautious regarding how to make use of this portion of Winnicott's thinking as well as the aspects of my own thesis regarding the significance of the 'biological mother' when considering mother-infant relationships that lie outside the focus of this article, for example, in cases of adoption. It is important to emphasize that this article's

28 A "mother-of-one's-own"

aim is to address the unique upbringing that occurred in the kibbutz. Adoptive mothers, although not 'biological] mothers, are certainly – by means of "primary maternal preoccupation' (Winnicott, 1958) – capable of being good-enough-mothers.
3 Bowlby adds the following footnote: "Although in this paper I shall usually refer to mothers and not mother-figures, it is to be understood that in every case I am concerned with the person who mothers the child and to whom he becomes attached rather than the natural mother" (p. 350)
4 This failure to differentiate the biological mother from other forms of maternal provision may also derive from the sociological–political changes in which egalitarian attitudes have become more popular. Although it might be thought that these egalitarian attitudes would influence the actual allocation of tasks within the private sphere in general, and childcare in particular, this is not the case. In almost all of the research on issues of maternal care-taking it is the biological mothers (compared to the fathers) who are the primary care-takers of infants and children in these studies (Baxter, 2002; Bianchi, 2000; Craig, 2006; Rabin & Shapira-Berman, 1997; and many others).
5 Toddlers learned from very early on that if they cry, the "night-keeper" will be able to hear them through the intercom and eventually come to check on them. The night-keepers will also take strolls throughout the communal children's homes to check up on the children.
6 The word "*Metapelet*" is the Hebrew word for both "caretaker" and "therapist."

References

Ainsworth, M.D.S. (1963). The development of infant–mother interaction among the Ganda. In B. M. Foss (Ed.), *Determinants of infant behavior* (pp. 67–104). New York: Wiley.

Ainsworth, M.D.S. (1968). Object relations, dependency, and attachment: A theoretical review of the infant mother relationship. *Child Development*, 40: 969–1025.

Ainsworth, M.D.S., Blehar, M.C., Waters, E., & Wall, S. (1980). Patterns of attachment: A psychological study of the strange situation. *Infant Mental Health Journal*, 1(1): 68–70.

Balint, A. (1949). Love for the mother and mother-love. *The International Journal of Psychoanalysis*, 30: 251–259.

Baxter, J. (2002). Patterns of change and stability in the gender division of household labor in Australia, 1996–1997. *Journal of Sociology*, 38(4): 399–424.

Beit-Hallahmi, B., & Rabin, A.I. (1977). The kibbutz as a social experiment and as a child-rearing laboratory. *American Psychologist*, (July), 532–541.

Bianchi, S. (2000). Maternal employment and time with children: Dramatic change or surprising continuity? *Demography*, 37(4): 401–414.

Bion, W.R. (1962a). *Learning from experience*. London: Tavistock.

Bion, W.R. (1962b). *Elements of psycho-analysis*. London: Heineman.

Bowlby, J. (1940). The influence of early environment in the development of neurosis and neurotic character. *The International Journal of Psychoanalysis*, 21: 154–178.

Bowlby, J. (1958). The nature of the child's tie to his mother. *The International Journal of Psychoanalysis*, 39: 350–373.

Bowlby, J. (1960a). Grief and mourning in infancy and early childhood. *The Psychoanalytic Study of the Child*, 15: 9–52.

Bowlby, J. (1960b). Separation and anxiety. *The International Journal of Psychoanalysis*, 41: 89–113.

Bowlby, J. (1973). *Attachment and loss, vol. 2: Separation: Anxiety and anger*. New York: Basic.

Bowlby, J. (1988). *A secure base: Clinical applications of attachment theory*. London: Routledge.

Chodorow, N. J. (2000). Reflections on the reproduction of mothering: Twenty years later. *Studies in Gender and Sexuality*, 1(4): 337–348.

Craig, L. (2006). Does father care mean father share? A comparison of how mothers and fathers in intact families spend time with children. *Gender and Society*, 20(2): 259–281.

Fairbairn, W.R.D. (1944). Endopsychic structure considered in terms of object-relationships. *The International Journal of Psychoanalysis*, 25: 70–92.

Fairbairn, W. R. D. (1952). Schizoid factors in the personality. In D. E. Scharff & E. F. Birtles (Eds.), *Psychoanalytic Studies of the Personality* (pp. 3–27). London, UK: Routldge & Kegan Paul. (Original work published in 1940)

Fraiberg, S. (1950). On the sleep disturbances of early childhood. *The Psychoanalytic Study of the Child*, 5: 285–309.

Freud, A. (1958). Child observation and prediction of development: A memorial lecture in Honor of Ernst Kris. *The Psychoanalytic Study of the Child*, 13: 92–116.

Freud, A. (1966). Interactions between nursery school and child guidance clinic. *Journal of Child Psychotherapy*, 1(4): 40–44.

Green, A. (1999). *The dead mother: The work of Andre Green*. New York: Routledge.

Grossmann, K.E., Bretherton, I., Waters, E., & Grossmann, K. (2013). Maternal sensitivity: Observational studies honoring Mary Ainsworth 100th year. *Attachment and Human Development*, 15(5–6): 443–447.

Kagan, J. (1997). Temperament and the reactions of unfamiliarity. *Child Development*, 68(1): 139–143.

Koren-Karie, N., & Aviezer O. (2017). Mother–child emotion dialogues: The disrupting effect of maternal history of communal sleeping. *Attachment & Human Development*, 19(6): 580–597.

Nachman, P.A. (1991). The maternal representation: A comparison of caregiver- and mother-reared toddlers. *Psychoanalytic Study of the Child*, 46: 69–90.

Ogden, T.H. (1985). The mother, the infant and the matrix: Interpretations of aspects of the work of Donald Winnicott. *Contemporary Psychoanalysis*, 21: 346–371.

Ogden, T.H. (1994). The analytic third: Working with intersubjective clinical facts. *The International Journal of Psychoanalysis*, 75: 3–19.

Ogden, T.H. (2004). On holding and containing, being and dreaming. *The International Journal of Psychoanalysis*, 85(6): 1349–1364.

Ogden, T.H. (2010). Why read Fairbairn? *The International Journal of Psychoanalysis*, 91(1): 101–118.

Ogden, T.H. (2016). Some thoughts on practicing psychoanalysis. *Fort Da*, 22: 21–36.

Oppenheim, D., Sagi, A., & Lamb, M.E. (1988). Infant–adult attachment on the kibbutz and their relation to socioemotional development 4 years later. *Developmental Psychology*, 24(3): 427–433.

Rabin, A.I. (1965). *Growing up in the kibbutz*. New York: Springer.

Shapira-Berman, O., & Rabin, C. (1997). Egalitarianism and marital happiness – Israeli wives and husbands on a collision course? *American Journal of Family Therapy*, 25(4): 319–330.

Sagi, A, Lamb, M.E., Estes, D., Shoham, R., Lewkowicz, K., & Dvir, R. (1982, March). Security of infant–adult attachment among kibbutz-reared infants. Paper presented at a meeting of the International Conference on Infant Studies, Austin, TX.

Sagi, A., Lamb, M.E., Lewkowicz, K., Shoham, R., Dvir, R., & Estes, D. (1985). Security of infant–mother, father, and metapelet among kibbutz-reared Israeli children. *Monographs of the Society for Research in Child Development*, 50: 257–275 (1-2, Serial No. 209).

Sagi, A., Lamb, M.E., & Gardner, W. (1986). Relations between strange situation behavior and stranger sociability among infants on Israeli kibbutzim. *Infant Behavior and Development*, 9: 271–282.

Sagi, A., van Ijzenndoors, M., Aviezer, O., Donell, F., & Mayseless, O. (1994). Sleeping out of home in a kibbutz communal arrangement: It makes a difference for infant–mother attachment. *Journal of Child Developmental*, 65: 992–1004.

Spiro, M.E. (1958). *Children of the kibbutz*. Cambridge, MA: Harvard University Press.

Van IJzendoorn, M.H., Sagi, A., & Lambermon, M. (1992). The multiple caretaker paradox: Data from Holland and Israel. *New Directions for Child Development*, 57: 5–24.

Winnicott, D.W. (1945). Primitive emotional development. *International Journal of Psychoanalysis*, 26: 137–143.

Winnicott, D. W. (1949/1975). Mind and its relation to the psyche-soma. In D.W. Winnicott (Ed.), *Through pediatrics to psycho-analysis: Collected papers* (pp. 243–254). New York, NY: Basic Books. (Original work published in 1949).

Winnicott, D. W. (1951). Transitional objects and transitional phenomena. In *Playing and reality* (pp. 1–25). New York, NY: Basic Books, In.

Winnicott, D. W. (1958). The capacity to be alone. In D. W. Winnicott (Ed.), *The maturational processes and the facilitating environment: Studies in the theory of emotional development (1965)* (Vol. 64, pp. 1–276, 29–36). London, UK: The International Psycho-Analytical Library.

Winnicott, D. W. (1960). The theory of the parent-infant relationship. In D. W. Winnicott (Ed.), *The maturational processes and the facilitating environment: Studies in the theory of emotional development.* (1965) (Vol. 64, pp. 1–276, 37–55). London, UK: The International Psycho-Analytical Library.

Winnicott, D. W. (1963a). Communicating and not communicating leading to a study of certain opposites. In D. W. Winnicott (Ed.), *The maturational processes and the facilitating environment* (pp. 179–192). New York, NY: International Universities Press.

Winnicott, D.W. (1963b). Dependence in infant care, child care, and in the psycho-analytic setting. *International Journal of Psychoanalysis*, 44: 339–344.

Winnicott, D.W. (1965). Primary maternal preoccupation. *Through Pediatrics to Psycho-Analysis.* (1975). *The International Psycho-Analytic Library*, 100 (300–305).

Winnicott, D.W. (1969). The use of an object. *The International Journal of Psychoanalysis*, 50: 711–716.

Winnicott, D. W. (1974). Fear of breakdown. *International Review of Psycho-Analysis*, 1: 103–107.

Chapter 2

"Love thy work"

From having no mother to being everybody's mother – re-examining the professional choice of women psychotherapists who grew up in the kibbutz[1,2]

Introduction

Many words seek to describe the unique and vital relationship that develops between mother and baby (Stern, 1992; Winnicott 1971); the most famous are, perhaps, Winnicott's words (Winnicott, 1960a), "There is no such thing as a baby." In these words, Winnicott seeks to outline the process of the infant's psychic formation as an integral part of his relationship with his mother.

The communal system (described in detail in the previous chapter), which was practiced in kibbutzim until the 1980s, required a significant physical and mental disconnection between the baby and her/his mother. In many ways, the child-rearing method of the Kibbutz is an outstanding example of a unique form of parenting, resembling to some extent the experiences of children growing up in boarding schools. The literature written on life in the kibbutz describes and emphasizes the various consequences of the childhood experience, following the communal educational system, on broad areas of one's life including relationships, parenting, intimacy, attachment patterns, personal resilience, self-image, and more (Levkovich, 2007). It can be assumed that the significance of the experience of growing up in the kibbutz, which accompanies those children in their adulthood, will influence many aspects, including their choice of profession and occupation.

Based on Freud's well-known statement that the task of the adult person concerns the combination of love and work, the personal choice of women who were raised in the kibbutz to engage themselves in dynamic–analytical psychotherapy is particularly interesting. I was specifically intrigued by this choice of career, given the connection that the analytical theories make, between the mother–infant relationship and the therapist–patient relationship.

In what way, if at all, is the communal child-rearing system intertwined with the considerations that led these women to choose their professional vocation? Does the mother's limited presence, or experienced absence, have any influence on their narratives, in general, and concerning the career choice, specifically? Is the communal system experienced as a trauma? And, if so, has the women's

DOI: 10.4324/9781003203193-3

experience with this "trauma" provided them with the strengths and resources required for the professional choice to engage in psychoanalytic treatment?

In this chapter, I will discuss women's choice to become therapists, based on the understanding and assumption that one's professional choice is influenced by many factors and motivations, some related to the environment and some related to one's personality. My understanding is based both on my clinical experience and on a study in which 11 women therapists, raised in different kibbitzes, were interviewed using in-depth, semi-structured interviews. The interviews were then analyzed systematically to provide the themes that will be discussed. All of the women who participated in this study were treated analytically, besides working analytically with their patients.

The conversations with the women reveal different links between their childhood experience in the kibbutz and the processes of professional self-development. The women discussed their perceptions and the meaning they attribute to their choice of becoming therapists. Most of the women we have interviewed experienced their profession as allowing them the experience of an ongoing personal growth and development. Most of them have also referred to the reparation that their professional choice allows them, focusing their energies on "making lonely people feel better." The discussion of the central themes that have emerged from these conversations is conducted concerning the clinical context of working with patients who were raised in various circumstances in which parents were unavailable, to various degrees. The unique experience of these women, who were put into the communal system at the age of three days, has relevance to some key issues that are themselves related to parental presence and absence, such as identity, self-development, and the tendency to direct one's self to others.

From two that are one to one that are two: basic principles in object relation theories

The framework of object-relations assumes, as an axiom, that the individual strives from birth to establish a meaningful relationship with significant objects (Noy, 2006; Solan, 2007). The infant and mother, which is the baby's primary attachment object, are intertwined in a unique relationship that evolves constantly (Stern, 1992; Winnicott, 1971, 1987, 2009). This tapestry, from "two" to one-which-is two, is gradually woven, from the primary maternal preoccupation and the continuity of good enough maternal care (Winnicott, 1960a). The mother provides the baby with the needed holding, care, and "oneness," under her physical presence and by being a responsive object. The reciprocity, between the mother and her baby, is created by the physical holding, the touch, the warmth, the look in the eyes, the smile, the facial expressions, the tone of speech, the feeding, the breathing, the rhythm, the interest, and the attitude. By doing so, the mother serves as a human "mechanism" for regulating, processing, and digesting the world and the external environment for the infant (Khan, 1963; Ogden, 1992). The mother's way of holding and handling the infant enables the regulation of the infant's self-experience and the continuity of being that the baby so desperately needs from the moment he is born. The infant must experience and grasp the boundaries of his body and separation, expanding his ability to contain the anxiety, vulnerability, and frustration involved in encountering objective reality. Self-establishment is a function of, among other things, the disillusionment and acceptance of breaking the omnipotent symbiotic unity of the mother–child unit (Mahler, 1975, 1976).

A premature separation, or the absence of this "one-ness" within the mother–infant unit (sub) condition, is described as having a traumatic potential (Winnicott, 1971, ; Klein, 1957, 1963; Bick, 1968; Bion, 1962, 1970; Balint, 1968; Mahler, 1976, 1975; Kohut, 1971, 1977; Anzieu, 1970; Bowlby, 1973, 1982; Ogden, 1992; Bollas, 1992; Tustin, 1986). These writers emphasize the importance of the "psychological envelope," whose role is to produce, for the infant, the sense of oneness, continuity, and consecutiveness. Anzieu (1970) conceives the psychic envelope, as the "skin-Ego," internalized through the infant's experiences, at the beginning of his life. The skin-Ego is, for the primordial psyche, a sack that contains the good and the whole-ness, serving as an interface between inside and outside. The skin-Ego can be thought of as a kind of physical–mental texture, which marks the boundary with the outer world and constitutes a buffer that protects the inner parts from the intrusion of external aggression. One's skin is a dimension of communication with others; a kind of "inscribing surface" on which the signs and impressions of the interaction with others are inscribed. Bion (1970) emphasizes the vitality of the mother's function as a container and a protective shield preserving the various mental processes of the infant. Under circumstances that are not traumatic, or when psychic strengths are intact, the infant may invest her/his efforts in avoiding the feeling of frustration. Under traumatic circumstances, or if the baby does not have the needed psychic strengths, organized thinking may be replaced by excessive use of rigid defense mechanisms such as rejection and denial. Excessive absence of maternal containing, what can be thought of as traumatic "no-thing-ness," can impair the development of the inner organization of the mind and evoke a self-experience of being "attacked," "helpless," or even "evil" (Segal, 1973).

In situations where the same protective shield, yielded by the maternal containing of the baby's anxieties, due to maternal poor care, negligence, or constitutional or inborn characteristics of the baby, the experience may be that of "nothingness," which is scalded into the baby's psyche and/or soma. Often, it may be experienced (and described) as a dull, albeit constant, pain that is difficult to define, express, clarify, or get rid of. The "nothing" may then become an abysmal space that creates a deep rift in the baby's psyche. Bollas (1992) who elaborated on one's experience of absence as a traumatic condition argues that when the child is left on her/his own (by the adults) (s)he is forced to contain the intensity of the pain and shock at a time that her/his strengths are not appropriate for carrying out this task. The result may often be one of psychic trauma, that may resonate throughout one's life. However, Klein (1963) has attributed significance to the experience of "nothingness," as facilitating emotional and mental processes that the infant is required to lead mentally. In her view, experiencing absence, to a certain degree, can strengthen the individual's mental functions.

The communal child-rearing system: in the absence of unity–uniformity

Stern and Bruschweiler-Stern (1998) note that although infant care can be carried out by any caregiver, no caregiver is in the emotional position to create the experience of love, interest, concern, and identification similar to the biological mother. Spiro (1958), who studied the communal child-rearing system in the kibbutzim, found that the infants' sense of estrangement from the mother created great difficulty in the early mother–infant dyadic relationship and argued that this could have been the cause of severe consequences in terms of other relationships later in life. Spiro found that the children of the kibbutz were exposed to rejection by the caregivers and experienced aggression from their peers, which led to the internalization of more rigid and unadaptable patterns.

Rabin (1965) compared, in his research, the children of kibbutzim to children of other types of settlements, concluding that a large number of caregivers from the earliest stages, as was the case in the kibbutz's communal system, was burdensome and hindered the normal development of the children of the kibbutz. Bettelheim (1969) found evidence of emotional shallowness in children raised in the communal system, attributing it to the multiplicity of caregivers, being a source for the individuals' mistrust of others and the difficulty they experienced within an intimate relationship. Consequently, this often led to the experience of difficulty in expression, specifically emotional. Sagi et al. (1985, 1994) based their study on Ainsworh et al. (1978) and found a significant prevalence of anxious attachment patterns among children who were raised in the communal system. According to Sagi's study, the unavailability of the mother especially at night, coupled with her substantial absence during the day, created an inconsistent attachment, which eventually led to the infants' anxious, avoidant, and ambivalent attachment. These findings have been supported by additional studies (Sagi, van IJzendoorn, Aviezer, Donell, & Mayseless, 1994; Donell, 1991; Rosenthal, 1988; Aviezer et al., 1999).

Other researchers have emphasized the differential parenting patterns that existed within, and despite, the uniformity of the kibbutz system (Lieblich, 1984; Oppenheim, 1998). Parents who were able to provide their children with a more personal approach, regardless of the strict rules of the kibbutz, hence facilitating a relatively flexible transition between the kibbutz laws and the needs of the child, enabled the child a wider range of emotions and adaptivity (meaning it was not always the child who needed to adapt to the "system" but that there were times that the parent was able to "convince" the system to adapt to the child's needs). However, these researchers also claim that often the kibbutz system was too rigid and was reluctant to take into account the emotional distress that was experienced by many children as a result of the communal system.

The caretaker as the maternal figure: the choice to become a therapist

Practicing psychotherapy exposes the therapist to a powerful multifaceted emotional experience (Neumann, 1991). The therapist–patient relationship is characterized by intimacy, and requires the therapist to be fully engaged, emotionally and otherwise (Fox, 1990). Psychoanalytic theories perceive one's professional choice as a possible way of expressing subconscious and unconscious impulses. The formation of a certain professional choice-tendency is regarded as the result of sublimation processes or identifications, among other factors (Drasgow, as cited in Brown, 1996). Neumann (1991), for example, emphasizes therapists' desire to be close to the unconscious and to experience mental suffering, as means of their struggle to better understand the psychic world and life. It is often the therapist's need to be able to organize, give reason to and cognitively master the unexpectable that drives her/him to this choice of becoming a therapist. In this regard, the therapist holds together his inner world by holding the patient, and this can be perceived as another means of self-holding (Winnicott, 1971) that was needed by the therapist during their childhood. Holland (1997, 1993) describes the personality of caregivers as based on the desire for personal contact and interpersonal closeness, a sense of responsibility, understanding, empathy, sensitivity to others, sociability, idealism, giving up, and self-giving. Others (Fox, 1990; Harari, 2002) talk about the need of caregivers for "controlled intimacy," a relationship that allows them to have better modulation of distance and closeness–intimacy.

Miller (1997) famously talks about the narcissistic aspect of the therapeutic profession, based on childhood experiences that have coerced the child into giving up her/his "self" for the sake of ensuring the maternal object's well-being. During childhood, the "gifted child" develops a special sensitivity to the signals and signs, expressing the maternal object's distress, shaping the child's internal object-relations. In this sense, the role of the therapist can be perceived as an "extension" of the parental role since the "therapeutic situation" allows the therapist to take upon her/himself a parental position, and experience, meaning that of being strong, caring, protective, providing the patient with parental functions, both nurturing and possessive (Doron-Yaron, 2001; Nadlin, 2002; Harari, 2002).

What did the women therapists tell us?

We were given away so small, not at all ready to be separated from our mothers. They did not allow us those moments of grace, the profoundly important experience of the attachment to the mother. It is something that can never be re-experienced, later in life. It became a distance that I was never able to build a bridge over. A gap that could not be fixed. It is as if parts were erased from my internal world, or rather they had never been established and were lost forever. These places inside me, are places of deep loneliness. There is a place that is empty inside me, and it can never be touched. Today I feel so much pain because of this distance and the feeling is of abandonment and terrible loneliness.

(Nina)

Nina was only one of many adults who were raised in the kibbutz, who spells out her profound sense of loneliness. It is probably the most common experience that I, as an analyst, encounter with my patients who were raised in the kibbutz and it is different than any other loneliness I have met with any of my patients. The women's descriptions of their childhood experiences are very much in accordance with object relations theories, which emphasize the infant's relationship with the mother as a crucial factor for normal development. According to Winnicott (1971), only the mother can give her baby the experience of "primary maternal preoccupation." The unity between mother and baby facilitates the experience of merging through which the baby can adapt to the external reality and create a healthy separation. Stern and Bruschweiler-Stern (1998) note that no caregiver is in an emotional position that allows for the creation of the experience of love, interest, and concern, which stems from the mother's ability to identify with her baby. One of the things that the women talked about was that the communal system did not allow the continuous experience of oneness that the baby needs to have with the mother. Separating the babies from their mothers and the fact that the caregivers alternated every few hours, throughout the day and night, allowed only brief encounters with unexpected caretakers whose familiarity with the singularity of the particular baby was rather tenuous. Babies, infants, and children lacked the experience of being "The One," and such discontinuous, inconsistent, and impersonal encounters weighed heavily on their ability to organize their inner world in a healthy way (Oppenheim, 1998). What the women who took part in this study, as well as many of my patients who were raised in a kibbutz, have told me follows the line of many other studies that have portrayed the experience of the communal system in shades of loneliness, abandonment, distance, and physical and emotional deprivation (Lieblich, 1984; Leshem, 1991; Balaban, 2001; Lamdan, 2004; Levkovich, 2007).

The question of "freedom" versus "negligence" was brought up by Ruth:

Growing up in a kibbutz is an experience that consists of all kinds of textures. Some connect and some don't. Perhaps this is what implies that there is a great difficulty, the disconnection between the things. Today, I can understand that this is the experience of trauma – that the various aspects remain dismantled and it is difficult to connect the parts to one coherent sequence. There is no doubt that during the day I was a happy girl. By day we were all heroes. We learned, we wandered in nature, we witnessed the wonders of the world in every sense of the word, we connected to the earth, to adventure. We did things that we couldn't tell the adults about. All kinds of childish nonsense and we could do them because no one stopped us. And that's the other side of the story. I did not feel this way as a child but I feel this today. There was no one to look after us. It was like the Wild West, no law to regard. We have done some horrible things that to this day no one knows about. I think to this day we are still afraid that the caregiver will give us a punishment, so we keep our mouths shut to this day (laughs). I laugh, but I get shocked every time I think about how we grew up, all alone, unattended, without anyone guarding us. It's scary, but we were happy children. I think. At least during the day, because at night.

Ruth, as Nina and the other women, talked about the complexity of her childhood experiences. Along with aspects relating to the same traumatic experiences, one can discern the different hues in the women's experiences, underlining different mechanisms of coping, psychic growth, and personal development. We could notice this split in the way the women recalled their childhood – in terms of memories their childhood was "beautiful" – but when attributing meaning to their experiences, they talked about them with profound pain and at times even anger and dismay. There seemed to be limited movement between the two ends of their experience and this was further illustrated by the common distinction many of them made between the "threatening nights" and the "beautiful, colorful days" which were basically about nature and freedom. There wasn't a single woman who did not talk about her experiences during the nights.

The night is a very sensitive subject. It was a real nightmare … and this nightmare continued into the morning when no one knew, or could have known, what had been going on with me throughout the night. I also could not know, at some point, because if I did "know" I wouldn't have been able to function during the day. I had to disconnect myself to survive. Here again, we are talking about aspects of trauma, and not just any trauma, but a continuous and ongoing trauma. We are talking about a small girl who had to dissociate to survive. The price of this is very high and I am still paying it, in all those places that I still feel inside. To this day there is a lot of pain that I am trying to work through.

(Rebecca)

"Days" and "nights" fluctuate in the women's narratives, in a pendulum movement, shifting between freedom and lawlessness and abandonment. Recalling the memories in itself involves the awakening of dimensions and aspects that were repressed and unfold during our conversations. Although this pendulum movement takes place partly at the conscious level, the constantly renewed consciousness is continuously overwhelmed by the pain of the women's experience of the communal system. It seems that there is a wild and jolting struggle between the desire to cling to the beauty that was "there" and the women's need to bring to light their experience of terror and loneliness. They struggle to express the various aspects, side by side, and it seems that my presence, as a witness to what has endured alone, is not easy for them. Despite the yearning for it, it is a foreign experience for them. At times, they can identify the split in which the experience has been preserved, but the processing of this split is long and slow. Partly it is so because the gaps between the meetings resemble the gaps that they have experienced during childhood, those that had forced them to make use of this split. The mechanism of splitting is necessary for the baby's initial adaptation processes and is recruited to cope with the overflow of anxiety-provoking stimuli (Solan, 2007). The split is also apparent in Alma's description:

> I saw the kibbutz as pastoral and beautifully, and declared myself "healthy," I decided that everything's okay: that my family and my parents are okay. I remember lots of friends and nature and a lot of "alone." These are things that I've been protecting for a very long time and they seemed lovely to me. I thought I wanted to raise my kids in the same way. But I also remember that we had to deal with being very lonely. I can hardly remember parents and family.

The fragmentation of the various aspects of the experience serves the child as a defense of his soul and stems mainly from one's need to maintain a benign memory. The split-off experiences are expressed in the way the experiences take on the opposite meaning during in-depth interviews. Often, the first mention of childhood was colored with feelings of warmth, freedom, space, and creativity, but as the conversations continued, we could feel how the experience loses its resilience, as different aspects of it were echoed. It seems that both the form and the order in which things appeared in the conversations reflected the mental processing that the women had gone through during their lives. As they said themselves, their childhood experiences reappeared differently in the face of various life events, allowing them to reconsider the complexity of their childhood.

The conversations we held with the women seem to have reflected the process of their coping itself; over time, their memories seem to have been pierced with "holes" that threatened the pastoral tranquility they have attributed to their childhood. Their sweet descriptions of freedom, nature, and creativity were overshadowed by the feeling of deep and painful loneliness that was also part of their experience. The recognition of the deep and early absence experience led them to a deeper introspection into their experiences. Their experience of "space" was lit up with the shadows of abandonment and neglect, and "freedom" was re-painted in hues of promiscuity.

> We were children of mother nature, we flew with the birds, but there was no one to catch us when we fell. Actually, we were very alone.
>
> (Nilli)

"Love thy work" 39

There were very promiscuous things that took place, things that happened to me that nobody knew about. There were stupid things that I did. Some of what had happened were like in those stories about orphans.

(Miri)

To this Nina added:

I had to hold everything inside, alone. I didn't think I was allowed to say I was scared. It's like black holes – this night where there's no one. Because they're black, they are blurry. I can only feel the anxiety that comes with it and nothing more. To this day, I dare not sleep alone.

Gradually, more memories are recalled, telling the story of the women's experiences of irresponsibility and of their sense of orphaning. This was not a harmonious process or a peaceful one. Rather, it is an evocative process of remembrance, bringing to life the two impossible ends of the original experience. The childhood movement of the pendulum and the jolts made it hard to patch and integrate the various aspects of their experience. Listening to the women, it was possible to see how the memory of the physical aspects of their childhood – the environment, nature, and space – preserved the positive and benign aspect, while the emotional experience contained the more traumatic aspects of neglect, abandonment, loneliness, and suffering.

Vered described it in the following way:

It was something a bit like an orphanage – the children's home. A feeling of being very lonely. At our parents' house, we felt like guests. We came over at 16:00 and by 19:00 our parents would say, "Let's go to eat dinner," and we would eat alone, in the children's home dining room, without our parents. And today when I think about it – it's just shocking! That experience of being so alone. I didn't share it with anyone because there was no one to share it with. No one was interested in how I felt or in what I was going through. I didn't grow up with my parents. The feeling was that the parents are not very significant. They were on the side, behind the scenes. There was something very, very alone. My internal experience was that of being rejected and it came with my experience with my parents – I felt they have rejected me, because where were they throughout my childhood?

The women's acknowledgment of their experience of the absent mother (or parents) provoked their anger. Regardless, many of the interviewees found it difficult to express direct anger toward their parents, and in many cases, they have even described their need to protect them. Often, there seemed to be a match between the motherhood experiences (of the women's mothers) and the women's own infancy experiences, as things have been told, over and over again, by the mothers to their daughters. When the women expressed their understanding and empathy

40 "Love thy work"

toward their parents, their blame was directed at the "communal system," and the kibbutz as a whole. This can be seen in Vered's words:

> When I was two days old, mom put me in the communal baby's home. The rules were very strict: Every four hours the mothers could breastfeed their babies and this was the only time the mother could spend with her baby. Throughout my life I have been followed by a story my mother had told me; because I was very little, I was also very hungry ... She would breastfeed me and then was required to leave. I had to wait for four hours until the next breastfeeding. She told me how she stood outside the baby's home and heard me scream. I screamed because I was hungry and they wouldn't let her in. This was how my life began. This is where I start. This is like my first childhood memory, which comes out of my mother's stories, but somewhere it is a part of me. I would have never done that to my kids, ever!

It is evident that as the women's experience of pain had been better worked through, their ability to express the anger and to have an honest and exposed dialogue with their parents improved considerably. Many of the women had attested that this ability had evolved over the years, often as a result of the therapeutic process they had been through. The birth of their children, especially the eldest one, often triggered the process of coping with their experiences of the communal system and of the role their biological parents had in their childhood. The encounter with the consequences of their experience of early abandonment had evolved over the years and was gradually exposed, depending on their ability to process it. The motion between the desire and the need to recognize and receive recognition of their experiences, the feelings of anger and pain, can be perceived as attesting to the mechanism of fragmentation whose function is to maintain the parent as a "good internal object." When these women gave birth to their children, their inner discourse with their (internal and external) mothers changed. Becoming mothers facilitated a new experience in which the women could identify not only with the "baby" but also with their mothers, who were forced to submit their babies in the communal system. Becoming mothers aroused much pain and anger, but also compassion.

> Ever since I became a mother, I think differently about things. From a mother's perspective, it is absurd to give away your baby to the children's communal home. Although I do not recall it as something "bad," when I became a mother myself I asked my mother how was it possible to give your child away, at the age of zero?! I cannot understand it and I am glad I didn't have to do it myself.
>
> (Nilli)

These early experiences, and their derivatives, obliged the children in the kibbutz to develop unique survival mechanisms. This need to survive the communal system living arrangements was brought up with all the women and is expressed in the women's diverse styles of coping. The various difficulties have led them to develop various strategies, recruiting and perfecting individual skills in the attempt to cope with feelings of pain and loneliness. From what the women said, it was evident that they needed to find their path to escape the daily distress they have experienced during childhood, and that in most cases the women, even at a very young age, operated a variety of intrapersonal strategies, often assisting the other children with whom they lived together. Alongside their social role, as "helpers," the women talked about their psychic withdrawal, which allowed them a refuge from the external reality and facilitated the opportunity to develop a rich internal world. This was often achieved and cultivated through reading, daydreaming and rich imagination. Some of the women were aware of the way they had used it as a means of repression and denial, and at times even as a dissociative mechanism:

> When I was little in a children's home, I couldn't handle everything, I didn't let myself know how I felt. At best I would cry alone into the pillow.
>
> (Yael)

A child's use of primitive defense mechanisms of repression, denial, and dissociation attest to the existence of a traumatic experience. The early separation from the mother, the unavailability of the parents from the beginning on, and I believe that more than anything else – the maternal absence that these women have experienced as children, profoundly bruises their object relations, both internal and external. The experience of early abandonment is scalded into the baby's mind (Bick, 1968; Tustin, 1986).

Naturally, the women cannot *remember* such early experiences, but the feelings of abandonment, neediness, loneliness, and helplessness that characterized their initial life experiences are awakened by future life events (Aviezer, Sagi, Joels, & Ziv, 1999). Early experiences of maternal absence scar the individual's psyche and soma, and are expressed throughout life, as they have echoed throughout the interviews. It can be assumed that in therapy the process of recalling and processing such early traumatic experiences will require a lot of time and patience as the patient will employ many of her/his initial defensive mechanisms.

Under circumstances of extreme absence, children are often required to employ a variety of coping strategies, from the use of primary defense mechanisms, through the adoption of parental functions (Winnicott, 1960b, 1963). The women described themselves as compliant and as young girls who put in a lot of effort into being "good" and keeping harmonious and conflict-free relationships, as is apparent in Nina's own words:

> I was a good girl. I didn't dare to be something else. I don't remember doing anything that could cause anyone to be mad with me. I didn't want to get in the way. I knew my parents were busy and I don't think I could bother

them. I knew you couldn't. I internalized the rules of the children's home very strictly. It was important for me to be good. Always. To be a good girl. I was so scared of my "metapelet."[3] When she was angry, I was sure the end of the world was coming. She was very authoritative, very, and when she was angry, you could feel that the world was falling on you and you were collapsing under it.

(Nina)

Alternatively, some of the women described strategies of self-harm, through severe feelings of rejection, guilt, and lack of self-worth:

I had a feeling of being very rejected, very unloved, lonely, compliant, and defensive. I had to take everything in and just keep it there, quietly. I didn't express my feelings. The initial experience was very, very, very difficult, very unconnected. Unconnected to emotions, with lots of anger towards the family and an inability to express any of it.

(Vered)

Many of the women's descriptions regarded how they had to deal with the pain on their own, alongside their feeling that their voice had been silenced, unrecognized, and as a consequence – their needs profoundly unmet. One's choice to hold one's self alone reflects the fracture in one's trust in the environment. When the child is overwhelmed by anger and anxiety that cannot be directed (or projected) externally, it becomes aggression that is directed at one's self (internally or employing self-harm). Often this would take the form of painful feelings of guilt, rejection, and lack of self-worth. Many of the women talked about their stubborn "self-holding," even at a very early age, as a way of coping with maternal absence:

With all the fears, you learn to manage. To Ignore them, repress them, overcome, without having to. So that's what I grew up to be – a person dealing with difficult things alone, by myself. I've been thinking about myself as a small child – waking up from nightmares, and there's no one around me. There were only beds with children. There's no mother to calm you down. My parents didn't even know. In the four quality hours we had in the afternoon I wouldn't tell them about the nightmares. If she wasn't there in the middle of the night, then she couldn't have known.

(Alma)

The self-holding and the need to function as a parent of one's own involves the elaboration of one's ability to listen to the parent's needs. Ehrenberg (1992) points to the suppression of the desire of such children. The child internalizes the knowledge of the danger involved in expressing feelings of independence, desire, anger, or any other expression of separateness, which may increase the aggression toward him. Therefore, common reactions in situations of distrust and lack of confidence in the relationship with the adult world will be obedience, submission, and convergence. Alice Miller (1997) notes that children whose parents fail to fulfill their emotional needs assimilate the talent to adapt and adjust to their parents' needs. Winnicott (1971) conceptualizes the "false self" as the suffocation of spontaneous emotions, following the parental unrecognition and maladapted response to the child's dependency needs. Under such circumstances, the child develops a "false self" that takes upon itself the role of the mother. The women's ability to care for themselves is a sign of both their strengths and the maternal absence they have suffered.

However, it was also evident from our conversations with the women therapists who were raised in the communal system, that the various coping mechanisms they had employed as small girls facilitated (and perhaps were enabled by) a rich internal world that had also served them as a significant refuge. In this sense, convergence into an inner world enables a unique and creative dialogue within one's internal world, serving also as a creation of a mental space that can facilitate better coping and relieve one's tension and distress. On the one hand, this internal psychic space served the women to connect with their feelings of pain and guilt, and on the other hand, it was also a place of refuge and a source for comfort and a sense of self-competent, value, and meaning.

Despite the separation from the parents and the nuclear family that sabotaged the sense of belonging, closeness, and security, some of the women were able to maintain a positive relationship with their parents whom they have perceived to be a source of support:

> My parents would always put us to bed, every night. In the middle of the night, I could not call the night-guardians[4] if I couldn't sleep, because I knew my parents would come over to check on me around midnight. And every morning, when they got up for work, they used to come over and say hello. So, they kind of covered the whole night.
>
> (Tamar)

Those who can internalize benign aspects from their relationship with their parents can establish it as a "safety net" that, in turn, can create an alignment that can assist the individual to better hold and contain various difficult situations in life, specifically those that lead to the feeling of loneliness. The women we have talked with were able to develop some object-consistency (Winnicott, 1971), despite the early separation and disconnection from their mother. Through the way they talked about their various childhood experiences, it was possible to note their empathy and the way it had served them throughout their life. Some of them did retain a sense that their mothers cared about them, regardless of their considerable absence and this was also apparent in the women's empathy toward their own mothers' suffering as young mothers who had to submit their babies to the communal system childcare arrangement. Some of them seemed to have been comforted by the thought that their mothers had suffered, not because of revenge, but rather as a sign of how much their mothers had cared about them. Some of the women talked about their "knowledge" of how significant they were to their parents, and this seemed to allow them to formulate a dialogue with their parents, which softened the women's painful experience following the parents' absence and unavailability.

Similar to the complexity of the experience with the parents, the always present peer group served both as a source of some difficulties and as the base for a very meaningful experience of *belonging*. The women's descriptions of this indicated the tremendous importance the peer group had in creating a holding environment, often protecting the children from their profound loneliness:

> I think I've been unconsciously a therapist almost since I was born. I've already taken care of her as a small child and a young girl. Somehow, I was able to "feel" people and know how to help them. Sometimes even at my own expense. There was something very basic that attracted me to people, and to the attempt to create harmony in disharmonious situations. In the kibbutz, you have to deal with it all the time … We had some difficult dynamics between the children. So, the same role of the compromiser the peacemaker, of making sure things are in harmony, and inquiring why things happen the way they do … I took all of this on myself, in this complex place that was the kibbutz and the children's home.
>
> (Miri)

In the case of these women who grew up and chose to care for others, as professional psychotherapists, the kibbutz children's home had provided them with as many interpersonal interactions as possible, in which they shaped their ability to give to others. In this sense, belonging to a group of children was an existential component in the establishment of one's attachment pattern, capacities of containment, and the need to protect others. In this sense, the maternal absence and the presence of peers were a cause for psychic growth (besides traumatic experiences). Ogden (1985) writes about the child who is required to adopt psychological coping strategies in the absence of a mother who can assist him in doing so. Shengold (1975) argues that ongoing loss and deprivation enable the child to develop coping strategies that can facilitate a reasonable mental existence. The relationships with the children as peers became, for some, a key force in developing coping strategies which served the women throughout their lives. Following the women who took part in this study, we could note a clear pattern of taking a parental and a therapeutic role concerning others, through which they could mobilize inner strength for the benefit of the other, thereby increasing the sense of self-worth and personal ability (Miller, 1991). In line with Miller's words, the women have described the "therapeutic role" as an internal mechanism that was constantly ingrained in them, and its use as a survival strategy that gave them a sense of strength and meaning, as well as a sense of control that was so vital for them in the various situations in which they felt helpless. Schafer (2006) argues that the basic transformation of the soul is created by recognizing the new abilities that become a part of the self. The process of self-discovery, as described by the interviewees, weaved together the intra-psychic took with the social and family environment.

The ability to act is portrayed as an existential choice that is essential for building a sense of competence. During their childhood, this choice was unconscious and the specific form varied. For some, it was in the form of social leadership, rebellion against the authority of the "system," social initiative, or by taking responsibility for peers. Either form was expressed mainly within the peer group and had a "parental" aspect to it. The women described their "choice" of childhood role as one which helped them to manage their loneliness and "make sense" of what was happening. In retrospect, they all attributed to their role, within the peer group, much of what has helped them through and led them to their career choice, as therapists.

The interviews indicate that the career choice was a complex process, some of which unconscious. The women found it difficult to relate to this issue and it required long and in-depth thought, albeit it was evident that the process of professional self-development began in early childhood and occurred mainly in two dimensions – the intrapersonal and the interpersonal. While the factors associated with the interpersonal–environmental dimension related mainly to their childhood and seemed to have been unconscious, the intrapersonal factors related both to their childhood and to the women's adulthood, and therefore were more conscious. Concerning the links between their childhood in the kibbutz and their choice to become therapists, they have said the following:

> I'm hypersensitive to loneliness and abandonment. And for some reason, all the abandoned patients always find me. I'm kind of inviting them into my life. It's like I'm giving them the feeling that I've been through this and that I understand them and therefore can help them. It could be the counter (transference), even though I'm more aware of these places. Today, however, in my countertransference, I feel their abandonment and pain as if it were mine.
>
> (Nina)

The children's communal arrangement intensified the social norms and values on which the kibbutz was founded. Individuals in the kibbutz were expected to give up any personal belongings and to reduce their personal space to a minimum. All was to be shared equally, and individualism was regarded as "not desired to say the least." Children were brought up to work hard, to not be weak which was equated to being emotional, to share everything with everyone. In many ways, "sharing" and "giving" were valued most highly and became one's "mother language." These norms and values that were universal to the kibbutz life, became a role for some of the individuals, such as the women we have interviewed, albeit they took on the values of sharing and giving and let go of the norms that prohibited the expression of emotions. Many of these women talked about having a therapeutic role when they were in kindergarten, and it seems that in many ways, they were "born" and "raised" to be therapists of others. Theories of learning (Krumboltz, Mitchell, & Johns, 1975; Lipset, 1962) emphasize processes of learning and the internalization of social values as influential to one's occupational choice. Social and cultural dimensions play an intermediary role in the individual's career choice and expectations. From a developmental perspective (Chartrand et al., 1990, ; Ginzberg, 1984; Super, 1953), the "professional self" develops during early childhood and is shaped over the years, relying on identifications with the adults and social structures surrounding the child.

Indeed, the women talked about their unique roles within their peer group, which had allowed them to establish a stronger social position and to express their unique selves within the group. The ability of these women to express themselves, even at the tender ages of kindergarten, and position themselves in a "therapeutic" caretaker role with their peers, created a rewarding dialogue between the external and the internal and strengthened their self-identity. In many ways, this role helped the women to solve the conflict built into the group situation; against the constant tension between the "collective" and the "personal," the therapeutic role acted as a bridge that enabled them to hold to both ends of the conflict, as it allowed them both their individuality and to conform to the fundamental values of "sharing." The women described how this position that they held within the group allowed them to simultaneously be individualistic and compliant to the social structures of the kibbutz in general and the communal system in particular. They took on themselves, from very early on, the complementary function of the "caregiver adult," making good use of personality traits of being (over)conscious and sensitive to their pain as well as that of others. They described similar dynamics in the context of their biological families, in terms of reversed roles. Often, in their relationships with their parents, these women described taking on themselves the role of the "responsible-caretaking adult," a role which was necessary for them not only because of perceiving their parents as "weak" and "helpless," but also as a means of protecting themselves from feelings of loss and pain. In many ways, these women have chosen to silence their crying in favor of listening to the crying of others.

The informal role of a "caretaker" that the women have adopted in childhood allowed them to experience the intimacy that they needed. Their capacity to "feel the other's feeling" helped them to silence their own, albeit creating an omnipotent sense of control over internal and external reality. The women have noted that, to a large extent, choosing to become a therapist allows them the same defensive structure, although more consciously. Encountering the pain of their patients touches their private agonies, stimulates deep identification, and feeds their nurturance needs. In many ways, they all say, becoming a therapist has enabled them to be the adult they did not have, as infants and children.

> We all know why we wanted to become therapists. First of all, it was a way of taking care of ourselves. And in the case of kibbutz children, who had so many caretakers but no one took care of them, it's ironic. I wanted to

build people's homes and obviously, I wanted to build my own house. But an emotional home. I believe I needed to feel at home inside me because I didn't receive it in my childhood. I've been working on this pretty much my whole life.

(Nina)

As Nina said it so bluntly, the need to take care of one's "self" was a major factor in choosing the therapeutic profession (Neumann, 1991). In contrast to the therapeutic role that was part of their childhood, one that had involved repressing and dissociation of significant parts of the self, the role of a therapist, in adulthood, requires the opposite and enables the individual to better contain one's psychic life. The reciprocity that is created within the therapeutic encounter makes it possible to recognize the needs that arise, simultaneously, in the therapist and the patient. Both require emotional intimacy. Within the therapeutic relationship, an endless variety of emotions may arise and be expressed, verbally and nonverbally, much of which was ignored or repressed during the patient's and therapist's childhood. Fox (1990) notes that therapists can experience a wide range of intense emotions, from the relatively safe distance between therapist and patient, and Harari (2002) found that many therapists are motivated by the desire to be close to the unconscious and experience mental suffering, as a mean of better understanding their inner world. Indeed, the women described the reciprocity created through the transference–countertransference and the links it creates between the various psychic aspects. Many of the women emphasized the aspect of "reparation" that the therapeutic relationship holds for them, specifically concerning their ability to work through the patient's issues with dependence, loneliness, and yearning for love.

My childhood and complexity of containing the external, the complexity with the peer group, with the "metaplot" [caretakers], with the "system," with the community, with all these people that you are constantly very exposed to … As a therapist, today, it's my complexities with myself, internally, interpersonal relationships. Understanding all sorts of things that I don't yet fully understand about my relationships with my closest family members, but today I can do it at my own pace, step by step.

(Noga)

Summary

Tamar said to us: *"You could say that the therapeutic work is all about listening, carefully, to the cry of babies … To cries that were unnoticed for years, of babies and children that did not receive the attention and care they needed."*

Listening to how the women describe their childhood dynamics in the kibbutz seems to indicate that the most central aspect of their choice to become therapists is that it allows them an experience of "reparation." This experience of reparation is created by the ability to be close to other people's needs of intimacy, and through the therapeutic working through of the patient's experiences of loneliness. Many of them recalled the significant childhood experience of being alone and afraid at night, often crying out for help, yet not being attended to. These unheard cries, and the cries the child ceased to cry, as a result, have impaired, to various extent, the child's ability to grow psychologically (Ogden, 2004). The women describe the therapeutic relationship as allowing them yet another encounter with their internal world, enhancing their dialogue with their experience of loneliness, rediscovering it, and the creation of a new reparative experience (Durban, 2004). Therapy is, thus, a space that allows psychological growth, for both the patient and them.

Shengold (1975) in his paper on Kipling's life argues that the more one "knows," the greater his degree of freedom. Given one's ability to say to himself and others, "I am the man. I've suffered. I was there," mental capabilities and self-image can be preserved (Whitman, 1855 cited in Seshadri 2002). These women therapists, who have all undergone extensive analytic therapy themselves, have gained considerable "knowledge" about their own childhood experiences and their significance. This, in turn, allows them to be in touch with their past, and also to be "free" to experience their presence. Their choice to become therapists, allows them to be continually (and constantly) in touch with their internal world and emotional experiences, constituting a reparation of the profound loneliness they have experienced as children. By attending to their patients' pains and suffering, and by their ability to offer intimacy and hope, these women attend to their own childhood experiences of loneliness. In many ways, they are the mother that was absent from their own lives.

Notes

1 This chapter was previously published in *Ma'arag: The Israel Annual of Psychoanalysis*, 2012, Volume 32. Magnes Press/The Sigmund Freud Center, The Hebrew University.
2 Based on the thesis of M. Valdman, supervised by the author
3 "Metapelet" is the Hebrew term for a "nannie" or the caretaker at the communal children's homes. It is also the Hebrew word for a woman-therapist
4 Night-guardians was a special role assigned to two women in the kibbutz who had to guard all the children during the night. The women in the kibbutz each had to fulfill this role for one week a year. During nighttime, these two women were responsible for all the young children in the kibbutz (around 200). They were connected to the various communal children's homes, by intercom, through which they could hear if any of the children cried or called for them.

References

Ainsworth, M.D.S., Blehar, M.C., Waters, E., & Wall, S. (1978). *Patterns of attachment: Assessed in the strange situation and at home*. Hillsdale, NJ: Erlbaum.

Anzieu, D. (1970). Skin ego. In *Psychoanalysis in France* (pp. 17–32). New York: International Universities Press, 1980.

Aviezer, O., van IJzendoorn, M.H., Sagi, A., & Scheungal, C. (1994). "Children of the dream" revisited: 70 years of collective early child care in Israeli kibbutzim. *Psychological Bulletin*, 116: 99–116.

Avieser, O., Sagi, A., Joels, T., & Ziv, Y. (1999). Emotional availability and attachment representations in kibbutz infants and their mothers. *Developmental psychology*, 35(3): 811–821.

Balaban, A. (2001). *Shivaa*. Tel-Aviv: The Kibbutz-Poaalim Pub. (In Hebrew).

Balint, M. (1968). *The basic fault*. London: Tavistock.

Bettelheim, B. (1969). *The children of the dream*. London: Collier-Macmillan.

Bick, E. (1968). The experience of the skin in early object relations. *The International Journal of Psycho-Analysis*, 49: 484–486.

Bion, W.R. (1961). *Experiences in groups and other papers*. London: Tavistock.

Bion, W. (1962). The psycho-analytic study of thinking. *International Journal of Psycho-Analysis*, 43: 306–310.

Bion, W. (1970). *Attention and interpretation*. London: Tavistock.

Bollas, C. (1992). *Being a character – Psychoanalysis and self-experience*. New York: Hill & Wang.

Bowen, M. (1986). *Family Therapy in Clinical Practice*. New York: Aronson. (1978).

Bowlby, J. (1973). *Attachment and loss – Vol. 2. Separation: Anxiety and anger*. New York: Basic Books.

Bowlby, J. (1979). *The making and breaking of affectional bonds*. London: Tavistock.

Bowlby, J. (1982 [1969]). *Attachment and loss – Vol.1. Attachment* (2nd ed.). New York: Basic Books.

Bowlby, J. (1988). *A secure base: Clinical applications of attachment theory*. London: Routledge.

Brown, D. (1996). Status of career development theories. In D. Brown, L. Brooks & Associates (Eds.), *Career choice and development* (pp. 513–525). San Francisco: Jossey-Bass.

Chartrand, J.M., Robbins, S.B., Morrill, W.H., & Boggs, K. (1990). The development and validation of the Career Factors Inventory. *Journal of Counseling Psychology*, 37: 490–501.

Donnell, F. (1991). *The impact of family based versus communal sleeping arrangements on the attachment Patterns of kibbutz infants*. Unpublished Master thesis, Haifa University, Israel.

Doron-Yaron, A. (2001). The *development of self identity of MA Students of Educational Counselling – the contribution of academic field work*. MA Thesis, Tel Aviv University.

Durban, J. (2004). Raparation – The place of the Third. *Sihot*, 19(1): 59–66. (In Hebrew).

Ehrenberg, D. (1992). Abuse and desire. In D. Ehrenberg (Ed.), *The intimate edge* (pp. 159–191). New York: Norton.

Eshel, O. (1998). 'Black Holes', deadness and existing analytically. *The International Journal of Psycho-Analysis*, 79: 1115–1130.

Ezra, A. (2001). *Being a Kibbutz mother to a child who is handicapped*. A MA Thesis, The Hebrew University of Jerusalem.

Fox, A. (1990). *The effects and consequences of being a family therapist on the family dynamics of the therapist*. A MA Thesis, Tel Aviv University.

Ginzberg, E. (1984). Career development. In: D. Brown, L. Brooks & Associates (Eds.), *Career choice and development* (pp. 169–192). San Francisco: Jossey-Bass Publishers.

Harari, Y. (2002). *Being an experienced counsellor*. A MA Thesis, Tel Aviv University.

50 "Love thy work"

Holland, J.L., Johnson, J.A., & Asama, N.F. (1993). The vocational identity scale: A diagnostic and treatment tool. *Journal of Career Assessment*, 1: 1–12.

Holland, J.L. (1997). *Making vocational choices: A theory of vocational personalities and work environments*. Odessa, FL: Psychologica Sassement Ressources.

Jannof-Bulman, R. (1992). *Shattered assumptions: Towards a new psychology of trauma*. New York: The Free Press.

Khan, M.M.R. (1963). The concept of cumulative trauma. *Psychoanalytic Study of the Child*, 18: 286–306.

Kleiberg, A. (2004). *Of a mother's love and the fear of the father – Another observation of the family*. Tel Aviv: Tel Aviv University Press and Keter Pub.

Klein, M. (1963). Mourning and its relation to Mani-depressive states*The International Journal of Psycho-Analysis*, 21: 125–153.

Klein, M. (1952). Some theoretical conclusions regarding the emotional life of the infant. In M. Masud, & R. Khan (Eds.), *Envy and Gratitude and Other Works 1946-1963* (pp. 61–93). The International Psycho-Analytical Library, 104: 1–346.

Klein, M. (1957). Envy and gratitude: A study of unconscious sources. In M. Masud, & R. Khan (Eds.), *Envy and Gratitude and Other Works 1946-1963* (pp. 176–235). The International Psycho-Analytical Library, 104: 1–346.

Kohut, H. (1971). *The analysis of the self*. New York: International Universities Press.

Kohut, H. (1977). *The restoration of the self*. New York: International Universities Press.

Krumbolts, J.D., Mitchel, L.K., & Gelatt, H.G. (1975). Applications of social learning theory of career selection. *Focus on Guidance*, 8: 1–16.

Lamdan, A. (2004). *From silence to a cry, to talking*. Ramat-Efal: Yad Tabenkin. (In Hebrew).

Lanir, Y. (2004). *The Kibbutz in the Israeli society – The pathology of a crisis*. Ramat-Efal: Yad Tabenkin. (In Hebrew)

Leshem, N. (1991). *The songs of the grass*. Ramat-Efal: Yad Tabenkin. (In Hebrew).

Lev-Wiesel, R. (2000). The effect of children's sleeping arrangements (communal vs. familial) on fatherhood among men in an Israeli kibbutz. *The Journal of Social Psychology*, 140(5): 580–588.

Levkovitch, R. (2007). *Two houses for one dream*. Jerusalem: Carmel Publication. (In Hebrew).

Lieblich, A. (1984). *Kibbutz, a place*. Jerusalem: Shoken Pub. (In Hebrew).

Lipset, L. (1962). Social factors in vocational development. *Journal of Counseling and Development*, 40(5): 416–503.

Mahler, M. (1975). *The psychological birth of the human infant: Symbiosis and individuation*. NY: Basic Books.

Mahler, M. (1976). *On human symbiosis and the vicissitudes of individuation*. New York: Library of Human Behavior.

Miller, A. (1997). *The drama of the gifted child – The search for the true self* (3rd Ed.). New York: Basic Books.

Miller, J.B. (1991). The Development of Women's Sense of Self. In J.V. Jordan, A.G. Kaplan, J.B. Miller, I.P. Stiver, & J.L. Surrey (Eds.), *Women's Growth in Connection – Writings From the Stone Center*. NY: The Guilford Press. (pp. 11–26).

Mitchell, S.A., & Black, M.J. (1995). *Freud and beyond*. New York: Basic Books.

Nadlin, A. (2002). *The prestige of being a social worker*. A MA Thesis, Tel Aviv.

Neil, A.S. (1960). *Summerhill school*. New York: St. Martin's Press.

"Love thy work"   51

Noy, P. (2006). *Psychoanalysis after Freud*. Ben Shemen: Modan Pub. (In Hebrew).

Neumann, M. (1991). The developmental phases of in a therapist's life. *Sihot*, 5(2): 62–81. (In Hebrew).

Ogden, T.H. (1985). The mother, the infant and the matrix: Interpretations of aspects of the work of Donald Winnicott. *Contemporary Psychoanalysis*, 21: 346–371.

Ogden, T. (1992). *The matrix of the mind – Object Relations and the psychoanalytic dialogue*. London: Marshfield Library.

Ogden, T.H. (2004). This art of psychoanalysis: Dreaming undreamt dreams and interrupted crics. *The International Journal of Psycho-Analysis*, 85: 857–877.

Oppenheim, D. (1998). Perspectives on infant mental health from Israel: the case of changes in collective sleeping on the kibbutz. *Infant Mental Health Journal*, 19(1): 76–86.

Rabin, A.I. (1965). *Growing up in the kibbutz*. New York: Springer.

Roe, A. (1957). Early determinants of vocational choice. *Journal of Counseling Psychology*, 4: 212–217.

Rosenthal, M. (1988). *Daily experience of toddlers, in three child care settings in Israel: Family day care, Center day care and Kibbutz*. Unpublished manuscript.

Rosner, M. (2004). *The Kibbutz at a time of change*. Tel-Aviv: The Kibbutz-Poaalim Pub.

Sagi, A., Lamb, M.A., Lewkowicz, K., Shoham, R., Dvir, R., & Estes, D. (1985). Security of infant-mother-father and metapelet among kibbutz-reared Israeli children. *Monographs of the society for research in Child Development*, 50: 257–275, (1–2, Serial No. 209).

Sagi, A., van IJzendoorn, M.H., Aviezer, O., Donnell, F., & Mayselles, O. (1994). Sleeping out of home in a kibbutz communal arrangement: It makes a difference for infant-mother attachment. *Child Development*, 65: 992–1004.

Segal, H. (1973). *Introduction to the work of Melanie Klein*. London: Routledge.

Seshadri, V. (2002). Rereading; Whitman's Triumph. *The American Scholar*, 71(1): 136–140.

Shengold, L. (1975). An attempt at soul murder—Rudyard Kipling's early life and work. *The Psychoanalytic Study of the Child*, 30: 683–723.

Solan, R. (2007). *The childhood's riddle*. Tel-Aviv: Modan Pub. (In Hebrew)

Spiro, M.E. (1958). *Children of the Kibbutz*. Cambridge, MA: Harvard University Press.

Stern, D.N. (1992). *Dairy of a baby – What your child sees, feels, and experiences*. New York: Basic Books.

Stern, D.N., & Bruschweiler-Stern, N. (1998). *The birth of a mother – How the motherhood experience changes you forever*. NY: Basic Books.

Super, D.E. (1953). A theory of vocational development. *American Psychologist*, 8: 185–190.

Super, D.E. (1996). The life-span, life-space approach to careers. In: D. Brown, L. Brooks & Associates (Eds.), *Career choice and development* (pp. 121–178). San Francisco: Jossey-Bass Publishers.

Tustin, F. (1986). *Autistic barriers in neurotic patients*. London: Karnak Books.

Winnicott, D.W. (1960a). The theory of the parent-infant relationship. In D.W. Winnicott (Ed.), *The maturational processes and the facilitating environment* (pp. 37–55). New York: International Universities Press, 1965.

Winnicott, D.W. (1960b). Ego distortion in terms of true and false self. In D.W. Winnicott (Ed.), *The maturational processes and the facilitating environment* (pp. 140–152). New York: International Universities Press, 1965.

Winnicott, D.W. (1963). Communicating and not communicating leading to a study of certain opposites. In D.W. Winnicott (Ed.), *The maturational processes and the facilitating environment* (pp. 179–192). New York: International Universities Press, 1965.

Winnicott, D.W. (1971). *Playing and reality*. London: Routledge.

Winnicott, D.W. (1987). *Babies and their mothers*. Cambridge, MA: Persues Pub.

Winnicott, D.W. (2009). *True self – False self*. Tel-Aviv: Dvir Pub. (In Hebrew).

Chapter 3

That which was "not"

Some thoughts regarding Oedipus's modern conflicts[1]

Introduction

There are important questions that did not even occur to our analytic ancestors, partly because they lived in an era where such questions and situations were beyond imagination. I am referring to questions concerning how the Oedipus complex applies in cases in which a child has two parents of the same gender, or has only one parent. It may be time for us to rethink or reconsider the modern Oedipus in light of the situations faced by our present and future patients. Although following theories of object relations, psychoanalysis has focused much of its attention on mother–infant relations, the father has remained a crucial figure in our understanding of the child's psychic development. Not only for Freud himself, as the monolithic "Father of Psychoanalysis," the Oedipus complex is still the focal point of much psychoanalytic theory and practice.

Nonetheless, since Freud, analytic writers have been intrigued by the various meanings and consequences of the Oedipus complex (Fenichel, 1931; Loewald, 1979; Searles, 1959; Britton, 1989; Celenza, 2013)[2].

Fenichel (1931) suggests simple solutions to two contradictory assertions that he makes in referring to the oedipal complex (p. 412). He highlights some significant assumptions regarding the oedipal conflict: "identification with the parents, by means of which the Oedipus complex is mastered, is in fact a decisive step in the formation of human character" (p. 414). And

> the danger so deeply feared unconsciously and thought to be bound up with the gratification of instinct is, first, that of the loss of the parents' love, and secondly – singularly enough – of physical injury to the genitals, i.e., of "castration."
>
> (p. 415)

These claims of Fenichel's point to external reality (identification with real external objects and the parents' communication of their love) as a significant factor in the development, resolution, and consequences of the Oedipus complex: There needs to be a parent that the child can identify with, and a parent whose love

DOI: 10.4324/9781003203193-4

54 That which was "not"

the child is afraid of losing, and manages not to forget, to healthily "master" the oedipal conflict:

> It is impossible to lay down a law as to why the Oedipus complex is, in practice, mastered in one case and not in another. But we can understand how, in certain individuals, through particular experiences, or experiences reacted to with their particular constitution, the Oedipus complex and castration anxiety were prematurely aroused or exceptionally powerfully stimulated.
>
> (Fenichel, 1931, p. 417)

The modern era allows, albeit ambivalently, for the diversity of marital and parental configurations. This is partly a reflection of changes in social norms and partly due to medical–technological advances in sperm/egg donations and IVF.

These social and medical changes should draw our attention, as psychoanalysts, to possible changes in the way the Oedipus complex, if the term is still useful, is experienced. Today, more children are born and raised by single-parent-by-choice, or by same-gender parents. These children do not have parents of two different genders, and we must look analytically into some of the issues that, as a result, may arise for our patients – whether they be children or parents. I owe much to Winnicott, Loewald, Ogden, and Warren Poland, who emphasize individuality and otherness. Poland (2011) states that "The psychoanalyst's task is facilitating the introspection and self-mastery of the analysand, paying particular attention to the exposure and exploration of unconscious forces, always working in the service of the other" (p. 355). Poland adds that "Reflection on years spent in the clinical laboratory has led me to hold a profound respect for three foundational principles: individuality, otherness, and outsiderness" (p. 355).

Building on Ogden's (2006) idea that "the task of each new generation is to make use of, destroy and reinvent the creations of the previous generation" (p. 651), I would like to rethink this delicate issue. Even today, few, I presume, would argue the importance of the father's presence and his possible effects on the child's development. Because a growing number of children are being raised in fatherless (or motherless) families, we must re-examine the very notion of the Oedipus complex.

While in Freud's era, the "family" consisted basically of a "mother"–"father"–"child" configuration, the modern family assumes a more complex unit. More often than men, women choose to be single parents (Javda, Badger, Morrissette, & Golombok, 2009). This is so, partly because women are often socialized to prioritize motherhood, and partly because technology allows them to require only a sperm donor. At the same time, men who wish to become single fathers, or gay parents, need an egg donor and a surrogate. Despite these social and medical–technological changes, psychoanalytic thinking has not changed its view of the father–mother–child family unit.

Most psychoanalysts still perceive the Oedipus complex as the core of psychoanalytic theory and practice (Etchegoyen, 1985, pp. 3–4).

In recent years a growing body of research has been concerned with the development of children raised within same-gender families, but these studies are mostly developmental in their orientation (Maccallum & Golombok, 2004). It is interesting to note that the study of Golombok, Tasker, and Murray (1997) indicates that

> children raised in fatherless families from infancy experienced greater warmth and interaction with their mothers and were more securely attached to them, although they perceived themselves to be less cognitively and physically competent than their peers from father present families.
>
> (p. 783)

Even these results indicated that there is a difference between same-gender families and two-gender families.

I want to emphasize that by suggesting that a male father is not the same as a "father construct," I am not, in any way, opposing parenting in gay marriages or single-parenting. Rather, , I am raising the question of whether the oedipal construct involving two parents of different genders *is* embodied in one's psyche–soma? It is, as Freud (1915, p. 269, 1917, p. 371) called it a "primal phantasy," an unconscious mental construct passed along biologically in ways that could not be explained then, and could not be defined now? While the evolution of a construct such as the mother–father family may exist, changes require additional time, regardless of how revolutionary or positive, or morally correct they may be.

Ehrensaft (2000) discusses the issue from a psychoanalytic perspective and cautions us to take into consideration that: "As we watch sperm transformed into men and men reduced to sperm, we witness both the construction and the destruction of the father" (p. 390). Ehrensaft further suggests that "Introducing a sperm donor into the creation of a family promotes a paradoxical construction and destruction of the father, both the real and the imagined one, the genetic and the social one" (p. 391). Ehrensaft stresses the role the sperm donor may play in the child's unconscious fantasy (p. 392) and discusses the child's possible construction of a "generic father" in fantasy. Corbett (2001) discusses some of the consequences of growing up within same-gender families, specifically about growing up "in the face of prevailing cultural norms" (p. 604). Like Ehrensaft, Corbett discusses the child's curiosity over the question of "father" vs. "donor" and his or her experience of often being caught up between the mother's explanation and his/her fantasies. Contemporary analysts, such as Aron (1995) have suggested the need to divert our analytic attention from the primal scene, in terms of parental sexuality, to "the child's experience, elaboration, and personal mythology of the interaction and relationship between the parents, which is often best symbolized by the child's image of the parents in sexual intercourse or some form of pre-genital sexual activity" (p. 206).

These studies offer valuable insight into the external–social–constructed lives of same-gender families and, of course, as the unconscious fantasies of both parents and children. Nevertheless, to the best of my knowledge, various essential questions are still left unanswered. For example, the gender of the "father" figure is seldom addressed, and we are accustomed to thinking of the "father" as a "man." The father's "otherness," regarding the mother's position, is enhanced by the fact that he belongs to a gender different from the female mother. Similarly, it is necessary to understand better the analyst and analytic setting's roles, concerning the creation of an intersubjective space in which the "third," as "other," can thrive.

Taking these social changes into account, the modern family calls our attention to some new questions: (1) Is the father figure's gender a given? (2) What is the essence of the father figure's "otherness"? (3) What may influence our patients' decisions to parent a "fatherless" or "motherless" child? (4) What is the role of psychoanalysis and the analyst in determining the patient's capacity to hold a "third" and an "otherness"? It may be too soon to conclude the experiences of children who are raised without a father or a mother – as is the case of children who are born via sperm-egg donations and who are raised either by a single mother or father, or children who are being raised by a gay couple. But it may not be too early to rethink our analytic conceptualizations concerning the new family configurations we are dealing with in our patients.

As an analyst, I have worked for many decades with lesbian and single mothers-by-choice (whose children were born from sperm donations). I have been intrigued by the possible "cooperation" (perhaps by means of inter-generational transference) of child and mother, in terms of the fantasy of the "killing of the father."

I am concerned about the possible unconscious fantasy that the child without a male father may have conspired with the mother to rid the family of a father. This may lead to excessive repression of aggression due to the child's fantasies that he/she has successfully killed his/her missing parent. I had to depend on clinical experience to begin to respond to my speculations concerning these matters. In what follows, I will discuss analytic work with two patients who have helped me weigh the merits of my thoughts.

Clinical material

Robin

"You certainly have a lot of pens," was the first thing Robin remarked, immediately upon entering my office for the first time. Robin had chosen me "carefully" after "checking me up" for more than two years of attending a program I was a part of. I can still recall my astonishment when she approached me and asked whether she could start therapy with me. I did not have the slightest idea that she liked me. I agreed to start working with her and noted that "secret love" might be an issue.

Robin's tendency toward self-holding was immediately apparent within the transference–countertransference relationship we established. She was the most

That which was "not"   57

dutiful patient I have ever worked with: She always arrived on time (although coming from afar), never missed a session, recalled her dreams, in detail, and often initiated intelligent interpretations. There seemed little I could add to the work she was doing by herself. Robin was very restrained in her behavior, and hardly ever looked at me. When entering my office, she walked straight to the couch, sat down, took off her shoes, put her socks on, and laid down. Robin would recline on her back, her hands folded on her chest. She did not move; she did not cry. It was always the same.

Robin's dreams had one exciting and unique feature in common – they were all monochromatic. I felt caught up in the detailed landscape of her unconscious life – buried beneath piles of conscious detailed self-interpretations, which she thought of before our session. Gradually, I came to experience Robin's loneliness and painful experience of exclusion. For a while, I abstained from saying much about the contents of her dreams. I referred to them mainly by telling her that she had done so much work, that there seemed little I could add, and also that doing the work by herself gave her a sense of security because she did not have to test her trust in me.

Robin was 29 and single when we started working together and struggling to come to terms with the end of a long-term relationship with her girlfriend, whom she plainly described as "disturbed." Our relationship turned "upside down" when war broke out in Israel in 2008. Robin lived in a remote town on the north border of Israel. When the war started, the area where Robin lived was targeted with numerous missiles. Robin demanded that I call her whenever there was a missile attack. Not only was that impossible (there were days of hundreds of rockets), but I was also reluctant to do so. I told Robin that she could call me whenever she wanted, but that was not enough; she insisted that I should be the one to initiate the calls. I had mixed feelings about accommodating her and felt guilty and privileged because I lived in a place that suffered relatively few missile attacks. Still, I was also angry for being pressured, as well as worried and concerned for her. I reassured Robin that I was there for her. She would reply by saying that calling me was not the same as my calling her. I sympathized with her wish, and said that indeed it is not the same, but added "why should it be?"

These exchanges remained a painful issue between us, and we repeatedly returned to it throughout the years. It took me a long time to realize that it was my refusal to "live with Robin" as a means of establishing an as-if-sameness that was a crucial turning point in our analytic work. I truly disappointed her, making her angry, perhaps for the first time. She refused to "forgive me" for not initiating the phone calls, and I told her I did "get" her disappointment and anger over my not behaving as she wanted me to. But I added, "We think differently about this." It was clear that she was asking me – understandably, from the transference perspective – to take care of her, while I, as her analyst, was asking her to take care of herself. Robin was determined not to negotiate this time around. Her previous compliant behavior was replaced by active rebellion and opposition – I was clearly, and aggressively, placed in the position of the external "other." It was

58   That which was "not"

difficult for me to be experienced as "not empathic," "tough," and "mean," and I wished I could have based my reluctance to call her on some "analytic" ethics or "rules" (as was suggested by my supervisor at the time) – but that was not the case. I was reluctant to "live" together with Robin and make-believe to act as if we were going through this war together.

My failure to reciprocate Robin's love became apparent during one Monday session, at which she confessed, "I love you." I hesitated, for a moment, trying to figure out what to say, and poof! The "magic" was over, and Robin disappeared (emotionally), refused to talk with me when she came to her next session three days later and announced that she had fallen in love, for the first time in years, with a married woman, mother of three children. I had been replaced in the blink of an eye. I felt as if I were a mere observer of an unfolding tragedy. Much of Robin and that woman's relationship was virtual'' and 'imaginary'. I was no longer the overt love object, pursued by Robin, and failing her by my refusal to be her spouse. Instead, I was recast as the "audience," and became the "other," to whom Robin could return, five times a week, to talk about her adventures, "out there in the world."

I felt compassion for Robin, and I was worried, angry, and sad for her. I was aware that both Robin and I were experiencing, to some extent, "our" love affair via a third person. Two years after this set of events, Robin told me she had done something she was feeling incredibly guilty about. She had been secretly reading some online emails. (These were emails sent regarding mundane issues of the Institute and a project I was involved in, which leaked into the internet.) There was nothing personally revealing about these emails; their significance for Robin, she confessed, lay in the fact that they involved a secretive, stolen penetration into my life. My immediate reaction was to thank her for telling me about it: "It must have been challenging for you to keep such a secret for so long." This enabled us to talk about her need to steal her way into my "other life" and about her anger at me for having "a full life" without her.

The struggle to take her place in somebody else's life was elaborated when she talked about her family background. Robin has three older sisters. She described herself as being her parents' last attempt to have a boy. Talking painfully about how it felt to fail her parents, she mentioned that her father chose a gender-neutral name for her and raised her to be "like himself."

She described her parents' marriage as "horrible" and talked at length about feeling that they should never have divorced. She blamed her mother for most of her parents' fights and could not understand why her father remained married to her. She described her mother as "depressed, spending whole days locked in her bedroom." She was angry with her mother, not only for being so depressed but also for sharing with her too much information regarding her hostile relationship with Robin's father.

"Sometimes," she said, "I feel so angry with her I wish she was dead."

All this unfolded as Robin and I were working through her confession about reading those emails. At her own pace and on her terms, she was able to face the fact that I had a life that did not include her. The pain she felt associated with this recognition could be so intense that it drove her to do things she had not imagined she was capable of, such as secretly "stealing" her way into my life. This enabled Robin to talk about her jealousy of her father's full life and her despair, and the rage she felt with her mother's reluctance (or inability) to live more fully. I thought of Robin's oedipal fantasy of rivalry with her mother as being profoundly compromised by her inability to enliven her mother (if only for the "joy" of re-killing her). To a much sadder extent, it was compromised by her gradual realization that she, too, was "dead" and lived her life without "real" love.

In time, Robin was able to deal with her own depression and better understand the way she used to defend herself, specifically by regressing to an imaginary life, in which negotiation and disappointments are to be tolerated. It was not easy for Robin to forgive me for having a full life since she often felt left out. When Robin began her analysis, she said that she had chosen me because I seemed to be a vivacious and busy woman, so she would not have to worry about my "deadness." Regardless of her perception of me as being entirely different from her mother, she did, of course, come to experience me, within the transference as both "other" and the "same" as her mother, especially when she experienced me rejecting her. Nonetheless, by not projecting on to Robin my reluctance to call during the missile attacks, and by not apologizing about it (i.e., taking it back), I was presenting myself as another who is not an extension of her desires and/or omnipotent control. By not encouraging her to believe that I could fulfill all of her needs, and not judging her for wanting me to, we were eventually able to make the gap between us, though a constant source of tension, tolerable.

I acknowledged Robin's profound and continuous disappointment with me, especially in terms of how she experienced our mutual investment in the relationship, to be so different. Robin traveled from afar, was on time, and very serious about her analysis, while I was not even willing to call her when she was bombed day and night. Robin was angry with me for being married, having children, taking vacations, and having other patients. More than anything, she was mad at me for not wanting her to be "everything." On the other hand, I wanted her to have a life of her own, and she experienced that as a rejection of her devotion to me. In one of our sessions, I told her, "I can be a lot of things, but not 'everything'." Robin was quiet for a few moments and then said, with a tense voice: "It's not that you can't, you don't want to." We sat in silence for a while, and then I said, as softly and gently as I could:

> I think you may be right, Robin. It's not only that I can't, but I also don't want to. I don't think I want to be anybody's "everything." I think being someone's "everything" sounds, even to me, like a very romantic idea, but in real life, it wouldn't be right for me.

I felt that I was not only telling Robin a profound truth about who I am, as a person, including my saying that I understood the appeal of the idea of being someone's "everything." I am no stranger to the desire to merge, but I do not believe it can work (except in profoundly destructive ways) in reality. It was vital for me to give Robin this truth about who I am and let her know that she is not alone in her struggle between the wish to merge and the wish to be free.

Robin took a few moments to think about what I had just said and replied, with a voice that at last sounded sadder than tense, that maybe it was time for her to find someone who would want to be her family.

It took three more years of intensive analysis to work through the various ways Robin sabotaged her wish to have a family, choosing, again and again, women unavailable and uninterested in a real romantic relationship.

Eight years into Robin's analysis, upon my return from summer vacation, Robin announced that she had decided to have a baby. I was amazed, but not surprised by how Robin made up her mind: She did so with minimal communication with me or self-reflection. Robin declined to have a male partner and went for a sperm donor, and within two months, she was pregnant.

She wanted no discussion with me whatsoever. I felt excluded from the process of her decision making. When she became pregnant, she did not express much happiness; all the excitement was shown by friends and acquaintances who were "absolutely ecstatic about it." She referred to her fetus, which she strongly hoped would be a girl, adding that she wouldn't have a clue about how to mother a boy. When she learned she was, indeed, having a boy, she said she felt "100% fit physically, but 100% closed off emotionally." During most of her pregnancy, Robin was detached from her baby and pregnancy, and we talked about this detachment as being, perhaps, a feature of her mourning process. Being a single mother was not something Robin wished for or wanted; she perceived it as a painful compromise and even a failure of some sort.

Robin was also worried that her single motherhood would make her more dependent on her mother's assistance. The pregnancy brought her a little closer to her mother, but nothing significant changed in her feelings. Although Robin was ambivalent about having a boy, she also expressed hope that having a boy would bring her and her father even closer, as her son would then be her father's only grandson. Robin's enmeshed ties to her parents, in which "love" and "hate" were mixed, in an unintegrated way, making it difficult for her to leave home and pursue a life of her own. One of the things we talked about at length was that by pursuing an unavailable love object, Robin was engineering a way to not ever be in the position of leaving her parents and, at the same time, hating them for leaving her on her own. This was apparent in her ambivalence regarding "difference," and I suggested that this played a part in our relationship. It was difficult for her to find the strength to contain our differences and still feel a loving connection. I suggested that part of her pain regarding her single motherhood was that it contained a realization that there are vital things that we cannot do together. Of course, it was a disillusionment of the stereotypical traditional family unit of mother–father–child, and even the kind that comprised two mothers and a child. Robin, who, throughout her life, had often felt that her mother was overly dependent on her, which made it too difficult for Robin to leave home, seemed to be repeating the unsolved dilemma by giving her son a fatherless existence. That fatherless existence placed her son in the position of not being able to leave home. There was no "other" to help him do so (leaving home is also a metaphor for the child's ability to differentiate him/herself from the parents).

It took Robin a while to feel attached to her son. Not surprisingly, she gave him a gender-neutral name (Charlie). After Robin gave birth, our relationship became closer, as her capacity to "use" me was gradually established to a greater extent. She could no longer continue the five-times-a-week analysis, and we reduced the sessions to two double sessions a week. Nonetheless, our relationship deepened and became more intimate. Robin's new motherhood was, yet again, an exciting and complex experience of both "same" and "other." Now both of us were mothers; we each had a son. There was profound intimacy in the fact that we each had had the experience of going through childbirth and building a relationship with a newborn. But, at the same time, I was the "other." Robin and Charlie were the "two," and I was the external "third," held by now within Robin.

Bella

I took to Bella from the first moment she entered my office. Perhaps it was her vigorous way of carrying herself, the mischievous expression on her face, or the combination of roughness and vulnerability apparent in the way she talked. Whatever it was, it was there from the first moment. Bella, thirty-four, was married to her girlfriend of eight years, with whom, for the past three years, she was trying to have a baby. She came to see me because "the procedure, naturally, has put her under a lot of stress."

Bella was the third of five siblings. She described her parents' marriage as "horrible" and placed most of the blame on her father with whom she hardly spoke. "He has hurt me profoundly. He is ashamed of me. He cannot forgive me for being a lesbian. When I came out, he told me that he would rather have a murderer for a daughter than a lesbian!" We both sat in shocked silence even though this information was new only to me. Bella went on to tell me the most astonishing story in a matter-of-fact tone:

> My maternal grandmother did murder two of her baby girls. It happened in the "Old country" before the family immigrated to Israel. My mother told me about it. As a little girl, she saw the murder of her baby sister.

This story became a core story in Bella's analysis, accompanying us for many years – a "symbol" for an essential structure of Bella's inner life and her external world. She found it challenging to differentiate myth from logic, unconscious fantasy from external reality or the danger babies may encounter and the father's possible role in the murder of babies.

During the third year of our encounter, Bella gave birth to a baby girl. She was ecstatic about finally becoming a mother, after years of IVF treatments. Within months of giving birth to her daughter, she decided to end her relationship with her partner and divorced her. There were preceding signs that not all was good between the two women, but what was shocking to me was that Bella so abruptly rejected her partner from the role of the other parent of "her" baby. She announced imperiously that she was the sole parent of the baby, and that her partner had no parental rights whatsoever. I found this extremely difficult to handle, both as a mother and as her analyst. It was clear to me that this was a very delicate issue. I perceived it as an enactment on behalf of Bella, and a repetition of the relationship she had with the partner of her past trauma, in which babies were murdered (in fact, or fantasy), and mothers/parents disappear.

Almost immediately after these sessions, Bella "disappeared" emotionally. It took me a relatively long time to acknowledge that I did not understand what she said. I could not make sense of how one sentence logically followed the preceding one. However, I slowly realized that the senselessness of her communications was what I needed to experience and understand – i.e., what it feels like to be the recipient of continuous, nonsensical communication. In retrospect, I am glad that I did not come to that understanding earlier because the experience of "not knowing which of us was 'crazy'" was very significant to our work. I often felt that whatever I had to say was irrelevant and even disturbing; I was beginning to experience myself as an external hazard of some sort.

The only time Bella related to me as a separate person was when she entered and left my consulting room. She would come into my office with her usual "joyful" and vigorous steps, often with a fragment of a song she was singing as if carrying a tail behind her. Then she would sit down on the couch and look at me with her mischievous facial expression and joyfully remark, "Good Morning!" Then, she would lie down and disappear, giving voice to her "internal pile of disconnected words," a way of talking to disguise the fact that she is lost and has no idea who and where she is. On her way out, she regained her posture, as if resuming her external armor, become vigorous again. She would leave with what often felt like a belittling, even somewhat sadistic comment, or form of relating to me.

Bella was much less confused and confusing in the way she spoke when we talked about the traumatic disruption of her former therapy. For confidentiality reasons, I cannot go into the details of what happened in Bella's previous treatment (which was conducted mostly by phone). I can only say that her therapist disappeared suddenly, and then reappeared a few weeks later, confusing Bella and providing no explanation of her abrupt disappearance. Later, the therapist seems to have had a mental breakdown, the details of which she shared with Bella. The therapist's breakdown occurred when Bella herself had fallen into depression. We later understood this not only as "present" trauma but also as a re-enactment of the family's ethos of babies being murdered by their mothers when they become "unbearable."

In one of these sessions, I told Bella I thought that her experience with E (her former therapist) was so painful and frightening for her that it shattered her ability to think and speak clearly. Bella cried quietly for a few moments before telling me how confused she felt and how she could not understand what was going on.

Bella talked at length of her anxiety when her therapist was not there to receive her weekly phone call and was terrified that I was going to do the same. She then recalled a traumatic separation she experienced as a young girl when her mother went to the hospital to give birth to her younger sister. The baby was born with a medical problem and had to remain in the hospital for a few weeks. Bella's mother returned home after a few days, but was naturally worried and preoccupied with the new, sick baby. Even after the baby came home, according to Bella, things never went back to the way they were, and her emotional experience was that her mother was gone, that she was no longer the way she was. In the following session, Bella was back in her incoherent way of talking, but now I knew she could speak differently. I stopped her and told her that I thought she was hiding beneath a pile of words and that perhaps she was afraid that I would find her and then leave or become tired of looking for her and would stop trying. Bella was quiet, and I could sense her shock, and then she said quietly, "No one has ever told me this. No one has ever told me that they could not understand what I was talking about. Who have I been talking to all this time if I haven't been talking to you?"

A flickering of the coherent talk was apparent when we talked about her relationship with her ex-partner. Bella was decisive about not allowing her "ex" to be a formal parent to her daughter. She allowed her to visit the baby, but nothing more. I felt distraught about this but had to find a way to talk with Bella about it without sounding judgmental or instructive. I told her that I felt it was very difficult for her to allow anyone else into the safe world she was trying to make for herself and her baby, and that perhaps she felt that everyone was a threat, especially if they had any claim on the baby. Often, Bella responded with sharp anger and would "kick me out." But in this instance, she gradually allowed her "ex" to have more presence in the child's life.

Bella was preoccupied with the possibility that her daughter might become angry later on for not having a father. We talked about the painful decision Bella had to make; having a father is not something that Bella felt safe about. She had "created" a girl who would need to process something that she had been struggling with throughout her life, feeling for many years, that her father had been nothing but bad memories and a threat. But this was not the whole truth. Another piece of the fact was that Bella loved her father, but had turned the pain into rage and aggression. This emerged as Bella's motherhood unfolded and when she was thinking about her daughter not ever having a father. She did not feel happy about this prospect.

Throughout her analysis, Bella was able to mourn the double-loss of her father – once when he was experienced as the father she did not want to have, and again when she felt that she was both unloved and unloving. Bella's mourning was followed by an ability to acknowledge that she had "killed" her father by kicking him out of her life, with the help of her mother. Bella's conviction that she did not love her father, aided by her mother's hatred of him, was a source of much guilt and the need to be, in unconscious fantasy, omnipotent, diminishing her need for a father. Much of Bella's mourning for her lost father became possible because of how sad she felt that her daughter would never have a father. In time, Bella's ability to mourn her losses improved significantly and allowed her, after years of analysis, to enable her ex-partner to have legal status as her daughter's "social" mother. It was also possible for her to accept, more fully, her choice of having a child without a "father."

Discussion

The clinical material I have presented is comprised of fragments from two analyses, both of which lasted more than seven years. Each analysis involved a woman who decided to become a single mother and choose an anonymous sperm donor. The decision to become a single mother was not the "reason" the two women gave for beginning analysis. Still, that decision did take center stage during certain phases of the analyses. Children and families play a significant social role in Israeli society, and women are "expected" to become mothers. Thus, becoming a mother is, in many ways, joining the "norm." Both Robin and Bella talked candidly about their feelings of "shame" and "guilt" concerning their choice, or, as they often perceived it, their inability to create a "normative" heterosexual family. Both needed to work through their individual experience of being "different," which seemed to be rooted in early childhood.

Klein (1928) added to Freud's notions by emphasizing the need to integrate "hate" and "shame" in the resolution of the oedipal struggle, which struggles and resolution is a part of the depressive position. Klein makes an interesting reference to the oedipal child's capacity to contain differences, utilizing unconscious fantasies about the parental (sexual) unit. Given that the child is unable to contain the extraordinary amount of hate he or she directs at the parental union, or, to put his "epistemophilic" impulse to good use, he may encounter difficulties (p. 169). Klein draws a connection between one's resolution of oedipal issues and the capacity to tolerate differences. This, I believe, has relevance to one's future choice of a partner and parenting styles (not only in terms of personality differences but perhaps also in terms of gender differences).

Exclusion and inclusion are significant themes in both cases presented here and I, too, was both excluded and excluding: Bella spoke to me in a way that was often incoherent, hence eliminating, and she often treated me with contempt and hostility, as a means of distancing herself from me and protecting herself from intimacy. Robin felt excluded from my "haven" during the war and for many years could not forgive me for not calling her on my initiative during the bombings. I could feel the tension between two of the patient's feelings states: her sense of being excluded from my life and her perception of living an inner life "crowded" with many internal objects with which she was embroiled. Robin was clear about her tumultuous relationship with her mother, as Bella regarded her relationship with her father. I perceived both patients as fatherless, and thus, in many ways, motherless.

In these two cases, it seemed that when a mother was unable to "hold" the father figure within her, she eventually became less of a "mother" to her daughter.

That which was "not"   65

This was partly because it is an outstanding role/obligation that a mother has regarding her child, and in part, because the mothers of both patients had forged a "vertical bond": mother–child, as opposed to mother–father. My experience with Bella and Robin led me to think that perhaps the idea of a male father, in the oedipal situation, is an evolutionary status quo, and that it will take a long time to change, despite the changes in current social–cultural norms.

Ogden (1987) suggests that the mother psychically holds the "other" (m-other), as an internal father-as-object whom the daughter (re)discovers as an external object, initially in the mother herself, and then as an external object in her own life. Hence, it is the mother, at the beginning of the infant's life, who is responsible for containing the "third" and the "other-ness" within her, postponing the baby's discovery of it until she is capable of coping with it. If the mother is unable to hold and withhold the "father" within her psyche, pathologies may develop, but the child's first encounter with the "father" is through the mother. Paradoxically, as Ogden (1987) describes it, the "transitional oedipal relationship in female development," the girl's first triadic object relationship, occurs between two people – herself and her mother. The internal paternal figure, held within the mother, is as important as the external father figure the child encounters. However, the father-within-the-mother takes the form of the mother's unconscious fantasies and psychic structures, such as her superego and ego ideal.

The transition from a father-within-the-mother to an external father is crucially important. As is suggested by Ogden (1987):

> The transition is not from one object to another, but from a relationship to an internal object (an object that is not completely separated from oneself) to a cathexis of an external object (an object that exists outside of one's omnipotence).
>
> (p. 486, italics added)

Hence, for Robin's and Bella's children to be able to mourn their persistent lack of a "father," both had to acknowledge their ambivalence regarding their decision to parent a "fatherless" child. In both analyses, it was crucial to recognize the significance of a "father." This was influenced by the patients' ability to contain and appreciate "otherness" within the transference–countertransference.

Feelings of "love," "hate," recognition, and acceptance of "otherness" go hand in hand. Klein (1940) suggests that at the onset of the depressive position and the psychic emerges from mother–infant "oneness," and it is following this emergence that a "transitional object" (Winnicott, 1953) is often needed to assist the shift from unity to separateness. This requires one's disillusionment of "sameness" followed by anger (or "hate") and then with the excitement and wonder that ensues in response to finding a "new world" outside of oneself and one's mother–child bond. Both Robin and Bella med to have difficulties integrating their "love" and "hate" for both their parents, and they consequently remained split consciously and unconsciously: "loving" the one, and "hating" the other.

Much hostility and ambivalence were directed by the two of them towards their parents' union. Both perceived it as a "bad" union and held the conviction that one of their parents was hurting the other, unjustly. Because of their intense identification with one parent, it was harder for Robin and Bella to establish a stable intimate relationship as adults. As a result of this fierce identification, they both decided to exclude an actual "father" from their child's life, not only in terms of not having a male father but also in raising their child as a single parent. Neither of them thought of this choice as an "ideological" matter, and both needed time to come to terms with the circumstances they felt forced them to make this decision.

Nonetheless, our analytic work revealed that the "choice" to parent a fatherless child was not a "conscious" choice, nor was it entirely coincidental. Instead, it seemed rooted in a more profound difficulty to contain a third, as an "other." Both women seemed to hold an unconscious psychic structure of a "deserting father" and a "miserable" mother. This was manifested in their intimate relationships as adults, as well as in the analytic relationship. I perceive male fathers to be of importance to their children. I believe that my holding of this notion, within myself – while not being judgmental regarding the patient's decision to have a fatherless family – served as a form of "father" (other) within me which was a necessary "third" (other) for both mother and child. I do not dispute Loewald's (1979) claim that "Insofar as human beings strive for emancipation and individuation as well as for object love, parricide – on the plane of psychic action – is a developmental necessity" (pp. 758–759). Still, for my patients' psychological growth (in terms of both individuation and object love), we needed first to restore to life the "father" so he could be killed in a growth-promoting way (Loewald, 1979).

I will now return to Ogden's (2006) idea about the tension "between influence and originality" (p. 654), which he views as lying at the core of the oedipal complex. I want to suggest that given Robin's and Bella's reluctance to fully (or unconsciously) acknowledge and accept their parents' union, it was harder for them to pursue an adult intimate relationship involving two separate people to parent a child with a partner. An exclusion, which was not worked through successfully, was, to my mind, re-enacted in their parental role as single mothers.

During my work with Robin and Bella, I have given a great deal of thought to their children, thinking about the possible emotional and unconscious fantasies that may result from their birth circumstances. I am especially concerned that as children born via anonymous sperm, they would be less able to contain the metaphorical "killing of the parent" as an unconscious fantasy or even as a "metaphor." As there is no "other" parent who has survived the child's murderous, unconscious fantasy, they might find it more difficult to gradually integrate their feelings of "love" and "hate" toward both parents. This may also be the case for a child whose parent has died, or who has left the family, or suffered severe depression, and so forth.

In the transference–countertransference, both patients positioned me initially as an internal, undifferentiated object, concerning which "there is not yet difference, for example, the difference between inside and outside, me and not-me, presentation and representation" (Ogden, 1987, p. 487). At first, I intuitively and only with time, more consciously, attempted, in these two analyses, to take the position of a subject-as-"third"/"father" to introduce "difference" and "otherness" (Poland, 2000a, 2000b, 2011). In retrospect, my reluctance to be in "unity" with Robin and Bella, regardless of how much I liked them, was a turning point in our analytic work. As their analyst, I was both the "mother" holding within me the loved father, assisting her "baby" to move from the pre-oedipal to the oedipal phase – and in which I, too, became an "external" object to the child – and the "father" facilitating the development of thirdness (Ogden, 1987, p. 488).

The role of the analyst as a "third"/"father"

Many of the analyst's roles may be perceived as reminiscent of the mother's position – being empathic to the patient's emotional experiences, containing her/ his anxieties, etc. I want to discuss the analyst's "paternal" role, as being the one who is responsible – even though she/he does not do it alone, but with the patient – to create the intersubjective analytic third-ness by means of being "other" than the patient and by being separated from the patient's experiences. When the analyst can be with the patient, as an external object, he/she facilitates another kind of shared experience, different from what is attributed to the "mother" – and hence, not a dyadic, but a triadic relationship. R. Green (2004) suggests that "there is no such thing as a mother–infant relationship" (p. 101). He points to the father that the mother holds for the infant:

> the good enough quality of the relationship with the mother hinges on the mother's love for the father and vice versa – even if the child's relationship to the father seems minimal in comparison to the bond with the mother in the earliest period of life.
>
> (p. 101)

Green attends to Winnicott's "transitional phenomenon" as embodying the "third-ness," taking place between the internal and the external. In Robin's analysis, it was the war that brought out the tension between similarities and differences. While Robin expected our experiences to be homogeneous (and they may have seemed so through an external perspective), they were, in fact, heterogeneous in my perception of them. It is not a coincidence that the war brought out the differences between us, facing the differences and the "otherness" of our experiences, and my reluctance to make them appear the "same" elicited Robin's anger. Perhaps, it was the most critical event that demonstrated to Robin that she had no omnipotent control over me (or the missiles). After much working through, Robin's anger changed into a more realistic perception of me, an external object, and our relationship. In Bella's analysis, the sharp turning point in moving from a maternal position to a paternal one, was when I realized that I did not understand what she was saying, and told her so. Moreover, I decided not to put so much effort into gathering up the bits and pieces of her fragmented speech. In both cases, I moved out of being an "internal object" into an (opposing) external object.

Ogden (2006) states that "In the oedipal battle, opponents are required" and that "when parental authority does not provide the 'brakes' for fantasy, the fantasied murder of those one loves and depends on is too frightening to endure" (p. 656). This is not only true of the child–parent relationship, but also the patient–analyst relationship. As Robin's and Bella's analyst, I had the crucial role of being an oedipal opponent. This is similar to how "parents are actively rejected, fought against, and destroyed, to varying degrees" (Loewald, 1979, pp. 388–389). I was rejected and attacked within the analytic relationship, but not "destroyed." Ogden (2006) suggests that "difficulty arises not from parricidal fantasies, per se, but from an inability to safely commit parricide and sever one's oedipal ties to one's parents." As illustrated in the material presented, the analyst took the place of the "third" as "other" to foster a space in which parricide could be re-enacted safely. This facilitated better use of the analyst-as-object.

Some final thoughts

I have attempted to present some of the questions springing from the analyses of two women who have chosen to mother a "fatherless" child. Both started their analyses for reasons other than their decisions regarding having a child. In both cases, it became clear that there was an issue, not only with their internal "Father" figure but also with the triangular construct arising from their relationships in their families of origin. Their struggles, although predominantly different, had some points in common. Both women struggled with "thirdness" and "differentiation," which were manifested in difficulties with establishing a mature and benign love relationship with a partner. In both analyses, transference and dreams revealed unconscious conflicts regarding the "Father" as a "third" "other" object. The movement from the dyadic relationship with the "Mother" was stalled for Bella and Robin, partly because of excessive marital conflicts within the "parental unit." Death, and in particular, "killing" were apparent in the ethos of both patients. In Robin's case, this seemed to have its roots in her mother's depression and suicidal ideation (at least in Robin's fantasies regarding the severity of her mother's depression), and Bella's case, in the family's inherited ethos of the fantasy of the maternal grandmother's murder of two of her daughters.

Compounding the difficulty in the triadic relationship between parents and children, each patient, consciously and unconsciously, had a highly ambivalent relationship with her father. For Robin and Bella, the paternal figure failed to be a "savior" for the mother or the daughter(s). In Robin's case, he was unable to save Robin's mother from her depression. In Bella's case, the maternal grandfather failed to keep his wife from becoming a murderer or his baby daughters from being murdered. Added to that was that both patients had unconscious, unfinished business with their fathers for "failing to choose them": Robin's father preferred a mistress. Bella's father was extremely distant and was perceived as humiliating her. Both daughters

That which was "not" 69

were "forbidden" by their mother to "love" their fathers. This took shape directly (in the form of accusations against the father/husband) and indirectly (in the way of the mother's "hatred" of the husband/father). For both patients, fathers were important: Robin perceived her father as a "good object," while Bella saw hers as a "bad object" and wished she had been more important to him. Nonetheless, both patients grew up "believing" that a woman/mother is "better off without a man."

Conscious family dynamics and unconscious psychic dynamics prevented Robin and Bella from establishing a more robust "triangular" construct. This dynamic was manifested in their object-choice (same gender) and their struggle to integrate their internal world with external reality. Robin's primary defensive mechanism was a schizoid reliance on fantasized love relationships (and the consequent inability to construct a "real" love relationship). In Bella's case, it was manifested, at its extreme, in the form of "psychotic" thinking and an incoherent way of talking. Both forms of defensive strategies played the role of "psychically enveloping" the patients to safeguard them from reality, consisting of a mother and a father, i.e., of a "third"-as-"other." Possibly, some of these unconscious factors played a role in Robin's and Bella's decision to mother a child without a father, or any other "third." There is, of course, significance to the parental configuration a person chooses. For both Bella and Robin, the decision to mother a fatherless child was rooted in the unconscious conflicts regarding the man/father-as-a-"third." Further analytic exploration is needed to determine how much this observation can be generalized to include the choice others make to create "fatherless" families.

Notes

1 This text was published in *Psychoanalytic Review* (2019), 106(3): 247–271
2 For a valuable feminist discourse with psychoanalysis and the fate of femininity in a patriarchal society, I recommend Chodorow (1978), Irigaray (1985), Dinnerstein (1987), and Flax (1993)

References

Aron, L. (1995). The internalized primal scene. *Psychoanalytic Dialogue*, 5(2): 195–237.
Britton, R. (1989). Chapter Two: The missing link: Parental sexuality in the Oedipus complex. *The Oedipus Complex Today Clinical Implications*, 54: 83–101.
Celenza, A. (2013). Maternal erotic transferences and merger wishes. *Rivista di Psicoanalisi*, 59(4): 821–838.
Chodorow, N. (1978). *The reproduction of mothering: Psychoanalysis and the sociology of gender*. London: University of California Press.
Chodorow, N. (1989). What is the relations between the psychoanalytic psychology of women and psychoanalytic feminism? *The Annual of Psychoanalsis*, 17: 215–242.
Chodorow, N. (1992). Heterosexuality as a compromise of gender formation: Reflections on the psychoanalytic theory of sexual development. *Psychoanalytic Contemporary Thought*, 15(3): 267–304.

70 That which was "not"

Corbett, K. (2001). Nontraditional family romance. *The Psychoanalytic Quarterly*, 70(3): 599–624.

Dinnerstein, D. (1987). *The mermaid and the minotaur: The rocking of the cradle and the ruling of the world.* London: The Women's Press.

Ehresaft, D. (2000). Alternatives to the Stork: Fatherhood fantasies in donor insemination families. *Studies in Gender and Sexuality*, 1(4): 371–397.

Etchegoyen, R.H. (1985). Identification and its Vicissitudes. *The International Journal of Psycho-analysis*, 66: 3–18.

Fenichel, O. (1931). Specific forms of the Oedipus complex. *The International Journal of Psycho-Analysis*, 12: 412–430.

Flax, J. (1993). *Disputed subjects: Essays on psychoanalysis, politics and philosophy.* London: Routledge.

Freud, S. (1910). Five lectures on psycho-analysis. In *The standard edition of the complete works of Sigmund Freud, Volume XI (1910): Five lectures on psycho-analysis, Leonardo da Vinci and other works* (pp. 1–56).

Freud, S. (1915). A case of Paranoia running counter to the psycho-analytic theory of disease. In *The standard edition of the complete psychological works of Sigmund Freud, Volume XIV (1914–1916): On the history of psycho-analytic movement, papers on meta-psychological and other works* (pp. 261–272).

Freud, S. (1917). Introductory lectures on psycho-analysis. In *The standard edition of the complete psychological works of Sigmund Freud. Volume XVI (1916–1917): Introductory lectures on psycho-analysis (Part III)* (pp. 241–463).

Golombok, S., Tasker, F., & Murray, C. (1997). Children raised in fatherless families From infancy: Family relationships and the socioemotional development of children of lesbian and single heterosexual mothers. Journal of Child Psychology and Psychiatry, Oct., 38(7): 783–791.

Green, A. (2004). Thirdness and psychoanalytic concepts. *The Psychoanalytic Quarterly*, 73(1): 99–135.

Irigaray, L. (1985). *Speculum of the other woman.* Ithaca, NY: Cornell University Press.

Javda, V., Badger, S., Morissette, M., & Golombok, S. (2009). 'Mom by choice, single By life's circumstances…' Findings from a large-scale survey of the experiences of single mothers by choice. *Human Fertility*, 12(4): 175–184.

Klein, M. (1928). Early stages of the Oedipal conflict. *The International Journal of Psycho-Analysis*, 9: 167–180.

Klein, M. (1940). Mourning and its relations to manic-depressive states. In M. Klein (Ed.), *Love, Guilt, andReparation: and Other Works 1921-1945 (The Writings of Melanie Klein, Vol. 1).* New York: the Free Press. .

Loewald, H.W. (1979). The waning of the Oedipus complex. *Journal of the American Psychoanalytic Association*, 27: 751–775.

Maccallum, F., & Golombok, S. (2004). Children raised in fatherless families from infancy: A follow-up of children of lesbian and single heterosexual mothers at early adolescence. Journal of Child Psychology and Psychiatry, Nov. 45(8): 1407–1419.

Ogden, T.H. (1987). The transitional Oedipal relationship in female development. *The International Journal of Psycho-Analysis*, 68: 485–498.

Ogden, T.H. (2006). Reading Loewald: Oedipus reconceived. *The International Journal of Psycho-Analysis*, 87(3): 651–666.

Perelberg, R.J. (2009). Murdered father; dead father: Revisiting the Oedipus complex. *The International Journal of Psycho-analysis*, 90(4): 713–732.

Perelberg, R.J. (2013). Paternal function and thirdness in psychoanalysis and legend: Has the future been foretold? *The Psychoanalytic Quarterly*, 82(3): 557–585.

Poland, W.S. (2000a). On discovering otherness of mind. *The Psychoanalytic Quarterly*, 69(1): 151–152.

Poland, W.S. (2000b). The analyst's witnessing and otherness. *Journal of the American Psychoanalytic Association*, 48(1): 17–34.

Poland, W.S. (2007). Oedipal complexes, Oedipal schemas. *American Imago*, 64(4): 561–565.

Poland, W.S. (2008). Outsiderness. *American Imago*, 65(4): 593–599.

Poland, W.S. (2011). Regarding the other. *American Imago*, 68: 355–359.

Searles, H.F. (1959). Oedipal love in the counter transference. *The International Journal of Psycho-Analysis*, 40: 180–190.

Winnicott, D.W. (1953). Transitional objects and transitional phenomena. *The International Journal of Psycho-Analysis*, 334: 89–97.

Chapter 4

The "choice" between illusory life and acceptance of the death of one's love object[1]

Introduction

The ability to remain alive psychically often requires that we let go of a lost love object. When separation is unbearable, a form of adjustment may develop in which the patient's attachment to their lost love object may staunch the desire to live his or her own life. In such instances, the patient may prefer to deaden major aspects of mental and emotional life in the effort not to leave the beloved object. Reality is then experienced as being at odds with the patient's survival, so they may fight, vigorously, to avoid the apprehension of external reality. The author presents an analysis of a young woman who lost her mother at the young age of seven.

This chapter addresses a conflict some patients exhibit in their relations with a lost love object. These patients hold on to their lost object in an unconscious effort to preserve the life of the object, although doing so threatens the very life of the subject. In other words, the subject may "go under" with the lost object as a swimmer may drown as she[2] clings to another swimmer already dead. Such patients unconsciously believe that by holding on to their lost object they can maintain a living relationship with them and that letting go of (accepting the death of) the object is equivalent to allowing the object to die (unnecessarily). The patient confuses her attachment to the lost object with "living with them" (being alive with them) while, in fact, the "life" they live together is illusory, a "life" that distances her from life in the world of external reality. This is, in my opinion, a different clinical picture (and perhaps theoretical one as well) from Freud's "melancholic" subject, as well as Green's subject who is suffering from the "dead mother complex," although there are, of course, overlaps between the two. The thesis I am putting forward is that, unlike Freud's subject whose reaction to the loss of their love object is basically narcissistic rage and withdrawal (both stemming from the death drive), or Green's subject who identifies with the dead mother's absence in the form of "psychic holes" (i.e., identification with the mother's death), my subject wants to live. This subject equates letting go of the lost object with death, whereas clinging to the object is a way for the subject, to stay *alive*.

In order to further elaborate on these similarities and distinctions, I will discuss two aspects of the individual's psychic struggle following the loss of a love

DOI: 10.4324/9781003203193-5

The "choice" between illusory life and acceptance of the death of one's love object   73

object. I will begin by introducing some overarching ideas concerning "mourning" and "traumatic loss" and will then elaborate on the differences between Freud's, Green's, and my own thinking regarding mourning and traumatic loss. I will then present clinical material from an analysis of a young woman whose mother died when the patient was seven years old.

The loss of a love object as trauma

Differentiating between mourning following an object loss and "traumatic" object loss is a delicate task. It is only the latter that forces the individual to use defenses in a pathological way. Most of the authors who have addressed this issue (for example, Freud, Klein, Fairbairn, and Winnicott) have attended to the possibility that an individual may find the loss of a (love) object unbearable, and will deny it, by various forms. But there seems to be agreement among almost all of the authors whose work I will discuss that the principal element that differentiates bereavement from trauma is that while the *main feature of bereavement is grief, the main feature of traumatic object-loss is anxiety.*

Freud's (1917) melancholic subject has lost a part of themselves; the reaction to that loss is, in fact, narcissistic outrage at that part being taken from them (Ogden, 1983, p. 229). Klein (1940), elaborating on Freud, states that a fundamental feature of mourning is "the testing of reality" (p. 126), meaning the testing of the mourner's capacity to face the reality of loss and the mourner's inevitable inability to fully face that reality. Always to a degree, the subject defends their "self" against the reality of the loss of the love object by means of manic defenses, which are ways of denying the dependency upon the lost object and the irreversibility of the loss (it is as if the subject proclaims: "If I don't need you it doesn't hurt to lose you").

The idea of the subject's avoidance of the unbearable pain of losing the object by denying the need and dependence on the object is also emphasized by Winnicott. He ties the degree of vulnerability of the infant or child to the extent to which a "holding" environment is available (Winnicott, 1960a, 1962, 1963a, 1963b, 1963c). What is traumatic to the infant's or child's psyche is a disruption of their going-on-being, and it is the maternal object's task to attempt to sustain this state of going-on-being in the face of the loss of the love object (Winnicott, 1965, p. 81). The child needs an environment which is expectable, one in which as little as possible is sudden or overwhelming. When there is a failure in holding (or when the lost object is the mother), the child's psyche must enter a defensive mode, which may disrupt the development of the psyche-soma. This is especially true in the phase of total dependence of the infant upon the mother, but remains true (albeit to a lesser degree) in the following phases of relative dependency. The individual defends against traumatic impingement by regressing to an unintegrated (psychotic) state or by forming a "false self" organization (Winnicott, 1960a). In both cases, the individual "gives up" on having a real and full relationship with external reality. In the "false self" personality organization, the subject denies their dependency and needs by heavily relying on the omnipotent fantasy of fully controlling the object, thereby obviating the experience of loss (Winnicott, 1960a, p. 586). Fairbairn (1941) suggests that what is catastrophic about the loss of the love object for the infant or child is being deprived of the experience of feeling "loved as a person and to have his love accepted [which] is the greatest trauma that a child can experience" (p. 39). He expands upon this set of ideas when he proposes that: "Any frustration in object-relationships is, of course, functionally equivalent to loss of the object" (p. 53–54).

How the patient presented in this article copes with her loss involves something of what each of these four theorists suggests, but is at the same time significantly different in nature. My patient's object-relations with the lost object are not narcissistic in their essence (Freud). She does not deny dependence on the lost object by means of manic defenses (Klein), or by means of false self-organization (Winnicott, 1960, p. 590). The principal form of my patient's coping mechanism is the creation of an illusory life in which the subject and the object keep on living together. Difficulties with differentiation prevent the patient from being able to let go of the (lost) object and pursue a life in external reality. My patient's illusory life is different from that of Freud's melancholic subject who engages in a purely narcissistic form of object relatedness (Ogden, 1983). By contrast, the essence of my patient's relationship with the lost object is only in part narcissistic. The relationship with the lost object is simultaneously realistic (in contact with the actual loss of the object) and "illusory" (an internal object relationship). This form of relatedness I have in mind is paradoxical in nature: the object is experienced simultaneously as lost/dead externally and alive internally. This is analogous to Winnicott's (1951) transitional phenomena in which the object is at the same time discovered and created; and analogous to Winnicott's (1969) conception of form of relatedness in early development in which the object is at once being destroyed and coming to life as a separate object.

Turning now to more recent contributions, Edna Furman's 1986 paper "On Trauma –When is the death of a parent traumatic?" poses a question that may cause many of us to uncomfortably "wriggle" in our chairs. Immediate instinct asks another question: *"When is the death of a parent in childhood not traumatic!"* But Furman is raising a significant and important point aimed at the delicate differences between "instances where a parent's death is traumatic from those where it is stressful [but not traumatic], because the impact on the psychic system and the means the personality employs in dealing with the tragedy differ" (pp. 191–192). Furman bases her differentiation on Anna's Freud (1960) perspective, which holds that children's vulnerability to trauma varies in accord with a number of factors including: "immaturity, anomaly, pathology, or individual variations in the level of tolerance for excitation" (A. Freud, 1960, p. 192).

It is not easy to differentiate between "traumatic loss" and "melancholia," on the one hand, and on the other, children's healthy "bereavement" following a parental loss. There is more than one feature they hold in common, but one of the most significant of these is the narcissistic aspect. Sacks (1998) states that

The "choice" between illusory life and acceptance of the death of one's love object   75

"the object loss in bereavement produces a special type of narcissistic disorder independent of any other diagnosis." Concurring with Freud (1917), Sacks holds that with "the loss of the object, libido is withdrawn back into the self" (p. 215).

The analytic literature indicates that a number of variables determine whether healthy or unhealthy bereavement will occur: (1) the subject's relations with the lost object (ambivalence, dependence, guilt, and so on); (2) the degree of self–object differentiation the subject has achieved from the primary childhood caretaker; (3) constitutional sensitivity to separations of all sorts; (4) vulnerability based on earlier infancy–childhood losses; and (5) the particular circumstances surrounding the loss (Sacks, 1998, p. 216). Over the years, numerous studies have been published regarding children's bereavement following object loss (Barnes, 1964; Blum, 2003; Lerner, 1990; Pollock, 1961; Scharl, 1961; Tyson, 1983) and most of them follow the theoretical–clinical guidelines of previous analytic work of Freud, Klein, Fairbairn, and Winnicott.

Of all of the papers in the analytic literature, I believe that the two most useful vantage points with which to compare my ideas regarding methods of coping with unbearable loss are those of Freud (1917) and Green (1993). To my mind, both Freud's and Green's conceptualizations of the methods of coping with the loss of a primary object are foundational to psychoanalytic thinking.

Freud's "melancholic" subject vs. Green's "dead" subject

Patients whose experience of object loss is traumatic present a somewhat different picture from those described by Freud in "Mourning and Melancholia" (1917) and Green in "The Dead Mother" (1993). Freud's melancholia, resulting from the loss of a love object, is a concept that logically follows from his ideas about narcissism (1914) and the ego ideal. In fact, it is not an "object loss" which is the focal point of Freud's "Mourning and Melancholia" (1917), but the narcissistic outrage of subjects whose "possession" has been "lost" or, more accurately, taken from them. Freud begins his paper with the statement that "Dreams having served us as the prototype in normal life of narcissistic mental disorders, we will now try to throw some light on the nature of melancholia by comparing it with the normal affect of mourning" (p. 243). Describing the main features of melancholia, he writes:

> The distinguishing mental features of melancholia are a profoundly painful dejection, cessation of interest in the outside world, loss of the capacity to love, inhibition of all activity and a lowering of the self-regarding feelings to a degree that finds utterance in self-reproach and self-reviling, and cukminates in a delusional expectation of punishment".
>
> (Freud 1917, p. 244)

What is most striking in the melancholic state-of-mind is the impoverishment of the ego: The melancholic's ways of "being," if carefully observed, lead to the conclusion that the loss they have suffered has to do with their ego, and not with their "object." "This picture of a delusion of (mainly moral) inferiority is completed by sleeplessness and refusal to take nourishment, and – what is psychologically very remarkable – by an overcoming of the instinct which compels every living thing to cling to life" (p. 246). It is important to take notice that the subject's melancholia is a "death wish" of some sort, as it exhibits their relinquishing of the desire to live. It is also worth noting that in Freud's conceptualization there isn't, in fact, a "lost object," as the object never actually existed, and what is, in fact, lost is a part of the subject's self.

Similar to Freud's subject, Green's subject, too, has lost a part of themselves and this loss serves as a means of clinging to the lost object. Unlike Freud's lost object, which is, in fact, a part of the subject's self, Green's "lost object," termed by him "the dead mother," refers to a mother who was psychically and emotionally lost, not physically lost. This mother, who was absorbed in her own mourning of some sort, was unavailable to her child. She did take care of the child, but "her heart was not in it," as Green puts it. Unlike Freud's melancholic subject who relinquishes the desire to live, Green's subject, who has been subjected to the "dead mother," does want to live and recuperate the lost-maternal-object, but the means they use are those of "killing of the self" by means of the creation of "psychic holes" that stand for the mother's absence. These holes fill in the gaps, which the mother has left behind by her absence. These psychic holes become the subject's ways of "holding" themselves. What Green has in common with Freud is that the two are describing a subject whose solution to loss is the deadening of parts of themselves. Both authors are describing a narcissistic organization in which identification with the object, and with the loss, is manifested within the subject's ego. While Freud discusses the subject's narcissistic rage, following the loss, Green discusses the "psychic holes" that not merely "represent" the mother's absence but are the inscription of it in the subject's psyche. The group of patients I am describing take on something from both Freud's and Green's narcissistic organization. Nonetheless, unlike Freud's subject and Green's, my subjects' aim is to continue their living experience with the (lost) object. By the reluctance to accept the object's loss, these patients can go on, as if living their life, renouncing the need to mourn the unbearable loss. Though their object-relating is narcissistic by nature (reflecting a lack of differentiation and separation from the object), the claim to the object is not narcissistic in essence, as is Freud's subject's reluctance to let go of the lost object. In this group, the reluctance to acknowledge the loss of the beloved object is mainly motivated by the conviction that their lives depend, literally, on the object's life. As a result of this conviction, letting go of the object is equated by them to their own death. These patients want, perhaps even desperately, to live. It is leaving the object that they find impossible. In their minds, leaving the object is equated to the death of the object and gives rise to the anxiety that the object's death is their own deed and fault. It can be said that Freud's subject is filled (and fueled) by (narcissistic) hatred and rage; Green's subject is filled (and fueled) with psychic holes. The patient I describe here is filled and fueled with illusions and

The "choice" between illusory life and acceptance of the death of one's love object   77

dreams of "living together" with the (lost) object – there is no narcissistic rage and there is no experience of psychic holes, as long as the illusion can be maintained of "living together" with the (lost) love object. Although this illusory life is disconnected from the reality of the loss of the love object, it is, nonetheless, connected to the (lost) object as an internal object and as means of connection to the subject's wish to live. It is the full acknowledgment of the object's loss (both externally and internally), the "leaving" of the object, that this subject is unable to bear. "Leaving" the object means that the patient needs to grow up (psychologically), let go of the desperate clinging to the object, and become a separate subject.

To summarize the major points of the differentiation I am attempting to draw between Freud's melancholic subject, Green's "orphaned" subject, and my subject, as illustrated by my patient: I have noted that all these patients experience: (1) vast difficulties in separation from, and mourning of, the (lost) object; (2) an inability to accept the reality of the object loss; and (3) an inability to symbolize experience with the lost object. But there are also important differences between the patients I am discussing and those of Freud and Green:

1. Freud's melancholic patient is engaged in a narcissistic relationship to the object and feels betrayed when feeling that the object is taking what the patient feels is rightfully their own.
2. In Green's patient, the object is equated with an internal void, a stand-in for the love object's vacuity. This object-as-void is then eroticized and cherished.[3]
3. The patient I discuss takes on the narcissistic quality of Freud's patient's relationship to the object, but holds onto her object not because of her narcissistic "right" to her claim on ownership of the object, but because she has come to believe that her own existence and that of the object are inseparable – the object will die without the subject, and the subject will die without the object. Thus, not letting go of the object reflects her desperate attempt to keep herself and the object alive. The patient believed she was leading a life with the (lost) object, not fully realizing it is an illusory life because the object had in reality already been lost.

In what follows I will present some clinical material drawn from an analysis of a young woman, followed by a discussion of the ways in which illusory life may result from the inability to let go of the lost object in cases where there has been traumatic loss.

Clinical illustration

Jane was twenty-two years old when she was referred to me by her psychiatrist who had given her the diagnoses obsessive-compulsive disorder and major depressive disorder. When we began our work, Jane was unable to work or study and spent most of her time at home with her immediate family (living there at that

78 The "choice" between illusory life and acceptance of the death of one's love object

time were her younger biological sister, her father and his second wife, and two younger step-brothers from the first marriage of her father's second wife). She said very little about her family, but did mention that she was the fourth of five children; she had three older brothers, all married and fathers to young children whom she loved dearly, and a sister four years younger than her. She only briefly mentioned the fact that her mother died when she was seven, and demanded that we "not make a big deal of it." Her mother had died several weeks after she was first diagnosed with a fatal illness. Throughout most of her analysis, Jane said little about her family or other aspects of her external reality, which lay in the shadows of her internal turbulences. But she seemed as cut off from her internal world as she was from her external world. She demonstrated little understanding of, or connection with, either world, internal or external.

For the first four years of our work together, Jane came twice a week, after which she began a four-times-per-week analysis using the couch. Throughout these years of analysis, she reported only a few childhood memories, one of which was of a time shortly after her mother had fallen ill, when she was asked to keep her distance from her mother because she (Jane) was ill with a respiratory illness (flu) that would harm her mother in her fragile state. I understood Jane's paucity of childhood memories not only as a reflection of her immaturity at the time of her mother's death, but also a reflection of her inability to face her mother's death as well as her inability to spend time with her mother during her final days. This one memory proved to be very significant. In the course of the analysis, she and I came to understand it as a symbolization of Jane's deep-rooted feelings of guilt concerning her "leaving her mother to die on her own," as well as the possibility that it was her own sickness that threatened her mother's life. Jane evoked warm feelings and an intense engagement in me. She asked many questions and, in so doing, made sure that I took an active position within our relationships. In identifying with her loss, I took up this active position for a much longer time than I would have otherwise. I had the feeling that there was something "real" that she needed from me, and so I was willing to answer some of her questions with "real" answers – such as answering her questions about my dog's name, or how many children I have. Intuition played a part in this, but also my compassion toward her deep loneliness. Most often I had the feeling of working with a very young child, expressing her need for "reality testing."

A few weeks after we started analysis, Jane came in and handed me a passion fruit which she found in my garden and said, "I brought you this because it fell off." For a moment I had the image of Eve picking up a fruit and handing it to Adam. I put the image aside, to be digested later, but – in retrospect – I think I had picked up something of Jane's abrupt exile. She lay down and after a minute got very anxious and said, "I have no idea what to talk about! What should we talk about?! I cannot see you! Can you see me?! What if you miss me? This is so hard!" [She looked back at me.] "I am afraid you won't know what I feel, because we cannot see each other." I said to her: "I think you're scared to death that I'm not still here, alive and well, and that I might drop you in a way that would leave

The "choice" between illusory life and acceptance of the death of one's love object   79

us unable to ever find one another again. The passion fruit, which you brought me, is, perhaps, like telling me, 'I am bringing you my fall, for you to hold,'" to which she responded, "I will not be able to handle it if you leave me. You have to promise me you will never leave." Although the content of her words was anxious, she became much calmer as she spoke, as if we were able to touch something that was very significant to her. So much passion (for life) had been dropped from Jane's life, and I thought, back then, that perhaps, most fundamentally, she came to see me for analysis to re-grasp her passion for life, whatever that might turn out to be.

Jane's experience with desertion and death struck a chord with me. I felt I was being given another "chance" to help a lonely girl whose mother had died on her. Although I did not lose my own mother to an actual death, I was no stranger to the experience of profound loneliness, and I have worked with other patients who have experienced profound loss and the extreme weight that absence carries with it. I felt compassion for Jane's struggle to bear the heavy weight of the dead. This allowed both of us to work through the differences between being "dead-while-alive" and "being-alive-in-death," as well as between "mourning" and "melancholia." Jane demanded that I be constantly awake and alive, while she was dissociating herself, often falling asleep, and not talking about anything that had meaning to it. I was to be there always, and to never ever lose my patience, no matter how hard she challenged it. Whenever I was about to lose it, I would imagine myself trying to allow a butterfly to walk all over me. This, as one can imagine, requires the quietest, calmest, most stable state, or else the butterfly will anxiously fly off.

The fear of "dropping" and "being dropped" was everywhere in the succeeding years of analysis, as Jane was haunted by the feeling that she was at the "end" of everything. In her sessions, when she was not asking me endless questions or recounting in minute detail the events of her day (for example, what she ate, to whom she spoke, how tired she was), she would disappear into long silences. She seemed to keep herself awake by dotting the silences with compulsive bursts of talking at me (as opposed to talking with me). I told her that I felt that she was "filling the gaps":

> It is unbearable for you to feel that there is a space between us. I think you are terrified by your feelings that you are losing me, or that I am about to "drop" you. It is unbearable for you to feel that there is a space between us, which amounts to a threat to your existence or mine."

Although, at that point, talking with each other was still rare in the analysis, Jane often said that my attempts to understand her made her feel much better: "It means a lot to me that you are trying so hard to understand what I am saying. The fact that you do not give up is very important to me." She felt the need to reassure me about my enormous value to her, and to encourage me to "keep on going." At that time, it often seemed to me that she was reassured by the music of my talking more than by the meaning of what I said. Speaking with her about

80   The "choice" between illusory life and acceptance of the death of one's love object

her intense fear of letting go, and perhaps also my endless efforts to find meaning in her anxious and meandering way of talking, helped Jane to gradually regain some faith in her own ability to experience and give meaning to her thoughts and feelings.

Separations and endings were everywhere for Jane. In one of our sessions, in the second year of the analysis, she said:

> I keep eating all the time. I can't stop it. When I get up in the morning it's better because I still have a whole day ahead of me, . The evening is the worst,because I have eaten all the food I have budgeted for myself, and there is nothing left.

I said, "Everything always feels as if it is about to end and be lost." In the following session, Jane went on to tell me: "I am never full. I am always hungry." I suggested that "there is always something vital that is missing" and Jane replied with desperation in her voice:

> It's so awful to eat openly! I am dying of fear of being in bed[4]. I am afraid of the bed! I miss you terribly. I wish I could have all the people that I love here in this room with me. But it is not possible. It is possible only in my imagination. The imagination is like my own room. It is where I can go to. Reality just disappears, In my imagination – everything is always destroyed and it will be the same with you. I cannot handle all the things that you are giving to me and I just know that I am going to destroy it all eventually."..

To this I said:

> I think that you are convinced that you are the cause of all destruction: You're afraid that you take everything in and you destroy it there. Nothing is left; not in your mind and not in the world outside. You feel you have nowhere to turn to, that you are nowhere and everyone else you love is also nowhere to be found. No one managed to survive your terrible destructiveness."

My interpretations were touching what I felt to be fundamental to Jane's terror – that in her (unconscious) phantasy she was responsible for her mother's death, not only by not saving her and even surviving her (living after her mother's death), but also because her anger had killed her mother or scared her away. One solution to the problem of preserving her mother's (and her own) life was to avoid life, to dissociate and detach herself from "reality." Unfortunately, this "solution" proved to be terrorizing her as well: detaching herself from external reality intensified her anxiety regarding her omnipotent aggressive phantasies and kept her from the "brakes" (Winnicott, 1945) that reality can put on fantasy.

I often had the feeling that Jane was frozen as a very young child, and this manifested itself in many ways: her childish tone of voice, her rather simplistic

The "choice" between illusory life and acceptance of the death of one's love object   81

way of understanding events in her life, the sorts of distinctions she made between "good" and "bad," her low tolerance for frustration, and her referring to herself as "Small Jane" (her father's second wife was also named "Jane" and she referred to her as "Big Jane"). Within the transference–countertransference, Jane's child-like states of mind manifested themselves in her endless questions and requests for advice concerning every aspect of her life, something that often made me feel like a human "Siri." These requests for advice were also manifestations of Jane's profound anxiety concerning "growing up"[5] Not only was I to be omniscient, I was expected to take part in all areas of her life, including cosmetic, medical, legal, and dietary matters. She found it extremely difficult to experience any form of separation from me, much less independence. Jane's conscious and unconscious anxieties overlapped with, and brought painfully to life, some of my own conscious and unconscious anxieties concerning separation, absence, and death, both as a daughter and as a mother. After four years of twice weekly psychotherapy, which we both found inadequate to meet her needs, I suggested that Jane begin a four-session-per-week analysis. My own experiences of significant object loss allowed me to feel close and compassionate, and to be able to contain many of Jane's "deadly" attacks. Jane expressed her anxieties and aggressions mainly by "disappearing," psychically, from the sessions. Handling voids and absences is both painful and something that I have had to become expert in. At that point, she wondered, aloud, whether the analytic couch was going to become her "bed" or her "death." I was quite surprised by her use of this word game, and considered it to be a very promising expression of her capacity for insightful thinking, one that would remain latent for a long time. She then said that death is always calling upon her, and she named this "ground zero," a quiet place of zero effort or struggle, a place of endless floating (a term also commonly used to refer to the place where the bombing of the World Trade Center took place). Later, she added, "this is mom's place." I commented:

> This 'ground Zero' is a place where nothing is required other than being together with your mother, whom you miss terribly. You do all that you can to keep her alive, because it is so terribly painful to let go of her."

To this, Jane responded, crying quietly, "I can't let her go. She is always there with me. Do you know that I often imagine her looking down at me from the skies?"

In the coming years of Jane's analysis this would be something that she and I would return to, again and again – to the way she lived her life by dying along with her mother, whereas living her life, truly, would amount to a desertion and betrayal of her mother. Jane would often feel guilty whenever she enjoyed herself, often saying how "unfair it is that I can do all these things, while my mother cannot anymore." Her greatest guilt was expressed whenever she and "Big Jane" would share some nice time together. She recalled

> I would never call her "mom." No way! I had a mother and there is no way that "Big Jane" could ever replace her. My younger sister, who has no memory of our mother, did refer to 'Big Jane' as her "mother" and I think this is why she is so fucked up! I could never do such a thing to our mother!

Being angry with her father's second wife was easier than being angry with her mother for dying.

Jane's anguished anger unfolded in the fifth year of her analysis. By then she was more capable of feeling the pain of her loss, as well as expressing some of her anger at her mother's death: "Why did she leave me so soon?! Why didn't she fight to stay alive?!" In one of our most significant sessions, Jane was dozing off, as she often did. I was extremely tired due to the hour of the day (noon), but also tired of my endless attempts to reach out to her and of my struggles to make sense of her "gibberish" – the endless, boring details of meaningless things. After sitting quietly, awake, safeguarding Jane's own sleep, I myself dozed off. It was barely a moment, but I was amazed to have a brief dream of a "mother." To my embarrassment, I woke up to hear Jane calling out my name. It was very common for Jane to call my name, checking to see whether I had fallen asleep. The only unusual thing was that this time, indeed, I had. Jane immediately said repeatedly: "Don't feel guilty! Please don't feel guilt! You have no reason to." I was quiet for a moment, more embarrassed than guilty. I said to her, "Amazingly I have had a dream about a 'mother.' I think I understand something new about falling off, and away, and who is there." We were both quiet and then she said again: "Please don't feel guilty." I said to her:

> Jane, you keep asking me to not feel guilty, which makes me think that not only are you angry with me for dropping off, and dropping you, but perhaps you have a need to forgive me for this. Forgiving me – for not being able to keep my eyes open, while you are laying here hour after hour, dozing off, not communicating with me, as if you are "dead" – is perhaps your way of (not) forgiving yourself for wanting to leave your own dead mother. It feels as if you cannot take it anymore, as I cannot take this anymore.

After a moment of quietness, Jane began to cry, saying "I want to leave her, but I can't. If I walk away, she will be dead, all on her own."

The truth is that to be *alive* is to be *limited*. I believe that by showing myself to be "limitedly human"– someone who, regardless of being deeply engaged and dedicated to Jane, can still drop off – demonstrated my aliveness as well as my limitations. This was one of the most significant "compromises" that Jane has learned to accept – that a relationship with a *living* object is, inevitably, a *limited* one. I do not know all the answers to her questions, sometimes I know the answers but I choose not to give them; I have other people in my life, I go away, and then I come back on my own terms; I am not a hallucination inside her head, but a real person with whom she has to struggle to form a relationship. Throughout

The "choice" between illusory life and acceptance of the death of one's love object   83

the endless variations of experiences, in the analysis Jane has come to realize the differences between being in a relationship with an object who is *really alive* and an object who is dead inside her, an object with whom she has established an illusory life. Our relationship, our warm engagement and the various frustrations that analysis, and life, impose, has enabled Jane to emerge from her "deep freeze" existence and bring to life her repressed emotional experiences with her mother and her mother's death. Very gradually, as Jane herself is able to choose life over death, her "mother" has awakened within her and became an object that has "life" to her, and thus becomes an object toward whom Jane has a variety of feelings, feelings that have been, until now, frozen (repressed, diverted, etc.).

Years into the analysis, in a very dramatic session, Jane cried out:

> My mother left me without saying goodbye. It was so painful for her to die and leave us, that she did not say goodbye, but, without this – I was left to wait for her, my whole life. I've waited and waited for her, every holiday, every birthday – but she never came. She should have said goodbye.

This was heart wrenching, but Jane's ability to at last express some of her anger, allowed her to start mourning the loss of her mother. In her unconscious phantasy, Jane was anxious and guilty that she may have damaged her mother (by being sick and not careful enough). She was also angry at her mother for leaving her, and that too, reframed itself into guilt. Staying alive, and leaving her mother to "die (and be dead) on her own" was a guilt-ridden burden that Jane was secretly carrying. These feelings of desertion and betrayal of her mother were mixed with the rage she felt toward her mother for dying and leaving her to live her life on her own. Jane's guilt was, naturally, bound together, unconsciously, with her anger, and vice versa. Much work was needed for Jane to be able to accept that both her guilt and her anxiety were manifestations of her unconscious aggression and for her to take responsibility for her share of it. External reality was something she was trying to avoid, at almost all cost, something which we came to understand, as her way of avoiding leaving/betraying her "mother."

At times I felt compelled to make interventions, particularly when I was tempted to leave her there on her own in her silence or in her empty verbiage. During her long silences (which could last a whole session), I often experienced an unfamiliar urge to let myself "drown" and "float" in my sleepiness. It was not boredom, but more a sensation of a warm thick, inviting blanket. These sensations were often interrupted by feelings of guilt for "leaving her to die there on her own." Under these circumstances, I found myself trying to draw myself out of the recognition that I was there on my own. I cared deeply for Jane. Her way of "being" and "not-being" was very consuming, though this often felt like a mixture of "everything" and "nothing." I became increasingly aware that Jane was eliciting in me feelings that were much like what it felt like to her, to be entirely alone – not being anyone, not having anyone – though Jane could not have put those feelings into words at the time.

84 The "choice" between illusory life and acceptance of the death of one's love object

Being attached to an object that is simultaneously everywhere and nowhere, it was never clear to Jane to what extent she could control her experience of her object, which led her to try to protect herself unconsciously by experiencing herself as both completely helpless and totally omnipotent. For years she presented herself, in the analysis, as a tiny baby who knows nothing about life, and who strives continuously to the deadly/heavenly state[6] – a place where all her needs are so fully supplied that they are non-existent and knowledge (thought) is in the hands of the (m)other. These experiences in the analysis are very hard to put into words, as it was almost impossible for me to reconstruct them and transcribe them, even immediately after the sessions were over. The sessions were a mixture of "gibberish" talking that carried no meaning – just piles of endless words, fragments of horror dreams, outbursts of rage directed at me for keeping quiet, or for ... saying the "wrong thing." She demanded that I advise her on everything, and when I would not, she would react venomously. Nothing I offered her was "right." Clearly, I was not the mother she needed or wanted and at the same time I reminded her, constantly, of all that she did not have. That was unbearable for her.

She was often reluctant to link thoughts to one another. Frequently she would "fall" into hypnogogic states of awareness–consciousness. In these states, Jane spoke in a way that sounded like "hallucinations." For example, in a session she said, "I am seeing now an old man sitting on the curb of the sidewalk." When I tried to understand the meaning of this statement, she said, "Oh, he is gone. Now I am seeing this beautiful flower and a butterfly on the wall." When I tried to relate to these states as "dreams" being told in vivo, I soon realized I had "no one" to talk with. As time went on I settled to silently witnessing the fragmented expressions of her "self," manifested by her way of talking – endlessly at times – not as means of communication but as means of evacuation (Bion, 1962). At these times, whatever way I chose to respond was not right for her; she could neither take it in nor let it go. Instead, she would "start a fight" and rage at me for daring to say what I had said. I felt that she was showing me a form of relatedness in which "being with" and "being without" occur simultaneously. Jane's rageful and anxious attacks may seem very different than the long silences and dozing off that were also so prevalent. Yet, I believe the origins were the same: an attack on life and living.

With time, I could speak with Jane *from* (and a bit *about*) my feelings of "being alone in the room," with her and without her, and about how afraid she was of losing me. It required years for Jane to be able to talk about her mother's death and throughout these years, I held inside me, what she had requested in our first session: "please don't make a deal of it. Everyone always thinks that everything has to do with my mother's death. It doesn't." Although her mother's death and her own life were known to her as a "fact," they were an "unknown experience" to her, and she needed perhaps to be a "Jane Doe" before she could begin to experience herself as someone about whom a "big deal" could be made. She asked (by inference) for a moratorium, a period of growth, during which she would be allowed to not-know who she was, what the meanings of her behaviors were, and

The "choice" between illusory life and acceptance of the death of one's love object   85

what connection, if any, there may be between them and the fact that she had lost her mother. There were long periods of times during which the lack of meaning, the lack of symbolic connection between present and past, led us both to the wish to give up. We both had to find the reasons to "go on," each digging into our own experience of loss-of-the-object that – however different – was put to use in this analysis. We each needed to better understand the differences and similarities between a living mother and a dead one, a living self and a dead one.

With time, Jane became more aware of the various, secondary losses attached to the "big" factual loss. Daily occurrences and life events, such as her sister-in-law's minor illness, an encounter with one of my daughters, falling in love with a new man, graduation – all awoke anxieties and intense emotions and were experienced within the analytic relationship; all being put to the test of her ability to feel, think, and communicate with me (as with all other external objects), as she was in the grip of them. Interpreting Jane's anxieties and her ways of handling these experiences played a major role in her ability to transform her way of holding-on-to-the-lost object to another way of living-without-it, a way that required that she leave the object despite fears that leaving would kill the object and herself. During a session in this period of our work, I said to her:

> When you get angry with me, you feel terrified of the possibility that you are hurting me and that I will be mad at you for this and leave you. You wonder if you are hurting me so much that you are actually killing me. You don't trust me to be able to stay and be with you even when you are so angry at me.

To this, Jane replied, "I am not really angry with you and I really don't want to hurt you. How can I tell whether you will stay with me? Eventually you will feel fed up and leave, like everyone else has." Exchanges such as this in which her fear of my death could be experienced in the context of my actual survival, helped Jane experience the reality of her mother's death, and separateness in general.

In Jane's experience, it was the process of "digestion" (food, thinking her thoughts, experiencing her emotions) that most endangered her and was felt by her to be a process of destruction (death), and not construction (life). The life she so often longed for was in "ground-zero-place" which she also referred to as "mom's place"; a heavenly place of zero efforts, movement or life, where no food, thoughts, words, or separations existed. Jane did not experience this "ground zero" as a place of death or dying, but rather as a place where she could live with her mother. Understanding this set of feelings became an important milestone in my understanding of Jane's perception of her situation and fundamental conflict. What we, as analysts often perceive to be a melancholic reluctance and inability to relinquish the lost object, was for Jane a way of being alive with her lost object. She felt that letting go of the object, in the sense of recognizing the reality of her mother's death, was to betray her mother and allow her to die (while imagining she possessed the power to keep her alive). Unable to let go of the lost object (that is, to acknowledge her actual loss), Jane could not mourn the loss and live life as a person with a life separate from that of her mother.

On being unable to leave and live

I am suggesting that Jane's management of her mother's death should be perceived differently from the way Green understands his patients who have a "dead mother," a mother-as-void (Green, 1993, p. 142). The major points of difference that I would like to emphasize are not those which have to do with the actual death of the mother versus her subjective death in the eyes of her child. Neither does the significant point of divergence lie in the difference between "brutal disappearance" and gradual loss. The point I would like to make is that there is a tie between the child's experience of inner aliveness and the ability to accept the actual death of the mother. When the experience of the mother's actual death is too much for the subject to bear, the individual holds to the unconscious belief that they hold the power to keep the object alive in their internal world if they do not let go of the object, do not allow separateness between self and object to be acknowledged. This results in the illusory life of the combined subject and object, as well as the threatened death of both if separateness is acknowledged. Thus, unconsciously, the subject and object live together and die together.

Lost and (not) found: losing one's self as a coping mechanism

Jane's denial of her loss requires powerful psychic defenses. It was necessary for Jane to keep her mother "not-dead" by means of dissociation and disconnection from reality, although she was not able to completely stifle feelings of guilt, anger, and most of all, a profound sense of helplessness. Jane's unconscious defenses not only served to deny the "real" loss of her mother – they also served to maintain the feeling that her beloved object was close by. For instance, her obsessive–compulsive defenses in the form of endless questioning of me and endless reporting of daily activities were meant to keep me in a state of being "as-if" awake, alerted, and alive. At times she seemed to be attempting to wake me up, revive or resuscitate me, for example, in the form of efforts to provoke me into anger by behaving like an infant, unable to talk and by refusing to think at a level we both knew she was capable of. Thinking requires the willingness to create and thus to leave what is already known in favor of something new (Amir, 2008). Both her silences and her endless meaningless talking were ways of obscuring the fact that there were two of us in the room, that our time together was limited and so was her control over me. Anger is an important feature of analytic work with patients suffering disturbances of the sort Jane was experiencing. Jane's experiences of profound feelings of numbness and fragmentation of thinking, and her obsessive–compulsive modes of defense, all were aimed at burying and deflecting – as much as possible – her fear of killing the object with whom her own life was fused. The patient's murderous impulses in part took the form of symbolic mental suicide – a killing of her own mental capacities and symbolic murder – in the form of a killing of my own freedom to think.

Falling (into) a sleep–quietness or quitting?

Jane's ongoing fight not to completely fall asleep, or to completely wake up to external reality, represented the working through of her endless encounter with the unbearable reality of being without her lost object.

As her analysis progressed, I could talk with Jane about the ways in which her various ways of "living" were, in many ways, a mental death. One of the interpretations that she found to be very meaningful was the idea that in her long silences, her dreadful attempts not to fall asleep, and her endless inquiries of me, we kept changing positions. At times she was the little girl who sits, in agony, beside her sick mother's bed and I was the about-to-die mother. At other times, she was the one fighting to stay awake and alive while I was the little girl who sits next to her, desperately trying to figure out how to help her "stay with me." She often felt very guilty about her silences and they were followed by endless, frantic apologies for "killing me with boredom." The understanding of the roots of these feelings, thoughts, and behaviors helped her to face and contain her feelings of frustration, anger, pain, and helplessness, as well as her sense of horrendous guilt and destructiveness.

Permitting patients like Jane to experience the diverse and complex emotions, feelings, conflicts, and thoughts that accompany being alive requires the analyst to be alive over long periods of time, even though the analyst may feel – for long periods of time – that they are the only one who is alive in the relationship. Much pain and frustration may be involved in this, as the analyst-as-a-real-object is far more limited than the lost love object who is an ideal "mythic object." Both the subject (patient) and object (the lost object/analyst) are expected by the patient to be omnipotent in their always-never-there presence, whereas the patient's real relationship with the analyst, as in the experience of mourning, requires the patient to relinquish this omnipotent "all-or-nothing" sense of the object. The patient's alive relations with the analyst, if successful, may allow him or her to put the lost love object "to rest" in the past tense; the object once existed as a "real-external-object," but no longer does. Their present and future presences can then be accepted in the form of psychical experience, such as memories, thoughts, fantasies, dreams, emotions, and imagination. This movement, between the tenses also implies a movement between knowing and not-knowing, as well as the emotional and mental acceptance of the limitation of "knowing."

Some final thoughts

We all have a love object we need to be able to let go of in order for us to grow psychologically and emotionally. The love object needs to be acknowledged as such, and this loss needs to be mourned. But, can a child, for example, really perceive the reality of their parent's death? Can a parent truly accept their child's death, not as an external objective "fact," but as a mental and emotional acceptance of their eternal absence? What mental solutions might a bereaved individual develop, consciously and unconsciously, in order to be able to go on living after such a loss? Can they leave their dead object to "be alive" on their own? How do they manage their sense of being left to live on their own? Some of our patients' losses are more traumatic than those of others patients, perhaps because of internal and subjective circumstances, or because of external and objective ones. The patient's ability to mourn and reestablish the good (love) object as an internal object depends on various conditions. Freud (1917) has described an inability to mourn in terms of a disorder of narcissism in which the object is felt to be an extension of the self, and its loss is felt to be an infuriating offense to the self (Ogden, 2002). Green (1993) has discussed an attachment to the object-as-void when the lost object is experienced as vacant. Here, I am adding to these ways of experiencing and responding to object loss, an experience of object loss in which the subject feels that they are "living" with the (lost) love object whose death is unconsciously denied. Such patients feel compelled, to various degrees and in various ways, to not let go of the object, as this is unconsciously experienced by them as deserting the lost object and causing the unnecessary death of the object and of the self (which is fused with the object).

Although the clinical material presented here is of a young woman who needed her analysis to construct a process of mourning the death of her mother when she was a very young child, I believe that the perspective offered is relevant to other patients whose love object was lost under less catastrophic circumstances. With patients like this, being alive as the analyst is vital. Just "surviving" (Winnicott, 1971) is not enough, in these cases. The determination to stay alive (in terms of being able to think (see Ogden, 2003)) is vital in order for these patients to be able to distinguish between living objects and dead ones, "current experience" (present) and "memory" (past), and to cherish both. Lucky are those who find it hard to understand what it feels like to be so devoted to a lost object that one's life becomes dependent on living–dying together, and how terrifying the possibility of leaving the lost object may be. For patients like this to be able to live life fully, they must agree to leave the lost love object and allow it to die (that is, accept the reality of the death). This may be, for some, the pain they must bear throughout their lives.

Notes

1 This text was published in *Contemporary Psychoanalysis*, (2020), 56(4): 562–585.
2 I am using "she" since the patient presented in this chapter is female.
3 It is important to take note of the significant difference between Freud and Green with regard to the subject's way of coping with the loss of the object. While Freud's subject forms an internal object representation of the external object, Green's subject forms (internalizes) an internal void (as a representation of the lost object/its void).
4 'Bed', in Hebrew sounds the same as 'death' ('Mitta'), although it is spelled differently.

The "choice" between illusory life and acceptance of the death of one's love object   89

5 See footnote iii -concerning the differentiation between Freud and Green, in terms of the subject's handling of the object loss as this meant leaving her mother.
6 By "heavenly" I am referring to a state that is "unearthly," meaning a state in which there are no needs that need to be fulfilled—something like "Eden" and this I equate to "death."

References

Amir, D. (2008). Naming the nonexistent: Melancholia as mourning over a possible object. *Psychoanalytic Review*, 95(1): 1–15.

Barnes, M.J. (1964). Reactions to the death of a mother. *The Psychoanalytic Study of the Child*, 19(1): 334–357.

Bion, W.R. (1962). The psycho-analytic study of thinking. *The International Journal of Psycho-Analysis*, 43: 306–310.

Blum, H.P. (2003). Psychic trauma and traumatic object loss. *Journal of American Psychoanalytic Association*, 51(2): 415–431.

Fairbairn, W.R.D. (1941). A revised psychopathology of the psychoses and psychoneuroses. *The International Journal of Psychoanalysis*, 22: 250–270.

Freud, A. (1960). Discussion of Dr. John Bowlby's Paper. *Psychoanalytic Study of the Child*, 15: 52–62.

Freud, S. (1914). On narcissism: An introduction. In *The standard edition of the complete psychological works of Sigmund Freud, Volume XIV (1914–1916): On the history of the psycho-analytic movement, papers on metapsychology and other works* (pp. 67–102).

Freud, S. (1917). Mourning and melancholia. In *The standard edition of the complete psychological works of Sigmund Freud, Volume XIV (1914–1916): On the history of the psycho-analytic movement, papers on metapsychology and other works* (pp. 237–258). London: Hogarth Press.

Furman, E. (1986). On trauma – When is the death of a parent traumatic? *The Psychoanalytic Study of the Child*, 41: 191–208.

Green, A. (1993). The dead mother. *Psyche*, 47(3): 205–240.

Klein, M. (1940). Mourning and its relations to manic-depressive states. *The International Journal of Psychoanalysis*, 21: 125–153.

Lerner, P.M. (1990). The treatment of early object loss: The need to search. *Psychoanalytic Psychology*, 7(1): 79–90.

Ogden, T.H. (1983). The concept of internal object relations. *The International Journal of Psychoanalysis*, 64: 227–241.

Ogden, T.H. (2002). A new reading of the origins of object-relations theory. *The International Journal of Psycho-Analysis*, 83(4): 767–782.

Ogden, T.H. (2003). On not being able to dream. *The International Journal of Psycho-Analysis*, 84(1): 17–30.

Pollock, G.H. (1961). Mourning and adaptation. *The International Journal of Psycho-Analysis*, 42: 341–361.

Sacks, A.M. (1998). Bereavement: A special disorder of object loss: A comparison of two cases. *Psychoanalytic Psychology*, 15(2): 213–229.

Scharl, A.E. (1961). Regression and restitution in object-loss—Clinical observations. *The Psychoanalytic Study of the Child*, 16: 471–480. 584.

Tyson, R.L. (1983). Some narcissistic consequences of object loss: A developmental view. *The Psychoanalytic Quarterly*, 52(2): 205–224.

Winnicott, D.W. (1945). Primitive emotional development. *The International Journal of Psycho-Analysis*, 26(3–4): 137–143.

Winnicott, D.W. (1951). Transitional objects and transitional phenomena. *The International Journal of Psycho-Analysis*, 34: 89–97.

Winnicott, D.W. (1960). The theory of the parent-infant relationship. *The International Journal of Psycho-Analysis*, 41: 585–595.

Winnicott, D.W. (1962). Ego integration in child development. In *D.W. Winnicott (1965). The Maturational processes and the facilitating environment: Studies in the Theory of Emotional Development*, 64: 1–276, (pp. 56–63). The International Psycho-Analytical Library .

Winnicott, D.W. (1963a). The development of the capacity for concern. In *D.W. Winnicott (1965). The Maturational processes and the facilitating environment: Studies in the Theory of Emotional Development*, 64: 1-276, (pp. 73–82). The International Psycho-Analytical Library .

Winnicott, D.W. (1963b). Morals and education. In D.W. Winnicott *(1965). The maturational processes and the facilitating environment: Studies in the Theory of Emotional Development, 64: 1–276*, (pp. 93–105). The International Psycho-Analytical Library.

Winnicott, D.W. (1963c). Dependence in infant-care, in child-care, and in the psychoanalytic setting. In D.W. Winnicott *(1965). The maturational processes and the facilitating environment: Studies in the Theory of Emotional Development*, 64: 1–276, (pp. 249–260). The International Psycho-Analytical Library.

Winnicott, D.W. (1965). A clinical study of the effect of a failure of the average expectable environment on a child's mental functioning. *The International Journal of Psycho-Analysis*, 46: 81–87.

Winnicott, D.W. (1969). The use of an object. *The International Journal of Psycho-Analysis*, 50: 711–716.

Winnicott, D.W. (1971). The use of an object and relating through identifications. In D.W. Winnicott *(1971), Playing and reality*, 17: 1–156, (pp. 86–94). London: Basic Books.

Chapter 5

Psychosomatic symptoms as physical dreams

Emotional experiences given expression through the body[1]

Introduction

Building on Winnicott's (1949) conception of the relations between the soma and the psyche, Bion's work on the analytic function of the personality (1962a, 1962b), and Ogden's (2004b) concepts of "undreamt" and "interrupted" dreams, I offer a view of psychosomatic symptoms as experiential phenomena that function as "physical dreams." I do not aim to address the neurophysiology of psychosomatic illness but instead offer an analytic understanding of psychosomatic symptoms appearing before or during the patient's analysis. Psychosomatic symptoms tell psychical "stories" about particular aspects of the individual's emotional experience. Thus, no generic interpretations exist or can assist us (Winnicott, 1949, p. 244). Instead, each analytic pair must find their unique way of dreaming the symptom and transforming the physical into an emotional experience that the patient can better contain. This process is both "internal" to the subject and "external" and "intersubjective," in that it requires the work of the two people's psyche-soma to effect change (Winnicott, 1945, p. 139; Ogden, 2004a).

Following Ogden's conceptualization of "undreamt" and interrupted dreams (Ogden, 2004b, 2007), a somatic symptom should be understood as either an emotional–psychic experience that the subject could not process appropriately or as one he or she could not handle at all. In Bion's terminology, these experiences remain in the form of beta-elements that cannot be linked in the process of dreaming and thinking (Bion, 1962a, 1962b).

Based on these ideas, I propose that psychosomatic symptoms may act as "physical dreams," which handle the emotional experience in two ways:

1. By creating partially contained beta-elements, i.e., "interrupted dreams," that serve as physical "stories," reflecting the patient's capacity to tell a pre-verbal story. In this case, the somatic symptom functions as a vehicle for rendering the unconscious conscious.
2. By transforming "raw" beta-elements, again "undreamt dreams," unpleasant emotional experience is cut off from both the soma and the unconscious mind into somatic symptoms, which have a connection with the unconscious mind and its capacity for psychological work.

DOI: 10.4324/9781003203193-6

Psychoanalysis and the soma: historical development

Gubb's review (2013) of the way psychoanalytic theorists have approached psychosomatic symptomatology emphasizes Freud's

> distinction, between the classic psychoneuroses (where the symptoms are symbolic and result from internal conflict, often based on early trauma, sometimes of a sexual kind, and where patients cannot take satisfactions available to them) and the actual neuroses (often related to frustration, which is the result of sexual satisfaction not being available in the real world, where the nervous system is bombarded with reality).
>
> (p. 107)

Freud (1893), very early on, seemed to emphasize the patient's attempts to – and struggles with – being *understood* by the doctor because the patient's psychic energy is attracted to and engulfed by the somatic symptom. For Freud, this is one of the major unconscious motivations underlying the formation of somatic symptomatology: shifting the patient's conscious attention from psychic conflict to the symptomatic somatic manifestation. Freud, when discussing his patient's condition, hints at a possible discrepancy between a somatic symptom that serves to disguise unacceptable thoughts, emotions, and sensations as a psychic "secret" with a somatic symptom that is a "foreign body" (p. 138). By these two terms ("secret" vs. "foreign body"), Freud refers to two different forms of relationship between the patient's consciousness and the psychic conflict that underlies the symptom. When the relationship between the conscious mind and the psychic conflict is a "secret," the patient retains some form of the unconscious remnant of the psychic conflict. When the relationship to the unconscious conflict is that of a "foreign body," the individual is unable to form any relationship with the psychic conflict and consequently is disconnected from that aspect of him- or herself.

After Freud rejected the actual neuroses concept, his method focused on unconscious conflict, primarily sexual content.

The psychoanalytic method was then based on the principle that unconscious conflict resolution occurs by making the unconscious conscious. This was made possible through the analyst's interpretation – and the patient's understanding – of the analysand's unconscious conflict. Ferenczi presents a somewhat different idea, which can be understood as a revision of Freud's ideas concerning somatic symptom formation. In "Transitory Symptom-Constructions during the Analysis" (1952), Ferenczi states that for patients to gain real conviction and faith in the analytic explanations regarding their symptoms, they must live "through an affective experience, to have – so to speak – felt it on one's own body" (p. 193). I understand this statement to imply that the somatic symptom has another role, other than disguising the unconscious conflict, as Freud would have it. For Ferenczi, the somatic aspect of the experience enhances and embodies the truth of an emotional experience, i.e., that which carries "conviction." Nonetheless, Ferenczi

Psychosomatic symptoms as physical dreams   93

does follow in Freud's steps, stating that somatic symptoms are real "representations, in symptom form, of unconscious feeling and thought-excitations which the analysis has stirred up from their inactivity (state of rest, equilibrium) and brought near to the threshold of consciousness" (p. 194). Like Freud, Ferenczi advocates the systemic analytic work of revealing the symptom's *meaning*, making the unconscious conscious and freeing psychic energy from the somatic symptom.

The Paris School has developed a more contemporary understanding of psychosomatic illness and symptomatology.[2] This perspective has its origins in the much earlier ideas put forth by Franz Alexander (1934). His revolutionary contribution was his idea that every physical illness is also psychosomatic, as it always involves both physical and psychological factors. In this way, he made all physical phenomena accessible to psychoanalytic work. His ideas became the fundamentals of the Paris School, which advocated an approach that "rejects any dualism between the psyche and the soma, and instead understands that these two entities are in a continuous interaction" (Gubb, 2013, p. 110). The Paris School, regardless of its strong attachment to Freudian theory, emphasizes the "type" of psychological functioning the patient presents us with – neurotic vs. non-neurotic – and prioritizes this over the revealing of the symptom's meaning. The symbolic meaning is thought to be retrospectively reconstructed by the patient and analyst. Gubb's analysis of the Paris School indicates that they perceive psychosomatic illness as related to the "death-drive." This idea is well described by Pierre Marty (1968) as a form of "progressive disorganization," which he relates to the "death instinct" in the sense that both describe a state in which the removing of the

> delicate libidinal systems which precede it, [is] giving way to the functional destruction of the subject. The unconscious becomes practically isolated, cut off from the preconscious activities as well as from manifest behavior. Organizing mental mechanisms, such as identification, introjection, projection, symbolization, association of ideas, condensation, and displacement, almost disappear and the fantasy and dream elaboration is interrupted.
>
> (p. 247)

To this Marty adds, "such a disorganization does not merely concern the mental functions; it is also pursued on the somatic level where it cancels the established hierarchy, causing a real physiological anarchy" (p. 247).

Marty (1968) relates somatic symptoms to the "death instinct" (pp. 247–248) by equating "somatization" to "disorganization." Regardless of the psychic solution to a problem, a patient may attempt – if it pulls away from "organization," i.e., is "disorganizing" – then it is a manifestation of the "death instinct" of the individual's psychic tendencies or forces that reverse psychic movement backward, toward disintegration and disorganization. Following this line of thought, somatization is a form of "psychic regression," a going backward, from the "verbal" to the "pre-verbal," from the ability to symbolize by using linguistic symbols, to physical manifestations. Both regression and somatization are related to an

94 Psychosomatic symptoms as physical dreams

earlier, less developed, phase of the individual's development. In sum, it seems to me that these authors tend to perceive the somatic symptom, either as a derivative of the instinct, which Freud (1915, p. 112; 1923, p. 56) positions at the frontier – between the mental and the somatic – or as acting in the service of psychic regression and disorganization (Marty, 1968), all in the service of the "death instinct."

Among the more contemporary analytic writers strongly influenced by the Paris School, McDougall's (1980) conceptualization of psychosomatic symptoms as a "foreclosure" is incredibly important. McDougall distinguishes between two types of symptomatology. She proposes that "psychosomatic phenomena, in contrast to hysterical ones, were devoid of repressed fantasy content capable of being verbalized and thus had no direct symbolic meaning such as we find in the unconscious structure behind neuroses" (p. 455). In some cases, McDougall suggests, the patient's psychosomatic symptoms may hold no symbolic meaning, mainly because he or she is entirely "dis-affected," disconnected from his or her feeling states. I understand these cases to be similar to Ogden's "undreamt dreams," in the sense that these patients lack the possibility of recruiting them in the service of doing any unconscious psychological work.

This brings me to Ogden's concepts of "undreamt dreams" and "interrupted dreams" (2004b, p. 860). The term "undreamt dreams" refers to actual and metaphorical night-terrors – states of mind. The individual seeks the analyst's assistance in doing psychological work with experience previously foreclosed from psychic representation. By this metaphor, Ogden refers to various experiences, emotional and psychic, that are entirely unavailable for unconscious psychological work, i.e., analytical work. These experiences, although they exist in the patient's psyche, are inaccessible to the patient psychically. They remain out of touch and need the analyst's assistance to become "psychic" material, which can then enrich the patient's psychic life. I view somatization as a prime example of undreamt dreams. By contrast with night terrors, actual and metaphorical nightmares are psychic experiences that can only be elaborated to a degree before becoming too frightening. At this point, the individual "wakes up in fear," which interrupts unconscious psychic/analytic work. This metaphor is used by Ogden to describe various psychic and/or emotional experiences that are limitedly accessible for some unconscious psychological work (i.e., dreaming) but which become too frightening at some point. When the patient's psyche is unable to elaborate these materials further, the patient then "wakes up," i.e., – ceases to do any further psychological work. In these cases, somatization would resemble what we are more familiar with – as in the case when somatic symptoms are being "used" by the patient to avoid further psychic and emotional elaboration of what he or she is bothered by. It is precisely when the patient is unable to carry on his unconscious psychological evolution that the analyst is most needed. However much the analyst may be attuned to the patient's psyche, the analyst is an external object, physically and psychically (to the patient). This may facilitate a new and different (dated) experience for the analyst and the patient. It takes two people to dream a new dream, as it takes two people to create a third (a baby).

Psychosomatic symptoms as physical dreams   95

Based on these thoughts, I would like to offer another perspective on the role the somatic symptom may play in our attempt to help our patients live their lives more fully. Understanding our patients' somatization naturally plays an important role in this attempt of ours, but I believe more can be said about how we think about this aspect of our work.

The interplay between the unconscious and the physical

I believe that there are two conceptions of psychosomatic illness that run through all of these theoretical perspectives: (1) the use of the body to symbolize psychic conflict; and (2) the foreclosure of emotional problems from conscious and unconscious psychological work, thus relegating the unprocessed experience to the body's realm in the form of somatic illness.

It seems appropriate to add Winnicott's work regarding the relationship between "psyche" and "soma" to these two conceptions of psychosomatic illness. Winnicott's (1949) work on the "overgrowth of the mental function reactive to erratic mothering" (p. 246) adds a critical thread of ideas to the psychoanalytic dialogue, which I take up in detail in the next section of this article. In his paper, "Psychosomatic Illness in Its Positive and Negative Aspects" (1966), Winnicott concludes that

> psycho-somatic illness implies a split in the individual's personality, with weakness of the linkage between psyche and soma, or a split organized in the mind in defense against generalized persecution from the repudiated world. There remains in the individual ill person, however, a tendency *not* altogether to lose the psycho-somatic linkage. Here, then is *the positive value of somatic involvement*. The individual values the potential psycho-somatic linkage. To understand this one must remember that defense is organized not only in terms of splitting, which protects against annihilation, but also in terms of protection of the psyche–soma from a flight into an intellectualization or a spiritual existence.
>
> (p. 515, italic in original)

I find this statement somewhat revolutionary, a declaration of the potentially positive, growth-promoting aspect of the somatic symptom.

Winnicott suggests that the person, however ill he or she may be, links psyche and soma via somatic symptom(s). This should be perceived as the positive side of what may too often be considered a psychological illness, expressed employing somatization. It is "positive" because the alternative may be that of a breakup between psyche and soma, i.e., dissociation, which Winnicott refers to as "depersonalization." It seems to me that what he is suggesting is that somatization serves as a refuge for the individual in some cases, either from over-intellectualization or a split between psyche and soma. Thus, the somatic symptom acts as a "bridge" between psyche and soma, safeguarding its close connection.

Gaddini (1987) contributes to this discussion by stating that

> for psychoanalysis, the body and mind form a functional "continuum," the main element of which is a process of differentiation going from the body to mind, but through which psychoanalysis, going by way of the mind, can ultimately arrive at the body.
>
> (p. 315)

Gaddini suggests that "the mind is extant throughout the body" (p. 315) and outlines the complex relationship between physiological and mental functioning, both of which, especially when the person is traumatized, accumulate (Khan, 1963) as somatization and can interfere with learning capacities. Lombardi (2016) suggests that the body appears to be the source of intensely disorganized emotions that press to be contained at the conscious level. He further states, "Bion's theory, centered on thinking and intersubjectivity, reaffirms, in a new way, the link between body and mind" (pp. 92–93).

Following these theoretical lines of thought, I, too, am suggesting that the physical is more "primordial" in nature and thus is relatively closer to the unconscious than the "mental." This offers a dual movement, meaning that some somatic symptoms need to be transformed into thoughts. In contrast, some thoughts need to be transformed and expressed as physical–somatic symptoms, enabling the analysand to use them for processing emotional experiences via unconscious psychological work. This idea is based on the assumption that it is the body that represents "reality." because the body, and the physical, have limits and limitations (Lombardi, 2016).

In contrast to the body, the "mind" holds within it both the more developed sense of thinking as conventionally conceived and the more primitive qualities of thinking, characterized by omnipotence, the uncircumscribed, and the infinite. Thus, some early experiences may be stored in the "mind" as reminiscences of the early "infinite," i.e., omnipotent state of mind. It is difficult to conclude where "experience" originates – psyche or soma – and is inscribed. When the development progresses well, the integration of the two spheres becomes possible. In less fortunate cases, when trauma (psychic or physical) predominates, the result may dissociate between the body and the mind (Balint, 1987; Krystal, 1988; Van der Kolk, 1996).

In such cases, the soma holds "unlived" emotional experiences (Ogden, 2016) that the subject cannot contain–dream–think. Still, the mind also, employing dissociation, may become the "host" of physical experiences that the subject is unable to process sufficiently (Winnicott, 1949, p. 246).

Psycho-soma vs. psyche-soma

At the beginning of life, the psyche and soma are indistinguishable. Winnicott (1949) suggests that the psyche is a set of "imaginative elaborations of somatic

Psychosomatic symptoms as physical dreams   97

parts, feelings, and functions," liveliness, which – at a later stage – will be felt by the individual to be located in the live body, forming the core for the imaginative self (p. 243). Only "gradually, the psyche and the soma aspects of the growing person become involved in the process of mutual interrelation" (p. 244). Winnicott conceives psychosomatic disorders as "halfway in between the mental and the physical" (p. 244). He goes on to say that when there is an

> overgrowth of the mental function reactive to erratic mothering, we see that there can develop an opposition between the mind and the psyche-soma since in reaction to this abnormal environmental state the thinking of the individual begins to take over and organize the caring for the psyche-soma.
>
> (p. 246)

This idea seems to correspond with Bion's (1962b) notion of the to-and-fro movement between the unconscious and the conscious aspects of the mind. I am suggesting that the analyst's provision of a good-enough holding and containing environment supports the analysand's ability to transfer conscious (primary or secondary process) experience back into the primordial physical and unconscious realms. In turn, this experience is rendered accessible to unconscious psychological work (dreaming and dream-thinking).

I want to elaborate on Bion's (1962a, 1962b) concept of "dreaming." Dreaming, for Bion, is synonymous with unconscious thinking, which is the richest form of thinking humans are capable of. It is considered the "richest" because we can simultaneously bring to bear on our experience linear and nonlinear thinking, primary and secondary process thinking, chronological time, and synchronic time, and so on. Bion, in *Learning from Experience* (1962a), introduces his ideas regarding the "dreaming" required for psychological growth, both while asleep and awake. In both states, emotional experiences need "to be worked upon by alpha-function before they can be used for dream-thoughts" (p. 6). In Bion's terms, alpha-function transforms unlinkable, a-symbolic, sense impressions derived from emotional experience into "alpha-elements." These can then be linked together to form symbolic dream-thoughts, which can be used in the process of dreaming. For Bion, to dream experience is to think it in its most generative and growth-promoting way. Not being able to dream experience, in Bion's terms, is not to do any psychological work with the experience.

In cases when dreaming is not possible, unresolved psychic pressure (i.e., beta-elements) can be relieved only by evacuation in such forms as projective identification, violent acting out, psychotic fragmentation, addictive behaviors. And as I will discuss in what follows – in the formation of psychosomatic symptoms. When the mother or analyst can contain the infant's/patient's evacuated, unthinkable thoughts, these thoughts may become thinkable.

I propose that experience could begin as purely physical and then be transformed onto a psychic–emotional conglomerate. The experience could also start as a psychic and then become an emotional–physical experience. A physical sensation, such as hunger, may be experienced as a psychic equivalent, in which the baby may experience himself or herself as being attacked (from with-in or with-out, as the internal and the external are undifferentiated at the beginning of life) (Klein, 1926, p. 40; 1930, pp. 24–25). This sensation could also be expressed as an emotion of fear/anxiety experienced via its physical equivalence, such as muscular contractions.

Whether the origin is the soma or in the psyche, the material needs to be transformed into "dreaming" and "thinking" to be utilized for mental growth. "Dreaming" the somatic symptom, i.e., doing unconscious psychological work with it, is different from "understanding" it, a more conscious form of analytical work. The analyst must have the ability to "dream–work–think" the symptom by using his or her reverie (Ogden, 2004b, p. 861). Whereas Ogden's emphasis is on the analyst's "capacity to sustain over long periods a psychological state of receptivity to the patient's undreamt and interrupted dreams as they are lived out in the transference–countertransference" (p. 861), I am applying this idea to the physical–somatic sphere. Somatic symptoms may be the "language" of patients whose object-relations require an even more primitive form of expression than those involved in transference–countertransference experience and locked within their body and ways of expressiveness. To the body, I am extending Ogden's idea that "The analyst's reveries [dreaming–dream work] are central to the analytic process in that they constitute a critical avenue through which the analyst participates in dreaming the dreams that the patient is unable to dream on his own" (p. 861).

Based on these ideas, to my mind, the patient may "know" something and be able to talk about it. Still, it will remain disconnected from a more "real," emotionally and physically "grounded" sense of experience. Unless the patient becomes able to transform his or her more superficial "knowing" into an emotional–sensuous (i.e., physical, somatic) experience, it is only "as-if" knowing and will remain detached: cut off from unconscious psychological work and genuine emotional growth. The baby (analysand) needs certain conditions to develop the ability to "dream himself into existence." This is true whether the shift is from the somatic to the psychic, or from a more limited psychic existence to a more prosperous, fuller psychic being – what Bion (1970) calls a healthy relationship of the "container–contained" and what Winnicott (1960) calls the provision of "holding" by the mother/analyst.

The somatic symptom: "breakup" or "makeup"?

The "perfect environment," states Winnicott (1949, p. 245), is one in which the mother actively adapts to the infant's newly formed psyche-soma. What makes an environment a "bad" one is the mother's failure to adapt, which the infant experiences as an *impingement* that requires the child to *react*. This may be later manifested in the form of a somatic symptom, which may reflect the individual's response to the impingement: That is, in cases where the impingements cannot be "processed" or "held" mentally by the baby, the child may react physically

Psychosomatic symptoms as physical dreams   99

and somatically. I perceive the psyche and the soma to have an interdependent relationship. In this relationship, the physical symptom may become the individual's hiding place, sheltering the patient from fully living emotional experience; and the mind may become a shelter in which the individual separates him- or herself from lived experience (Winnicott, 1965, p. 143). This suggests that a bi-directional movement between the psyche and the soma is required to process lived experience. When the mother contains the baby's raw experiences, even when they are manifested in somatic symptoms, the baby will transform these experiences into "thinking" or dreaming. This "dreaming" often takes the form of making the unconscious available to the conscious and its secondary process, "finite" thinking) or to "dreaming" (in the form of making conscious' experience available to unconscious' thinking/dreaming). In the former (unconscious / physical-to-conscious), I view the somatic symptom as an "interrupted (physical) dream" in which primordial physical experience has yet to adequately confront the real external world with all of its limitations and finite qualities. In the latter case (conscious to unconscious /physical), I am conceiving of the somatic symptom as an undreamt (physical) dream (Ogden, 2004) in that the physical symptom is inadequately connected with its primordial unconscious/physical origins and is "unthinkable" in purely conscious terms. The second idea is also based on Winnicott's (1949) idea:

> In these terms we can see that one of the aims of *psychosomatic illness* is to draw the psyche from the mind back to the original intimate association with the soma. One has also to be able to see the *positive value of the somatic disturbance* in its work of counteracting a "seduction" of the psyche into the mind.
>
> (p. 254)

Building on Winnicott's conception of the psyche-soma and its relation to the mother–infant unit (1949), McDougall (1974) offers the notion that the breakup between the mind and the body may appear in the form of a psychosomatic symptom. It represents, among other things, the breakup of the mother–infant unit, not allowing for healthy separation to occur. The untimely separation between infant and mother shows itself in the "ill-separation" of the subject's mind and body, which may take the form of a fused or split-off relationship of mind and body. Winnicott believes that the infant's mental activity allows for the child's adjustment and management of the mother's deficiencies. Nonetheless, this is possible only when the mother protects her baby from encountering too many stimuli, too early. The infant's mind is engaged, and in fact develops, when compelled to bridge normal, manageable, and inevitable impingements; should the impingements be too much for the infant to handle via his or her mental capacities, the baby may need some aid from the physical sphere[3]. This is where psychosomatic symptoms are of value. *Hence, it is relatively safe to suggest that the subject's somatic symptoms tell a story of the patient's earliest object relations in general, their relationship with the mother in particular, and – even more – with the mother's failure as a perceived good-enough environment.*

When the infant's adaptation is *not* gradual and exceeds the child's mental capacities, the "mental functioning might become 'a thing in itself'" (Winnicott, 1949, p. 246). I believe that in such cases, the appearance of a somatic symptom in the course of analysis actually indicates *progress. The progress is* in the form of returning to the psyche-soma of mental material that was ill-located in the mind (as will be illustrated in the clinical material I present later in this article). The analytic process can serve to re-locate the mental content to its "correct place," moving it either upward from the unconscious to the conscious aspect of mind or the other way around, from the conscious. to the unconscious /physical domain. One must keep in mind that the physical unconscious is the earliest psychic realm and may need to be revisited in order for the individual to work with as yet "unlived life" (Winnicott, 1971; Ogden, 2016).

I wish to offer an alternative perspective to that of McDougall. McDougall suggests that "psychoanalytic processes are the antithesis of psychosomatic processes" (p. 438). I want to borrow Bion's concept of the contact-barrier functioning to safeguard both conscious and unconscious mental functioning from undoing interference from the other (Bion, 1962a, p. 17). Ogden's idea (2001) of re-minding the body, it can be said, is that "in health, the experience of being bodied and the experience of being minded are inseparable qualities of the unitary experience of being alive" (Ogden, 2001, p. 155). Drawing on Bion's (1962a) concept of "binocular" vision (p. 103), Ogden (2001) suggests psychosomatic symptoms may be yet another expression of our process of dreaming:

> the psychological work done at the frontier of dreaming [ought not] be thought of as a linear "forward" progress from unconscious to preconscious, from it-ness to I-ness, from thing-in-itself experience to higher-order symbolization and reflective self-awareness. Such a linear conception badly misrepresents the psychological work to which I am referring, which is most fundamentally dialectical in nature.
>
> (p. 8)

Hence, dreaming is the experience of one's ability to do unconscious psychological work with one's disturbing emotional experiences. This psychological work is dialectical in nature as Ogden states:

> *Unconscious experiences and pre-conscious experiences, "it-ness" and "I-ness," raw sensory experiences and verbally mediated experiences, are all without meaning except in relation to one another; and once differentiated from one another, they continue throughout life to stand in conversation with one another, each creating, negating, preserving, and vitalizing the other.*
>
> (2001, p. 8, italics added)

Hence, I am suggesting that psychosomatic symptoms tell a story in its rawest form. Before the infant's words began to carry symbolic meanings, raw meanings are held exclusively in the form of "thing-in-itself" experience, including bodily experience. These primitive states should not be treated as a "problem" that needs to be solved, but as stories that could benefit from being translated into dream imagery or verbal symbols. From this perspective, psychosomatic symptoms are stories that need to be told, a tune that is a wordless rhyme of our most profound emotional experience. With the integration it offers, the analytic process may enable the analysand to have a broader and more profound experience of him or herself.

The soma as the core of one's true emotional experience

At the core of contemporary psychoanalysis lies a conception of a process in which patient and analyst endeavor to gain a sense of what is "true" to the patient's core "self" and experience (Winnicott, 1955, 1956; Bion, 1958, 1962a, 1962b, 1965; Ogden, 1985, 1991). This may be harder than it seems. Ogden and Gabbard (2010) suggest that although contemporary psychoanalysis positions the search for the "truth" as its principal goal, it is often "difficult to not succumb to both external and internal pressures to measure the therapeutic success in terms of symptom relief" (p. 534). Hence, analysts, too, may feel the pressure to define the diminishing of somatic symptoms as a central goal of the analytical work, thus overlooking their importance to the analytical work of uncovering the more profound emotional "truth" of the patient's unconscious life.

Winnicott (1949) has suggested that at the beginning of life, psyche and soma are indistinguishable. It can be presumed that the "truth" of the baby's experience may be physical or psychical in its origin, and will often be expressed in and through the soma. Since the baby, at that stage of life, lacks not only words, but also images as well, the various sensuous, emotional, mental, and physical events will be inscribed in the infant's soma and the psyche. Bion (1962a, 1962b), too, emphasizes that the most basic "truth" is not only an emotional one but – even more so – a sensory one, when he talks about beta-elements as "raw sense impressions." Those will become accessible to the infant's thinking only by the transformative function, carried out for the child by the (m)other. Hence, both Winnicott and Bion suggest that the physical sphere holds, within it, the most fundamental of the human's "truth," which is not only an emotional truth but also one that is directly connected to the care one receives. This primary–raw "truth," which is inscribed in the body, can be transformed into a psychical "truth" only through a process of "transformation" requiring the participation of (an) other human being (for example, the baby's mother, the patient's analyst). Without this transformation, the primary-raw "truth" may remain physical, manifested primarily in psychosomatic symptoms. Bion (1962a) and Ogden (2003a, 2007) equate the process of transformation to "dreaming"; the patient needs to be able to dream his or her raw experiences into a psychic-emotional experience which then can be used by this patient for further unconscious thinking/dreaming and further psychological growth.

Winnicott, Bion, and Ogden offer complex conceptualizations of the "truth" as an emotional experience that lies at the core of the subject's sense of self, stating that this core truth, of one's personal experience, is crucial and integral to the formation and stabilization of the experience of the "self." It makes it possible for the individual to experience an internal moral compass with which to measure every encounter the person has with her or his own thoughts, feelings, and behavior, as well as those of others. There is a constant dialogue/movement between psyche and soma in which one attempts to locate oneself. A "truth" may originate in the psyche and be expressed via the soma, and vice versa. It may arise in the analysand and be sensed and verbalized by the analyst, or the other way around.

In *Learning from Experience* (1962a), Bion presents some of his most notable concepts, on which I would like to base my ideas regarding psychosomatic symptoms. The first of these ideas is his model of the transformation of raw sense impressions via alpha-function into alpha-elements, which can be linked to unconscious thinking. The second of his key arguments is his conception of the "contact-barrier," which functions as a semi-permeable membrane that governs mental contents' movement from the conscious to the unconscious aspect of mind, and vice versa. A third critical concept is his notion that dreaming, which occurs both while awake and asleep, is a medium for processing emotional experience. Bion sums up these essential ideas in the following passage:

> Alpha-function operates on the sense impressions, whatever they are, and the emotions, whatever they are, of which the patient is aware. In so far as alpha-function is successful alpha elements are produced and these elements are suited to storage and the requirements of dream thoughts. If alpha-function is disturbed, and therefore inoperative, the sense impressions of which the patient is aware and the emotions which he is experiencing remain unchanged. I shall call them beta-elements. In contrast with alpha-elements the beta-elements are not felt to be a phenomenon, but things in themselves.
>
> (Bion, 1962a, p. 6)

Psychosomatic symptoms, I am suggesting, may begin either as beta-elements or alpha-elements. Thus, it can be utilized to bring mental contents from the unconscious to the conscious mind or bring mental contents from the conscious to the unconscious mind. In the latter case, the movement to the unconscious is what will enable the waking thought to become dream-thought, thereby making it available to unconscious psychological work (dream-thinking) and our richest form of thinking.

I find three theoretical conceptualizations to be of importance:

1. Bion's idea of the container–contained and the mother's alpha-function;
2. Winnicott's theory of the mother as a "holding environment" (1945); and
3. Ogden's ideas regarding the patient's and analyst's capacity for dreaming.

Psychosomatic symptoms as physical dreams   103

These conceptualizations all emphasize the process that raw, primary material has to undergo for it to be "thought," "held," "contained," or "dreamt" by the subject. All of these concepts, regardless of their differences in what they emphasize, are related to how the subject becomes an integrated whole, including the integration of psyche and soma. For that to happen, another human needs to be aiding the subject in this complex task of "coming together." In the absence of another human (mother/analyst) who can help the baby/analysand hold, contain, and dream his or her bits, the raw, primary experience may remain buried in the unconscious and/or manifested in the physical. Although Ogden (2004) differentiates "holding" from "containing" and "dreaming," I would like to suggest that all three forms of relations (i.e., Bion, Winnicott, and Ogden) of mother–infant (and analyst–analysand) have an inherent transformative function. In a sense, they all contribute, albeit differently, to the emergence and development of a more coherent and alive "self" that can experience its sensuous and emotional sensations and feelings and be better equipped to think/dream them.

The analyst's role (of holding, containing, and co-dreaming) the analysand's raw experiences is indisputable. It seems to me that Bion, Winnicott, and Ogden, as well as many others, agree that at the beginning of the infant's life, there is no way he or she can differentiate between physical and psychical-emotional experiences. The infant/analysand needs them to be held and contained by an (m)other. The two mutually interact and transform one other. This is perhaps best demonstrated in the act of breastfeeding, where the baby's act of crying fills the mother's breasts with milk, and the mother's act of breastfeeding transforms the baby's physical and emotional experience (hunger–distress) into a good feeling that is the sense of fullness.

Clinical material: "the body does not rule"

"The body doesn't rule!" was one of Mrs. T's frequent declarations, referring to one of "the most fundamental values of my childhood – no matter what goes on, you always get up in the morning to feed the ducks." She was brought up in a detached kibbutz and raised by a teenage mother whom she described as "anxious about everything, unable to love anyone, certainly not me," and a father who was "all over the place – a total mess." When I asked Mrs. T why she was seeking my help, she replied, "I am looking for someone to witness my death." My heart skipped a beat at the bluntness of her answer. She sounded so sincere, sad, and quiet that I could not tell if she meant it concretely or as a metaphor.

In the initial few sessions, Mrs. T dutifully described her life, from infancy to the present. In her late thirties, she was very successful in her profession, married for fifteen years, and a mother of two. She had been in therapy before and felt that "they were good and helped me quite a bit, but something vital is still missing. I have achieved everything I ever cared for and valued, but I am not happy, to say the least." Many of her complaints were about her husband's "emotional unavailability," However, she did say, repeatedly, "as difficult as the marriage is, sometimes even worse, I will never divorce. There has to be another solution." This puzzled me, as she often felt miserable, but her insistence did not weaken,

104 Psychosomatic symptoms as physical dreams

and it did square with what I felt to be true about her attitude toward her analysis. From the beginning, it was clear that she was a "serious, hardworking patient" who would come to her sessions, "no matter how hard it is."

Six months into her five-session per week analysis, Mrs. T began to feel ill. Several of her symptoms bore some resemblance to those of a stroke: She experienced pains in the right side of her body, which was only apparent in how she lay on the couch, reclining as she clutched her right arm with her left one. At these times, she found herself unable to retrieve words. Once during a weekend break in the first year of analysis, the patient collapsed at her home, possibly losing consciousness, and was rushed to the emergency room by her husband, hospitalized for a week, and released without an exact diagnosis.

She resumed her sessions immediately upon her release, looking very ill. Of her collapse, she said, "I thought I was going to die. I couldn't control the trembling of my right side, and I couldn't think clearly. All I cared about was to not be left crippled. I thought I was having a stroke. I did not want to die." She was quiet for a moment and then added, "next to that, my greatest fear was that I was making a fool of myself. The worst thing that can happen is that they will not find anything wrong and tell me that 'it's all in your head.'"

Mrs. T, although continuing her very high-level functioning outside the analysis, was indeed having great emotional difficulty in the analysis. She regressed to a non-verbal state, unable to articulate her tremendous separation anxiety and profound depression. She shed silent tears in the sessions, never moving on the couch. She referred to her tears as "drops of acid burning my eyes." She came dutifully to all her sessions, and after some weeks, she was able to tell me about her sleepless nights and her feeling of being utterly alone in the world. She told me she felt like "a lump of pain hanging on the edge of a cliff, I am afraid to let go because I might fly away like a helium balloon and disappear into space."

It became more and more difficult for Mrs. T to contain her physical pain and psychical pain. At times it was heart-wrenching to be with her. It was clear that she was doing her best to trust me and try to let me help her, but I was "never enough," I was always "missed," and she was still terribly lonely. When I asked her to try to tell me what she felt during the painful silences, she said:

> I can't. There is no one with me in this hell. I am all alone here. You can come with me when I step into this place and be here when I come out of it, but in the hell itself, I am completely alone.

I told her that I was concerned that she was returning to work too soon after her hospitalization. She said, once again, "the body does not rule." I was beginning to realize that Mrs. T's ill health was presenting us with an important opportunity for productive work in the analysis. I told her that I thought that the spread of physical pain that she called "bone cancer stage 4" was an expression of a "story," "the story of an illness you had during your infancy that you felt to be incurable and deadly." Mrs. T "recalled" being left alone, as a baby, without her mother's care. It was not only her mother who was not there, but also neither was there any one *specific* maternal figure. As a baby, the patient was utterly alone,[4] for long periods, during which, I surmise, she felt unbearable loneliness and terror, all of which went unwitnessed, and were "shell-shocking" both her mind and body.

Despite her remarkable achievements, hidden beneath them she was "very sick and about to lose my life." Her body was held by her mind – that is, her mind was working excessively to disguise her physical experience of abandonment. The patient's dictum, "The body does not rule," was true in a sense she did not recognize: Her body could not even experience pain that was of its own making and was instead transformed into psychic pain (terror and loneliness). Her mind relived her "death" with me, this time as a witness and a trustworthy person to care about her and for her. This "care" had a lot to do with my active presence in her mortal world, capable and willing to experience what was not yet impossible for her to experience.

I accepted the role assigned to me as a "witness to her death," in the sense of not urging her to quickly return to her rigorous job as a way of proving to herself that she was "okay." But I was not a "silent witness." I affirmed my presence by sharing my feelings and thoughts about what I imagined she was experiencing – feelings that could not be translated into words. During the patient's silence, I told her of my understanding concerning her horrible despair's roots. I said to her that I think that her feeling that she was about to die, or even worse, that she must stay alive and would find herself unable to do so was because she was utterly alone and unable to do a job that required two people to do it. Her attempts to make genuine contact with her mother by telephone failed again and again. With each failed attempt, her depression deepened, but she seemed unable to give up on her mother, endangering her own life, psychically (and physically, as well, at times).[5]

I said to her:

> You are endlessly and desperately calling your mother, and each time you try to find her, you feel she disappears even more. She feels to you like an insubstantial "hologram." This is tremendously painful and makes you feel that no one in the world loves you and wants to care for you. Everyone in your life disappears along with your mother – your husband, children, and me.

Here, even as she was silent with Mrs. T, I hoped to initiate a conversation between her body and mind. As she began to find herself able to resume talking with me, she was, in an important sense, speaking for the first time. Her words were now connected with the agony of her body. She responded to my comments by saying, "That's right" or "There is no one to take care of that baby." I then could tell her, "How terrifying this is, to feel that you are all alone in the world with no one to care and mind for you. Experiencing me as someone who cares for you, enables you to experience this torment, in the context of being together with someone."

My role as a "container" (Bion, 1970) was manifested in the way I used words of my own to give form to her "untranslatable," unverbalizable, physical pain. I

106 Psychosomatic symptoms as physical dreams

think that it was my effort to *find* words for her pain as much as my actual *use* of words to describe the problem that was of value to Mrs. T. Just being "two" was very important. I have no doubt that she knew and felt how deeply touched I was by her suffering, and this awareness was echoed in her gradually developing trust that her pain had an effect on me. I said to her:

> "Your pain, which is "all over the place," is an expression of your terribly sorrowful feeling that you are critically wounded; you did not die as an infant, but you were left in critical condition. You have lost your faith that you can affect anyone in a way that allows the other to know what you are going through, to stay with you, and help you hold your experience. No one can do this alone. Even if there is one body who suffers, there must be two people to hold it, to go through it together.

I would tell her:

> You cannot believe and trust me to be present and to care about you during her long silences. Even when I am here with you, you feel you are utterly alone, all by yourself, with no one to hold you or understand what you are going through. It feels as if every spot that was not held when you were a baby is aching now.

I added, "Feeling so alone is terribly painful; it's as if your whole being and self are being attacked and that results in terrible pain which is 'all over the place.'" Neither of us needed to refer to her condition as "merely" psychical, or "merely" physical. Instead, we allowed it to be both, as well as in an intermediate area between the two (Winnicott, 1971). It was a way of telling a story that can be said in no other way.

At the outset, Mrs. T referred to the analysis as a "zoo," that is, something built for the purpose of "locking up the animals." She experienced the animals' cages and the analytic "setting" as places where insufficient attention was paid to her needs that was similar to her experience in infancy and childhood. As far as I could determine from what she had been told about her early life and based on my own experience within the transference–countertransference, "attention" in infancy and childhood amounted to little more than physical handling. Her fights, anger, and high level of achievement in the world allowed her to feel that, at least in one part of her life, "there has to be something I can do to stand up for myself." I understood that her rage concerning me and the analytic setting was not an attempt to "destroy" the unsuitable setting, as she has experienced it to be. By referring to the analysis as a "zoo," leaving some sessions in the midst, and especially by voicing her feeling that it is "never enough," Mrs. T was desperately attempting to reconstruct the setting to suit her particular needs. This made her too anxious, "believing" she may have destroyed me and my ability to be with her. I offered Mrs. T these thoughts and also suggested to her the following:

Psychosomatic symptoms as physical dreams   107

I think that although you keep saying, "the body does not rule!" you are at the same time protesting against the silencing of the body. The body has to count. Your body is giving you a "fight" and reclaiming its rightful place. It has been deprived of the holding it needed when you were an infant, and is now in danger of collapsing.

By this, I was trying to express my understanding of the "fight" that had developed between her psyche and her soma. Her infant psyche was trying desperately to "hold" her emotional experience of the lack of physical holding, as well as mental and emotional. It was as if I could hear her psyche saying to the soma, "the body does not count." To this – her soma replied with a fight, forcing the psyche to acknowledge its existence through the constant physical pains.

Gradually, Mrs. T talked in her own words about her feeling of not being entitled to live and her sense of "living through hell with no one around to attest to it." This was one of her most fundamental experiences of infancy and childhood. Although she could verbalize some of it earlier in the analysis, some fundamental aspects of it needed to be physically expressed in physical pain. She had been told, and in that sense, "knew" about the circumstances of her care during infancy and early childhood, but she did not "know" – in the most primitive physical way – how terrified and lonely she was as a baby. This aspect of her life was pre-verbal and beyond her capacity to contain, comprehend, and verbalize. It had to await a deep regression to be experienced by her in the analysis. She was held by a concerned human being (me as her analyst) for it to be converted into a form that she could make available to unconscious thinking (dreaming). Her willingness to "accept any diagnosis as long as they don't tell me that 'it's all in my head'" echoed her experience in infancy (which she could not remember or verbalize) of being entirely unattended to during nights of terror. Only after her profound regression in the analysis, which took years to work through, could she "find" the strength to approach the relevant medical experts and receive a diagnosis of a specific syndrome that turned out to be the physical and psychical origin.

It may be that the syndrome she suffered from was left undiagnosed for almost seven years because Mrs. T needed to tell her story and needed to experience it, for the first time, with me as her analyst. The chronic pain was finally identified as a physical syndrome, fibromyalgia, which is often connected to prolonged exposure to trauma in early childhood. By the time it was finally diagnosed, Mrs. T no longer needed it "to tell a story" and attain proper treatment for her medical illness.

This case illustrates how somatic symptoms may help to transfer psychic material from the unconscious to the conscious mind, acting as a sort of intermediary between soma and psyche. Mrs. T was unable at the time her symptoms appeared to think (do psychological work with) the emotional experiences of abandonment and neglect that occurred during her infancy. These unprocessed experiences, which were both psychic and somatic, needed to be expressed physically before taking psychic form. Mrs. T (and I) required the physical expression of her early

108 Psychosomatic symptoms as physical dreams

experience to "know" what she had been through. These early and primordial experiences were not, and could not be, registered in her memory; thus, they were inaccessible for any working through. The somatic symptom, acting as a mediator between soma and psyche, was "both" physical and psychical. Our work ultimately enabled the integration of the soma and psyche.

"A woman afraid of dying"

Mrs. O was a married woman, in her early fifties and a mother of two when she came to see me, complaining about "depression, lack of vitality, loneliness, and boredom from life." Although she seemed to have struggled with a fear of death throughout her life, she was one of the liveliest patients I have ever worked with. Mrs. O was born prematurely and had to stay at the hospital for the first month. Since her family's home, in the kibbutz, was a great distance from the hospital, her parents visited her only a couple of times during her hospitalization. Because she and her family lived in a kibbutz at the time (the early 1970s), when she was finally released from the hospital she was brought back to the communal childcare unit of the kibbutz, in which babies and children grew up separated from their parents. Although she was a fragile baby who suffered from chronic respiratory problems, no special care was given.

Mrs. O had achieved the ability to experience being separated from her mother (both as an internal and an external object) and felt quite satisfied. The achieved differentiation from her mother was manifested in her decreased levels of anger and anxiety toward her mother. She was more capable of being in touch with the mother, without being overwhelmed with guilt, whether she was a "good-enough" daughter. This was also expressed in her decreased self-criticism levels and her increased capability to tolerate feelings of disappointment, perceived failures, and general frustration, all of which took an intense positive toll on the transference–countertransference aspect of our relationship. One of the main changes within the analytic relationship was her enhanced ability to withhold the gaps between our sessions: Her nightmares decreased significantly, and she was much less depressed. Clearly, Mrs. O had done a lot of work with her depression (i.e., her unconscious "hope" that her mother would come back to take care of her); and had processed much of her unconscious identifications with her "dead mother" (Green, 1986). Her ability to use me as her analyst and participate more fully and deeply in the analysis improved tremendously. Her love and hate were integrated to a much greater degree. Regardless of her severe separation anxiety, Mrs. O could by this time envision an end to the analysis. However, she could still not handle the fact that this would also terminate our relationship.

Around the time she was improving psychically, Mrs. O developed an allergy to lactose and shortness of breath. Some of the latter took place during her sessions. These attacks of shortness of breath caused her great distress, mostly when they occurred during sleep. In a session following one of these attacks, she said,

Psychosomatic symptoms as physical dreams   109

"I felt as if I might have been having a heart attack, and that terrified me." We both viewed this as a good development, making her fear of dying real and "readable."

> You still wake up afraid of dying, but now you find someone (referring both to her husband and to me as her analyst) next to you who is there to help you, and you can go back to sleep, knowing that this was "only" a bad dream.

By this time, she and I had talked at length about her tremendous loneliness as a child. In those days, she was often afraid for her life, feeling that there were external threats and her inability to contain her anxieties and loneliness, which were "killing" her.

I said to her:

> It is *so* scary not to be able to breathe and to fear that you are about to die. If it scares me to see you like this, I cannot imagine what it was for you to be so afraid and not have anyone by your side when you were very young.

Ms. O responded with a quiet silence. After a few moments, she said, "Yes, I have always had vivid memories of those nights, as if they were inscribed on my soul. I wish they were just imaginings." It took me a moment to realize that perhaps she was not referring only to what she wished had been possible in the past, but also to what she hoped would be possible now, with me. I said to her:

> Perhaps this is something that you can imagine now because it is not so dangerous anymore. You are not that lonely child anymore, who was so desperate for her mother to come. You have built yourself a life with people you love and who love you. Life is not dangerous anymore. I think that you, too, know this by now, but this is also scary because it brings up your wish to be a grown-up and leave me and the analysis.

As I noted, the attacks were clearly connected to Mrs. O's budding capacity to endure separation from me and the analysis: "Your ability and wish to breathe on your own is being attacked. You are not sure you can make it out there in the world." By now, we both knew that the most intense issue of her analysis, manifesting differently at each phase, was the separation anxiety that originated in her infancy and childhood. We could view her attacks on herself (for example, calling herself incompetent, crazy, and infantile) as a fearful response to our mutual feeling that the analysis was progressing very well and that its ending could be seen on the horizon.

Following one of the weekend breaks, Mrs. O began her session, saying:

> You know, my mother has told me, years ago, that she has had a tough delivery with me. She said that I did not want to come out and that I was born with

110 Psychosomatic symptoms as physical dreams

the umbilical cord tied tightly around my neck. I never thought about it – that I actually started my life on the verge of dying, and I don't think she thought about it much either. I must have been a terrified little baby.

I thought that she might be afraid that I would not let her go or be hurt by her growing up. I said to her:

I think leaving without fearing death, yours or mine, would be an entirely new experience for you. You are caught between your wish to grow up and leave and your fear of the possibility that this will destroy us. Leaving a mother who stays alive and who can be happy for your aliveness is not something that you trust easily.

Mrs. O nodded and said:

Yes, I am petrified, and I have no idea what's on "the other side." I may die – how can you tell? But maybe I need to agree to die, so I can live. I mean, that no matter how afraid I am that I will die if I decide to live, I have to give it a chance. Maybe there is an "other side," and you *will* be there for me.

Surprisingly, the lactose intolerance Mrs. O suffered no longer caused her anxiety; instead, she approached the condition with curiosity. After a few weeks, she came in smiling broadly and said:

I think I have figured out the lactose thing! I have been wondering about it, especially because I love ice cream too much to be willing to give it up … I just realized that R [her elder daughter)]had just turned eighteen, which is the same age my mother gave birth to me! It's amazing because looking at R – and you know how much I love her and how mature she is – I cannot imagine her having a baby at this age! What were they thinking?

Although she sounded almost cheerful as she said this, she fell quiet and after a few moments, said sadly, "What chance did she have with me? She was so young and miserable. Perhaps she did do her best – and that *was* the best she could do." We were both quiet for a while after she spoke these words. Following her hard work in analysis, Mrs. O was able to feel much greater compassion, both toward her infantile self and toward her mother as a young woman struggling to cope with a difficult delivery and a new baby.

After considerable analytical work, Mrs. O was able to *re-locate* her "near-death" experiences (both attacks of shortness of breath and allergic responses to lactose) as not only in the past but also in the "physical" present, i.e., the actual life of her body/mind. Throughout years of analysis, the working through of this enabled her to re-locate her conscious anxiety about separation back into her body/

unconscious where it was first experienced. As Winnicott (1949) put it, the mind is a pathological entity when disconnected from bodily experience. Her separation anxiety, manifested now as somatic symptoms, became reconnected with physical experience and was at the same time becoming genuine dream-thoughts, available and accessible for the unconscious work of dreaming.

Although the two "physical" symptoms (shortness of breath and lactose intolerance) did not disappear entirely, they did improve.

After further work on Mrs. O's struggle to "breathe on her own" and be alive and separate from her mother's severe depression, we came to understand the lactose allergy as her way of saying: "I want to live and this (milk) is not good for me." I understood the symptoms not as a symbolic representation of unconscious conflict, but as the functioning of a capacity to enter into a conversation between body and mind. For Mrs. O, at this moment in her analysis, the principal development involved enhancing the role of the unconscious/physical sphere through our conversation. The somatic symptoms served, in this case, to transfer primitive material, which was registered in the psyche but was inaccessible to unconscious psychological work (dreaming), from the psyche to the soma. What had been predominantly psychical (fear of dying) was being re-located to the body, where these fears originated in infancy. During her infancy, she had been unable to process the emotional aspect of the physical experiences, which led to the psychic's physical disconnection.

This terrifying experience, torn as it was from its original context (the body), persisted as an over-generalized and rigid psychic entity (psychosomatic symptom), unavailable for dreaming. The analysis provoked a new movement, enabling Mrs. O to dream, for the first time, the disturbing infantile experience in the context of a living psyche-soma and a facilitating intersubjective matrix (the analytic relationship).

These two clinical examples illustrate the dual movement of psyche-somatic material, enabling it to be utilized for psychological growth through unconscious working through, that is, dreaming. The somatic symptoms serve as an intermediate zone, between soma and psyche, transferring material either from the unconscious to conscious, or from the conscious to the unconscious, in both cases enabling better integration of psyche and soma.

Notes

1 This text was published in *the Contemporary Psychoanalysis*, 54 (3), 560–589, 2018
2 For an excellent introduction to the 'Paris School', see Gubb, 2013
3 On the other hand, if there is not enough frustration of the infant's appetites, the infant will have difficulty developing an autonomous self (Winnicott, 1963).
4 As I have detailed in previous chapters, babies and children in the kibbutz spent almost 21 hours a day (including nights) separated from their parents, from birth on. The patient, along with her peers, was taken care of by various caretakers from the kibbutz
5 For example, when deeply distressed, she would leave her home at night, driving aimlessly for hours, despite being very tired. Also, she sometimes refused to take the medication prescribed by her physician

References

Alexander, F. (1934). The influence of the psychologic factors upon gastro-intestinal disturbances: A symposium on: General principles, objectives, and preliminary results. *The Psychoanalytic Quarterly*, 3: 501–539.

Balint, E. (1987). Memory and consciousness. *International Journal of Psychoanalysis*, 68: 475–483.

Bion, W.R. (1958). On arrogance. *The International Journal of Psychoanalysis*, 39: 144–146.

Bion, W.R. (1961). *Experiences in groups and other papers*. London, UK: Tavistock.

Bion, W.R. (1962a). *Learning from experience*. London, UK: Tavistock.

Bion, W.R. (1962b). The psycho-analytic study of thinking. *International Journal Of Psychoanalysis*, 43: 306–310.

Bion, W.R. (1965). *Transformations: Change from learning to growth*. London, UK: Tavistock.

Bion, W.R. (1970). *Attention and interpretation*. London, UK: Tavistock.

Bollas, C. (1978). The aesthetic moment and the search for transformation. Annual of Psychoanalysis, 6: 385–394.

Bronstein, C. (2011). On psychosomatics: The search of meaning. *International Journal of Psychoanalysis*, 92(1): 173–195.

Ferenczi, S. (1952). Transitory symptom-constructions during the analysis. In *First contributions to psycho-analysis* (pp. 193–212). Authorized Translation by Ernest Jones. London, UK: Karnac.

Freud, S. (1893). Fraulein Elisabeth von R, Case histories from studies of hysteria. *The standard edition of the complete psychological work of Sigmund Freud, Volume II (1893–1895): Studies of hysteria* (pp. 135–181).

Freud, S. (1893–95). Studies on hysteria. *Standard Edition*, 2: 1–305.

Freud, S. (1915). Instincts and their Vicissitudes. *Standard Edition*, 14: 109–140.

Freud, S. (1923). The Ego and the Id. *Standard Edition*, 19: 1–66

Gaddini, E. (1987). Notes on the mind-body question. *International Journal of Psychoanalysis*, 68: 315–329.

Green, A. (1986). The dead mother. In A. Green (Ed.), *On private madness* (pp. 142–173). London, UK: Hogarth Press.

Grotstein, J.S. (2007). *A beam of intense darkness*. New York, NY: Karnac.

Gubb, K. (2013). Psychosomatics today: A review of contemporary theory and practice. *Psychoanalytic Review*, 100(1): 103–142.

Khan, M.R. (1963). The concept of cumulative trauma. *Psychoanalytic Study of the Child*, 18: 286–306.

Klein, M. (1930). The importance of symbol-formation in the development of the ego. *The International Journal of Psychoanalysis*, 11: 24–39.

Klein, M. (1926). Infant analysis. *International Journal of Psychoanalysis*, 7: 31–63.

Krystal, H. (1988). *Integration and self-healing*. Hillsdale, NJ: Analytic Press.

Lombardi, R. (2016). *Formless infinity: Clinical explorations of Matte Blanco and Bion*. London, UK: Routledge.

Marty, P. (1968). A major process of somatization: The progressive disorganization. *International Journal of Psychoanalysis*, 49: 246–249.

McDougal, J. (1974). The psychosoma and the psychoanalytic process. *International Journal of Psychoanalysis*, 1: 437–459.

McDougall, J. (1980). A child is being eaten. *Contemporary Psychoanalysis*, 16: 417–459.

Ogden, T.H. (1985). The mother, the infant and the matrix: Interpretations of aspects of the work of Donald Winnicott. *Contemporary Psychoanalysis*, 21: 346–371.

Ogden, T.H. (1991). Some theoretical comments on personal isolation. *Psychoanalytic Dialogues*, 1(3): 377–390.

Ogden, T.H. (2001). Re-minding the body. *American Journal of Psychotherapy*, 55(1): 92–104.

Ogden, T.H. (2003a). On not being able to dream. *International Journal of Psycho-Analysis*, 84: 17–30.

Ogden, T.H. (2003b). What's true and whose idea was it? *International Journal of Psycho-Analysis*, 84: 593–606.

Ogden, T.H. (2004a). The analytic third; Implications for psychoanalytic theory and technique. *Psychoanalytic Quarterly*, 73: 167–195.

Ogden, T.H. (2004b). This art of psychoanalysis: Dreaming undreamt dreams and interrupted cries. *International Journal of Psychoanalysis*, 85(4): 857–877.

Ogden, T.H. (2005). *This art of psychoanalysis: Dreaming undreamt dreams and interrupted cries.* New York, NY: Routledge.

Ogden, T.H. (2007). On talking-as-dreaming. *International Journal of Psychoanalysis*, 88: 575–589.

Ogden, T.H. (2009). Rediscovering psychoanalysis. *Psychoanalytic Perspectives*, 6(1): 22–31.

Ogden, T.H. (2016). *Reclaiming unlived life – Experiences in psychoanalysis.* London, UK: Routledge.

Ogden, T.H., & Gabbard, G.O. (2010). The lure of the symptom in psycho-analytic treatment. *Journal of The American Psychoanalytic Association*, 58: 533–544.

Smadja, C. (2011). Psychoanalytic psychosomatics, . *International Journal of Psychoanalysis*, 92(1): 221–230.

Van der Kolk, B.A. (1996). The body keeps the score: Approaches to the psychobiology of the post-traumatic stress disorder. In: B.A. Van der Kolk, A.C. McFarlane, & L. Weisaeth (Eds.), *Traumatic stress*, (pp. 214–241). New York, NY: Guilford Press.

Winnicott, D.W. (1945). Primitive emotional development. *International Journal of Psychoanalysis*, 26: 137–143.

Winnicott, D.W. (1949). Mind and its relation to the psyche-soma. In *Through paediatrics to psychoanalysis – Collected papers*, (pp. 243–254). London, UK: Karnac.

Winnicott, D.W. (1955). Metapsychological and clinical aspects of regression within the psycho-analytical set-up. *International Journal of Psychoanalysis*, 36: 16–26.

Winnicott, D.W. (1956). On transference. *International Journal of Psychoanalysis*, 37: 386–388.

Winnicott, D.W. (1960). The theory of parent-infant relationship. *International Journal of Psychoanalysis*, 41: 585–595.

Winnicott, D.W. (1963). Communicating and not communicating leading to a study of certain opposites. In D.W. Winnicott (Ed.) (1965), *The maturational processes and the facilitating environment: Studies in the theory of emotional development*, (pp. 179–192). London, UK: The Hogarth Press and the Institute of Psycho-Analysis.

Winnicott, D.W. (1965). *The maturational processes and the facilitating environment: Studies in the theory of emotional development.* London, UK: The Hogarth Press and the Institute of Psycho-Analysis.

Winnicott, D.W. (1966). Psycho-somatic illness in its positive and negative aspects. *International Journal of Psychoanalysis*, 47: 510–516.

Winnicott, D.W. (1971). *Playing and reality.* London, UK: Tavistock.

Chapter 6

When hunger strikes

Re-thinking Kafka's "A Hunger Artist" in light of Winnicott's theory of the psyche-soma[1]

When I first read Kafka's short story "A Hunger Artist" I was shocked by it. There are many ways of reading this story, I took it to the issue of witnessing versus participating, as different modes of presence. We all face dilemmas concerning witnessing and participation, from the personal to the social. It may be injustice that we encounter within our families, between colleagues or other people we know, it may be on the social level, and at times – it may even be about atrocities.

As analysts, this issue is even more complex: To what extend do we witness our patient's stories? And when is it that we should step in and "participate"? And what does it mean to witness versus participate? It is not simple to make the distinction between the two – when an analyst interprets – does this account for witnessing or for her/his participation?

These concepts are related to one of the fundamental and highly-valued values of psychoanalysis, that of "neutrality." Alvarez (1985) undertakes the meaning of the analyst's neutrality, especially when working with psychotic and borderline children, hoping that it is relevant to neurotic children as well. Alvarez refers to both Etchegoyan (1983) and Bion's (1962, 1965) thinking, focusing on one point they share in relating to the passive–active aspects of psychoanalysis and the analyst's role. Grotstein (1983) discusses Tustin's theory concerning "the experience of the senses and their relationship to the development of mind" (p. 491). For her, Grotstein suggests:

> the sense organs of these hapless children turn in upon themselves and engender autochthonous (self-creating) sensations so as to re-create an autistic sensory world independent of the external one, but one, interestingly, which still maintains the memory of the great catastrophe when the infant, presumably, *felt prematurely ripped away from its primary at-one-ment with its nurturing mother and consequently experienced a most traumatic detachment from her.* The legacy of this catastrophe is the experience of a perennial hole or wound.
>
> (p. 491, Italics added)

Grotstein asks us to pay attention and reconsider the forms that thinking and feeling take in a mind that has not yet differentiated from one's body. Children who have been awakened to the world too early may find it extremely difficult to adjust

DOI: 10.4324/9781003203193-7

to it: "they can only respond reflexly and mechanistically as in the limited digital computer *language of yes or no, and generally no because no is safe and yes is dangerous*" (p. 493, italics added). In the case of anorexia nervosa, saying "no" functions as a defense against the overwhelming absence. The "hunger artist" who refuses to eat denies his need of others. Yet, he chooses to do so in front of an audience. The artist, who "performs" holds, in fact, his audience as "captive," locked in a moral conflict; should they intervene and stop the artist's dangerous self-starvation or should they let him die, if this is what he insists on?

Taking the dilemma back to the analyst–patient relationship – should interpretation be our most active participation in our patients' lives or should we, at times, do something else, that may account for something that is "not analytic," yet we believe it is for the benefit of the patient's growth?

Introduction

Winnicott's perspective on psychosomatic illness as a phenomenon that bridges the unconscious and the conscious will be discussed using clinical material and Kafka's short story *A Hunger Artist*. The author makes use of Winnicott's ideas in discussing the idea that psychosomatic symptoms, or illness, are not necessarily a form of acting out in need of elimination, but a nonverbal "language" in need of a listener. I will describe clinical cases in which the psychosomatic symptom was treated as a sign of something that went wrong within the mother–infant relationship, which has awaited a good-enough environmental provision to enable the creation of a new meaning.

Since Kafka's (1926) "A Hunger Artist" was published thirty years before Winnicott's 1949/1975 paper "Mind and Its Relation to the Psyche–Soma," I was intrigued by Kafka's observations about the relationship of the mind and the psyche.

I read Kafka's story with Winnicott's ideas (1949, 1966a, 1966b) in mind, along with my own experiences as an analyst, a mother, and a child. Two struggles struck me as vital to understanding both Kafka's story and Winnicott's conceptualization of psychosomatic illness: (1) the struggle between anonymity and being "known" (to someone in particular), and (2) the individual's struggle to differentiate and integrate what otherwise would be chaotic and split off. These vary from one person to another, and weigh differently throughout our lives, depending on one's developmental stage, personal strengths, and external reality.

Mother and infant, psyche and soma, silence and word

Winnicott (1949) states: "*I do not think that the mind really exists as an entity*" (p. 243, emphasis in original) conditioned on satisfying "very early developmental stages" (p. 243). He adds that, given an unsatisfactory early development, "the mind will often be found to be developing a false entity and a *false localization*" (p. 244, emphasis in original), thereby locating the somatic disorders "half-way between the mental and the physical, [which puts them] in a rather precarious position" (p. 244). I understand this to mean that the somatic disorder acts as a bridge between the unconscious and the conscious aspects of the mind, similar to Green's (2010) differentiation between psyche and mind when he observes, "the split psyche/soma – which is part of normal experience – can take a very pathological turn. This is what we observe in psychosomatics" (p. 4). This means that the somatic illness not only "bridges" the unconscious and the conscious, but is also a "bridge" between the patient's inner world and external reality. Nonetheless, this comes at a cost, as the individual is engaged from his or her psychic reality.

Lombardi (2003), referring to Ferari's theorizing of the body–mind relations, adds another crucial dimension, that of psyche–soma language. He suggests that "it is possible to distinguish between the corporeal and mental levels, a prerequisite for the distinction between concrete and abstract and hence between object and word" (p. 1019), emphasizing Ferari's theory of the body as "*the concrete original object* (COO), which provides both basic sensations and the perceptual structures of the mental apparatus" (p. 1035, emphasis added). According to this theory, the body is equivalent to the unconscious, in the sense that it is "hosting" the concrete object (Lombardi, 2008): "The presence of the concrete body in session draws attention to itself as a concrete event which – as such – is not yet thought, but is on the point of becoming so" (p. 92). Lombardi (2008) suggests that the body (soma) inhabits the pre-thought material, which can be referred to as unconscious, and further elaborates on the connection between the body and the unconscious:

> I find the emphasis on the "concrete" particularly significant because it seems to link psychoanalytic research on the body with the clinical manifestations of concrete thinking to be found in serious cases, and with the assessment of the unconscious with which we are confronted when the whole train of thought is dominated by the element which has for its content a bodily innervation.
>
> (p. 93, emphasis in original)

Hence, Lombardi is making a unique connection between the soma and the unconscious and one's concrete thinking. Somatization may thus have a significance similar to that of dreams, acting as important "messengers," or carriers of psychic-emotional information.

The relations of psyche, soma, and mind are, of course, at the center of Winnicott's (1949) paper since he includes the soma *within* the psyche and the psyche within the soma: "I suppose the word psyche here means the *imaginative elaboration of somatic parts, feelings, and functions*, that is, of physical aliveness" (p. 244, emphasis in original). In other words, in health, the psychic apparatus includes imaginative elaborations of the soma. "Gradually the psyche and the soma aspects of the growing person become involved in a process of mutual interrelation," so that eventually, "the live body, with its limits, and with an inside and an outside, is *felt by the individual* to form the core for the imaginative self" (p. 244, emphasis in original).

When hunger strikes   117

In a state of health, the development of the psyche–soma is conditioned on the fact that "its *continuity of being is not disturbed*" (Winnicott, 1949, p. 245, emphasis in original), which is itself conditioned on "a good environment, which is absolute at first, [and then] rapidly becomes relative" (p. 245). The complete responsibility of the environment for the infant's needs is crucial to the understanding of the well-being of the infant's psyche-soma at first, as well as, in the long run, of the mature individual, meaning somatization is perceived by Winnicott as the present indicators of past failures in the individual's early environment. Each and every infant requires the active adaptation of its environment, maternal or analytic (Winnicott, 1953, p. 93, 1960b, p. 594, 1963a, p. 343).

In a later paper, "Psycho-Somatic Illness in Its Positive and Negative Aspects," Winnicott (1966b) elaborates his major ideas about the psyche–soma. Suggesting that there are some positive aspects to a psychosomatic illness, he emphasizes the "the patient's *pathological splitting of the environmental provision.* The split is certainly one that separates off physical care from intellectual understanding; more important, it separates psyche-care from soma-care" (p. 511, emphasis added). By this, Winnicott restates what is most significant to his thinking: (1) What is pathological about psychosomatic illness is the (excessive) employment of *splitting.*. (2) What is split is the *environmental provision.* This conceptualization is crucial, as Winnicott positions psychosomatic illness *not* within psyche and soma, but *between subject and object*, perceiving the psychosomatic illness as an expression (manifestation, symptom) of another split, between infant and mother. (3) The split is, specifically, between the maternal holding of the infant's mind (that is, psyche, cognition) and the handling/holding of the infant's body. This original split is then manifested in the infant's splitting of his psyche from soma.

The way I understand Winnicott's ideas is that the psychosomatic symptom, or illness, is the patient's way of exhibiting something that has not yet been formed as "psychic information" within one's mind. This "information" does not yet exist in the patient's mind – only in one's soma. For the patient to be able to overcome his or her somatic illness (or to handle it better), the latter will need to become psychic material, meaning it will need to be transformed from somatic information into psychic information.

This is a revolutionary idea, implying that, at least for some patients, psychosomatic illness can promote psychic health. Indeed, for some infants/patients, the unity and personalization can be achieved without somatic illness, but for others, somatization may be needed. For such patients, relationships with their mothers in early infancy did not facilitate the needed unity between psyche and soma; under the circumstances, the best that they were able to do was to develop a psychosomatic illness. In analysis, a psychosomatic illness may facilitate – or result from – a regression to the most primary state possible, from which the patient, with the aid of the analyst, will be able to (re)establish a better unit status (with/ via the analyst) and a unity of soma and psyche.

Hunger strike: the individual's need of an "other"

Kafka's "A Hunger Artist" is about a man mastering the "art" of self-starvation. By referring to him as an "artist," Kafka is labeling "self-starvation" as an "art," which like any other form of art, can be thought of as sublimation. The artist struggles with and sublimates, first and foremost, two basic human needs: first, his need of food, which he is unable to accept, and second, his need to be acknowledged by an "other." I find Winnicott's theory, of both the psyche–soma relationship and the early mother–infant relationship, to be very relevant to this story. Not only is physical nurturance (food) connected with emotional nurturance, it is also noteworthy that the artist starves himself to death in front of an audience, which acts as a witness to the artist's physical self-destruction. The artist (infant/patient) and the audience (mother/analyst) are mutually dependent on one other – but, while in a healthy relationship, infant/patient and mother/analyst are mutually dependent "until life does them part"; given the pathological dependence (of the artist and his audience) it is "until death does them part." Kafka's story, like Winnicott's theory of psyche–soma and its relations to the mind, embodies the paradoxes of death in life, presence in absence, total dependence in omnipotence.

Kafka leaves it to the reader to comprehend what could possibly cause a person to willingly give up his life and cause people to witness and actively participate in such an act. By describing various characters, "witnessing" and "participating" in the artist's performance (the audience, the two ladies, the overseer), Kafka raises the question of "responsibility." As in the case of a dream, I conceive all of this to represent the dreamer's struggles. Within analysis, patient and analyst may each play any of these different roles, interchangeably.

Working with patients who express some psychic aspects through their soma requires the analyst to take responsibility for both the emotional and the physical well-being of the patient. The analyst's capacity to take responsibility has to do with his or her ability to contain feelings of guilt and concern, which Winnicott (1958) refers to as "ruth." (Winnicott's concept of "ruth" refers to "concern," and ruthlessness to lack of concern.) Although he states this in regard to the development of the infant's concern for his mother's well-being, I would like to suggest that this concept can be applied to one's guilt and concern regarding one's ruthlessness toward one's psychic or somatic self. Important information has to do with the way the patient refers to his or her somatic symptom, in a sense regarding the symptom as an "object" with which the patient has a "relationship." I am equating the somatic symptom to the individual "sick baby-self," and the way he or she takes care of the symptom may be, for the therapist, another source of information regarding the patient's early object relations. Hence, somatic illness represents not only the ill adaptation of the mother to her infant, but also the ill adaptation of one's psyche and soma. The analyst, like the mother, needs to survive the patient's ruthless attacks, both those directed inwardly (psyche ↔ soma) and those directed at the analyst.

There is little doubt that self-starvation is an act of ruthlessness and that the individual lacks concern for this or her physical needs, which are disposed of and thrust on someone else – a parent or physician – who is then not only responsible for literally feeding the individual, but often has to force it upon him or her, thus becoming an "aggressive" other. As in Kafka's "A Hunger Artist," a somatic (anorexic) patient forces the analyst to decide where the line between witnessing and participating should be crossed. Winnicott (1949) refers to the crucial role of the environmental provision, which facilitates the development of the psyche–soma relationship, including the vital role held by one's feelings and expressions of "ruth." In the absence of a good enough environment, fully adapted to the infant's needs, the relationship of psyche and soma, mother and infant, (patient and analyst) cannot develop healthily. In terms of responsibility, with its intimations of "witnessing" and "participating," the mother, at the early stages of life, and the analyst, within the analytic relationship, need to find a way to achieve the delicate balance of dependence and independence needed by the infant/patient, at each specific phase of development. Too much or too little are experienced as impingement – that is, a disturbance of one's continuity of being. This, in turn, may lead to disturbances of one's psyche–soma and self–other relations. As analysts, we often master the art of witnessing: participating in our patients' lives, at times struggling with patients' self-destructive behavior. We are often torn about when to intervene and what might be the best way to engage in the analytic relationship. This is true with all patients, but is even more crucial with "difficult patients" and those who suffer from psychosomatic illness.

The somatic symptom, or illness, may be perceived as "pulling" psychic pain to the (physical) "surface," making the invisible psychic pain physically apparent, transforming it into a relational medium of communication. There is a paradoxical interplay of "anonymity" in the relationship of the psychic pain and the somatic symptom, as the latter may seem more concrete, or more "real," than psychic pain. At the same time, the somatic symptom obscures the psychic pain to which it is in some Unknown way connected. The somatic symptom has an important role in revealing (and hiding) the psychic pain to the external world. The analyst is an important "witness" to the patient's somatic and psychic pain, and the patient needs the analyst to be his or her audience, before whom he or she performs. Analysts must transform each patient from "a" patient to "the" patient, for as the patient's caring audience we do not merely "witness" the patient's suffering, but are emotionally engaged in his or her life. In cases of more extreme somatic illnesses, such as anorexia nervosa (e.g., Kafka's hunger artist), the analyst may need to consider a more active engagement. Often, extreme somatic illnesses are meant to test the mother/analyst's capacity to maintain the delicate balance between "witnessing" and "participating," testing the analyst's own capacity to care ruthlessly for the patient.

Winnicott (1960b) relates the physical act of feeding to the emotional maternal care of the infant:

> It would be wrong to put the instinctual gratification (feeding etc.) or object relationships (relation to the breast) before the matter of ego organization (i.e., infant ego reinforced by maternal ego). The basis for instinctual satisfaction

and for object relationships is the handling and the general management and the care of the infant, which is only too easily taken for granted when all goes well.

(p. 592)

By this, Winnicott seems to imply that the mother, who is responsible for providing the infant with all of his or her physical, emotional, and environmental needs, is the one who can facilitate the development of a healthy psyche–soma. For example, a mother's way of feeding her baby is never just "physical." A good emotional feed establishes one's internal good object which, in turn, enables the infant/patient to be "alone," that is, with one's self. "The capacity to be alone depends on the existence in the psychic reality of the individual of a good object" (Winnicott, 1958, p. 417).

Where there were "mother" and "infant," there shall be "psyche" and "soma"

The final scene in Kafka's story describes the artist's physical death, wrapped in the arms of the overseer. The overseer is the only character who is emotionally engaged and who talks with the hunger artist. He is the only one who asks him why he is not eating, and the artist's answer is surprising: He tells the overseer that there is nothing else he can do, besides fasting. It is not entirely clear from Kafka's way of telling the story of the artist whether he is struggling to die or to live. The artist explains to the overseer that he was fasting because he could not find any food (nurturance) that was "good enough" for him. You cannot but think of Winnicott's good-enough maternal care, one that nurtures the child in a benign way that makes one *want to live*. We can only imagine the sort of disappointment one has to have endured, for such an elimination of hunger to be necessary. With his final words, the artist is suggesting that fasting is not, for him, an *ideology*, but a by-product of *unsatisfactory circumstances*.

Winnicott (1941) discusses the "physiology of anxiety" (p. 62) stating:

To understand what is happening when we watch these symptoms, I think we have to know something about the child's feelings and phantasies, and therefore about the amount of excitement and rage that is admixed, as well as the defenses against these.

(p. 62)

This is another reference of Winnicott to the issue of the psyche's (emotions) relations with the soma (symptoms). He then adds, "He [the individual] unconsciously fears specific bad things which exist somewhere in him. 'Somewhere' means *either outside or inside—ordinarily both outside and inside himself*" (p. 62, italics added). For Winnicott, psychosomatic symptoms, or illness, belong to a layer in which differentiation has not yet been achieved; the individual cannot tell whether it is from the "outside" or the "inside" of him or her, nor whether it is "somatic" or "psychic." The somatic symptom "can be exaggerated or inhibited in accordance with the unconscious phantasy which happens to affect the particular function or organ" (p. 62). Winnicott seems to move back and forth, from the internal environment of impulses, anxieties, and feelings of love, hate, and rage, to the external reality where objects resign, "good" or "bad," either subjectively or objectively (as in cases of deprivation). The somatic symptom lies in between, perhaps like a valve of a pressure cooker, aimed to relieve excessive pressure.

Somatization, as in the case of Kafka's hunger artist can be perceived as outlining the absence (of nurturance), going against life (nature), and can reflect the mother's absence from her infant's life. Kafka's artist fits Winnicott's (1966a) description of what distinguishes "privation" from "deprivation." "Deprivation," suggests Winnicott, "means that someone was not letting the child down, and then this failed" (p. 6). The hunger artist is depriving himself of food, which is essential for life. This is connected to a good-enough and reliable environmental provision, which failure leads "to a reaction in the child to unpredictable impingements from external reality. This reaction breaks the continuity of the child's being and there follows a change in the child and in the child's capacity to rely on the environment" (p. 6). Paradoxically, Winnicott states: "The antisocial tendency is a symptom of a return of hopefulness" (p. 7), and I suggest that this can be applied to somatic disorders as well.

Excerpts from a case study

Sharon's communication of her hunger

Regardless of her intelligence, Sharon was very childish, compliant, and aggressive. The most apparent feature of her behavior was her extreme anxiety and edginess. She seemed always to be on the verge of exploding, and she actually often did, leading me to feel anxious and eventually tired of trying to have a conversation with her. She often seemed to observe her own patterns of communication, but even when her communications did seem like genuine self-reflections, it was impossible to talk about them. I was prohibited from joining her self-reflection, and when I tried, I was usually attacked viciously. After trying for a couple of years to have a discourse with Sharon, which included talking about her extreme anxiety and the way it turned into rage, perhaps as a means of not feeling so "little" and helpless, I began to feel that it was, in fact, quite futile.

Around the fourth year of her analysis, Sharon started eating less. This seemed to develop subtly and gradually but was declared aloud and often, unlike other anorexic women I have worked with. She would come to her session and account for everything she ate that day, often recounting what she had eaten since our last meeting. She was extremely proud of not eating and dressed in rather tight clothing, so that her loss of weight would be visible. I was surprised when I realized that Sharon's attempts to not eat did not evoke worry but rather compassion for her attempts to appear as sick as possible. It is not, of course, that I wanted her to

122 When hunger strikes

do better at fasting, but that even her attempts at fasting seemed unsuccessful. It felt as if even her anorexia was an "as if" anorexia.

Sharon herself expressed frustration over not being a "good anorexic," and each time she was "complimented" for her thinness, she was elated. I found this to be unusual as well. In my experience, anorexic women more often felt distress when they were complimented (on being thin), which caused them often to lose more weight. These women did not want to look good; they wanted others to acknowledge their illness, not their "good thin look." On those occasions when Sharon tried to engage me in talking about her food intakes and about how sick she is, I often refused, telling her that she was using food and eating to pull me into an interaction that would be more of an as-if engagement. "I do not want to as-if talk with you. I want to really and truly talk with you about the things that bother you. It is not food." For a long time, this made Sharon very angry with me: "You don't care about me! How can you be so calm and relaxed when I am not eating!" I felt that Sharon was "playing" with her food, similar to a way a toddler, seeking attention, might do so – not for the sake of curiosity and creativity, but for the sake of driving his or her mother "crazy."

This lasted for almost a year, at which point I contacted her dietitian and explicitly asked her to gradually stop treating Sharon. I shared with her my feeling that, in this specific case, paying attention to Sharon's eating disorder was like joining her in her ill attempt to be sick. Soon after the dietitian told Sharon that her weight was stable and "good enough" and that their relationship should be discontinued, Sharon's symptoms subsided significantly. We worked through her need to be sick as an expression of her profound anxiety to be an adult, or should I say, an adult woman. Not eating was Sharon's way of expressing her fear of living: Life as an adult was too heavy for her to carry, psychically, and by means of diminishing her body, leading to a constant physical feeling of weakness and nausea, she hoped she would elicit in me – as her analyst–mother – the wish to keep taking care of her.

Feeling she was "pushed" into therapy by her mother allowed Sharon to maintain her ambivalence, acting as a psychic dis-integration, similar to the role the somatic symptom has, physically. Her ambivalence was communicated everywhere: in forever trying to change the times of her sessions, in almost never bringing up something she wished to talk about, in "undoing" everything she said in the sessions, in being so extremely erratic it was impossible to talk, and in bringing up the option of quitting her analysis a couple of times a month, but never agreeing to discuss it more seriously. In her fifth year of analysis, I was on the verge of losing my patience. I told Sharon, "You have to *make up your mind* whether you want to be in analysis, or not." I did contemplate this statement for quite a while, but it still felt "impulsive" when it came up. I cannot recall ever giving a patient an "ultimatum," as I did with Sharon. Nonetheless, it felt like the most authentic thing I could say, and I felt that our most fundamental struggle was about authenticity. I felt that I could no longer carry on with the kind of communication Sharon was forcing upon us: It felt like waiting for a volcano to erupt, keeping still and silent.

Neither did it feel helpful to talk with Sharon about "what she ate." I experienced this as useless and at times even harmful, as it moves too quickly toward the differentiation between "soma" and "psyche."

More questions than answers

Treating patients who exhibit psychosomatic illness raises significant questions regarding which analytic intervention is best. The answers to this are complicated and are based on the analyst's own personal psychosomatic experiences and perspectives: Is it the patient's way of destroying the analysis? Is it the patient's way of not communicating? Is it the patient's way of communicating some truth regarding his or her emotional state? Is it a way of committing suicide? More urgent, perhaps, than these questions is the analyst's question: "What should I *do* about it?" Because whatever may be our preferred way of perceiving our patients, we should consider our position as the patient's "audience," and ask ourselves what role we play in patients' acting out, psychic and/or somatic.

I perceive somatic disorders to be the patient's wordless communication, a way of relocating his or her original trauma, which was originally unthinkable and unspeakable. The psyche's ability to live within the soma is conditioned on the infant's ability to establish an "I am" state (Winnicott, 1962b, p. 62), and this is followed by an establishment of the infant's capacity to acknowledge a "not-me" which leads in turn to persecutory anxiety. The psychosomatic illness often acts as a defensive mechanism against the anxiety of losing the union between psyche and soma, meaning differentiation. Hence, the successful differentiation of psyche and soma, followed by a successful integration, is conditioned on "good-enough active and adaptive handling," without which "it may actually prove impossible for this development of a psychosomatic inter-relationship to become properly established" (Winnicott, 1962b, p. 62).

An external environment that fails the infant's individual need for adaptive care, and fails to address the infant's authentic needs and features, elicits the danger that the infant will accommodate his or her unique characteristics to fit the environment's needs. The result, which Winnicott (1960a) has referred to as a "False Self," is "an attempt on the part of the individual to solve the personal problem by the use of a fine intellect" (p. 144), while "in the healthy individual, it must be assumed, the mind is not something for the individual to exploit in escape from psycho-somatic being" (p. 144).

Under less fortunate circumstances,

> A particular danger arises out of the not infrequent tie-up between the intellectual approach and the False Self. When a False Self becomes organized in an individual who has a high intellectual potential there is a very strong tendency for the mind to become the location of the False Self, and in this case, there develops dissociation between intellectual activity and psychosomatic existence.
>
> (Winnicott, 1960a, p. 144)

Both Kafka's hunger artist and Sharon insisted they needed nobody, and exhibited a "false self" in their denial of psychic and somatic needs, while both desperately needed an audience and were unable, in fact, to lead full, independent, and interconnected lives.

Sharon was unable to use words creatively, with personal, intimate connotations, either with me or with others. The capacity to use words is extremely significant in establishing the relationships between psyche and soma, since it mobilizes intellectual forces (Winnicott, 1962a). Winnicott, relates psychosomatic disorders to two states: (1) the preverbal, and (2) a much later one in which verbalization fills the "gap" in a way that, in fact, dissociates between "psyche" and "soma." As much as the true self has to do with authenticity, it may be safe to suggest that personalization does also, since it is a word "that can be used to describe the achievement of a close relationship between the psyche and the body" (Winnicott, 1963b, p. 223).

In the case of Sharon, self-starvation acted as a mechanism of the false self that "gradually become[s] a 'caretaker self'" (Winnicott, 1955, p. 18), replacing the environmental good enough provision. In such cases, the somatic illness serves to make the absence present, while allowing the individual to exhibit his or her caretaking capabilities. The psychosomatic disorder may serve to hide the individual's mental illness (Winnicott, 1963b), breaking the link between psyche and soma, resulting "in various clinical states which receive the name 'depersonalization'" (p. 224). What is crucial to understand about the false self is that: "The false self cannot, however, experience life, and feel real" (Winnicott, 1956, p. 387). The feeling of unreal-ness was significant in Sharon's analysis. I often felt as if I was "forced" to witness a poorly acted show.

Final thoughts: psyche ↔ soma, a two-way transformation

Choosing to fast is a symptom of a wider "breakup" between psyche and soma. This breakup will appear, later on, in the individual's relations with his or her caretakers and cathected objects, as well as in the transference and countertransference within the analytic relationship (Lombardi, 2008). Another frequent expression of this breakup in the mother–infant relationship is commonly expressed in the form of somatization, which, unfortunately, may be perceived by the analyst as "acting out," or as an obstacle to the analytic process. Lombardi speaks of these misunderstandings of somatic expression in which the body and the somatic symptom may act as an object with which the patient has a complex relationship (Gedo, 1997), including that of love–hate. It is wise for the analyst to observe the ways the patient treats the somatic illness as an object and to take notice of whether the patient dismisses the symptom, cares for it, expresses hate or compassion, and so forth – all of which may be reminiscent of the patient's early object relations. Unable to tell his story verbally, the patient needs to express his or her unconscious experience in such nonverbal terms as somatic symptoms, or other physical means, like extreme body-building, extreme sport activities, eating disorders, and self-harm.

Excessive use of somatization might also be understood as "representing" the individual's experience of early maternal care, which was more physical than psychic-emotional. In cases of excessive somatization, the mind either transforms a nonverbal psychic experience into a concrete embodied one, or may sustain an early physical experience within the body-soma, unable to transform it into a psychic-symbolic and verbal one. In both cases the patient maintains the split between psyche and soma. On the other hand, the somatic symptom allows the patient to experience something Ih is crucial to him or her, which was unavailable for psychic-emotional working through in the here and now of the analytic setting. This allows the patient to transform the somatic experience into an alive, emotional experience. The somatic symptom thus acts as a grounding force onto the reality of the concrete body (Lombardi, 2008) and allows for the unconscious to be further elaborated in Current emotional experience, as in Ogden's (2003) "dreaming" oneself into fuller existence (p. 598).

Working with patients, like Sharon and the hunger artist, who rely on somatization as their primary form of communication may be extremely difficult. Sharon was often suspicious of me and perceived me (rightfully so) to be outside her omnipotent control, which made it extremely difficult for her to "use" (Winnicott, 1969) me, or to make use of verbal *symbolization* as a means of communicating her feelings and thoughts. Sharon often perceived our exchanges as dangerous as eating: "You will use what I say against me. Nothing good will come of it. I will disappear if I talk with you." For Sharon, taking in my words was similar to taking in food. Both were perceived as eliminating her individuality and subjectivity; neither food nor words was experienced as nurturing. Furthermore, for Sharon, fasting and being silent made her feel more visible, and elicited her hope of being better cared for. Eating and talking both amounted to taking in a "bad," even destructive, object, which threatened her by diminishing her omnipotent control over me, as her external object. It took years of analysis for Sharon to be able to accept me as someone whom she cannot control, and it was only then that I could be given a role as an external subject (Winnicott, 1969). Within the analytic relationship, Sharon was gradually able to differentiate herself from me, as her realization of her inability to control me was established. I also believe that the fact that I was not alarmed by her fasting forced her to find other ways to communicate with me. I refused to join her somatic language and dwell in endless, pointless accounts of what she ate and how many grams she has lost. I insisted on talking with Sharon about her need to have me in a constant alert state of mind, and suggested to her that the only way she could feel that I cared for her was my being anxious. I perceived this need of Sharon that both she and I will be constantly alert and anxious as her regression to an early state of object relations.

Our patients' reliance on somatic symptoms or illnesses can be understood as a form of regression (Winnicott, 1955), not only because they have found

126 When hunger strikes

the reliable environment they so need, but often because they have not found it. Sharon, who was unable to use me as a good object, narcissistically cathected. The somatic symptom became her main object of relatedness (not yet separate from the self), coming at the expense of object-usage. Sharon's, as well as the hunger artist's, soma (and self-starvation) served them as a primitive replacement of an external other, while preserving the other as merely an "audience" to their acted-out somatization (self-starvation). There is a world of experiences occurring between the patient and his or her somatic symptom, and if we manage to listen carefully and not interrupt too much or too soon, we will discover (some of) the bodily centered "music" of the patient's early life.

Note

1 This text was published in *Psychoanalytic Review*, 106(4): 325–341, July 2019.

References

Alvarez, A. (1985). The problem of neutrality: Some reflections on the psychoanalytic attitude in the treatment of borderline and psychotic patients. *Journal of Child Psychotherapy*, 11(1): 87–103.

Bion, W.R. (1962). *Learning from experience*. London: Heinemann.

Bion, W.R. (1965). *Transformations*. London: Heinemann.

Etchegoyan, R.H. (1983). Fifty years after the imitative interpretation. *International Journal of Psycho-Analysis*, 64: 445–459.

Gedo, J.E. (1997). The primitive psyche, communication, and the language of the body. Psychoanalytic Inquiry, 17(2):192–203.

Green, A. (2010). Thoughts on the Paris school of psychosomatics. In M. Aisenstein & E. Rappoport de Aisemberg (eds.), *Psychosomatics today: A psychoanalytic perspective*. London: Karnac.

Grotstein, J. (1983). Autistic states in children. By Frances Tustin. London: Routledge and Kegan Paul, 1981, pp. 376. *International Review of Psycho-Analysis*, 10: 491–498.

Kafka, F. (1926). *The metamorphosis, a hunger artist, in the penal colony, and other stories*. Arlington, VA: Richer Resource.

Lombardi, R. (2003). Catalyzing the dialogue between the body and the mind in psychotic analysand. *The Psychoanalytic Quarterly*, 72: 1017–1041.

——— (2008). The body in the analytic session: Focusing on the body-mind link. *International Journal of Psycho-Analysis*, 89: 89–109.

Ogden, T.H. (2003). What's true and whose idea was it? *International Journal of Psycho-Analysis*, 84: 593–606.

Ogden, T.H. (2009). Kafka, Borges, and The creation of consciousness, Part I: Kafka – Dark ironies of the "gift" of consciousness. *The Psychoanalytic Quarterly*, 78(2): 348–367.

Winnicott, D.W. (1941). The observation of infants in a set situation. In D.W. Winnicott (Ed.) (1975). *Through paediatrics to psycho-analysis* (pp. 52–69). London: Hogarth Press and the Institute of Psycho-Analysis. .

—— (1949). Mind and its relation to the psyche-soma. In D.W. Winnicott (Ed.) (1975). *Through paediatrics to psycho-analysis* (pp. 243–254). London: Hogarth Press and the Institute of Psycho-Analysis.

—— (1953). Transitional objects and transitional phenomena: A study of the first not-me possession. *International Journal of Psycho-Analysis*, 34: 89–97.

—— (1955). Meta-psychological and clinical aspects of regression within the psycho-analytical set-up. *International Journal of Psycho-Analysis*, 36: 16–26.

—— (1956). On transference. *International Journal of Psycho-Analysis*, 37: 386–388.

—— (1958). Psycho-analysis and the sense of guilt. In D.W. Winnicott (Ed.) (1965). *The maturational processes and the facilitating environment: Studies in the theory of emotional development* (pp. 15–28). London: Hogarth Press and the Institute of Psycho-Analysis.

—— Psycho-analysis and the sense of guilt. In D.W. Winnicott (Ed.) (1965). *The maturational processes and the facilitating environment: Studies in the theory of emotional development* (pp. 15–28). *The International Psycho-Analytical Library* 64, 1–276, 1965.

—— (1960a). Ego distortion in terms of true and false self. In D.W. Winnicott (Ed.) (1965). *The maturational processes and the facilitating environment: Studies in the theory of emotional development* (pp. 140–152). London: Hogarth Press and the Institute of Psycho-Analysis.

—— (1960b). The theory of the parent-infant relationship. *International Journal of Psycho-Analysis*, 41: 585–595.

—— (1962a). The aims of psycho-analytical treatment. In D.W. Winnicott (1965) (Ed.). *The maturational processes and the facilitating environment: Studies in the theory of emotional development* (pp. 166–170). London: Hogarth Press and the Institute of Psycho-Analysis.

—— (1962b). Ego integration in child development. In D.W. Winnicott (Ed.) (1965). *The maturational processes and the facilitating environment: Studies in the theory of emotional development* (pp. 56–63). London: Hogarth Press and the Institute of Psycho-Analysis.

—— (1963a). Dependence in infant care, in child care, and in the psychoanalytic setting. *International Journal of Psycho-Analysis*, 44: 339–344.

—— (1963b). The mentally ill in your caseload. In D.W. Winnicott (Ed.) (1965). *The maturational processes and the facilitating environment: Studies in the theory of emotional development* (pp. 217–229). London: Hogarth Press and the Institute of Psycho-Analysis.

—— (1966a). Becoming deprived as a fact: A psychotherapeutic consultation. *Journal of Child Psychotherapy*, 1(4): 5–12.

—— (1966b). Psycho-somatic illness in its positive and negative aspects. *International Journal of Psycho-Analysis*, 47: 510–516.

—— (1969). The use of an object. *International Journal of Psycho-Analysis*, 50: 711–716.

Chapter 7

What do faith and trust have to do with psychoanalysis?

Introduction

I have chosen this topic to be the last chapter of this book for more than one reason. First of all, I perceive trust and faith to be some of the most important issues in human life, a fundamental condition, as well as a developmental achievement (trust) that should not be taken for granted, as well as a given source (faith). Another reason is that as an Israeli secular Jew, I cannot repudiate the unique context of the society in which I live. The majority of the population in Israel is Jewish, but a significant portion of it comprises Muslims and Christians. Many of the citizens (of all three religions) are religious and observe the laws of their religion. I think that regardless of my secularity (which I share with most of my fellow analysts and researchers at academia), there is no way you can live in Israel and be mindless about the significance faith has in people's lives.

Yet, my interest in the issues of trust and faith is completely secular. Trust, as I perceive it is acquired within the infant–mother relationship, hence it is a developmental achievement. I think few will disagree with me about this, or about its significance to our lives, in good times as well as when we encounter difficulties. Trust is also profoundly significant to the therapist–patient relationship, often put to test within the transference. Faith is a more complex idea, often because it is immediately related to religion, but not only because of that. It is also an abstract notion, difficult to measure scientifically or to conceptualize. Psychoanalysis's relationship with the concept of "faith" has always been rather tensed, not welcome for various reasons. In what follows, I will attempt to illustrate its relevance and significance to the analytic process, conceptualizing it as an inborn potentiality. I will try and plant this concept, of "Faith" in a flowerbed that has already been cultivated by Winnicott, Bion, and Eigen, to mention just a few.

"Healing" is a big word that often evokes one's fantasy of eliminating past pains and traumas, becoming a completely different person, than before. This is of course not possible, regardless of the profound faith I have in the possibilities that psychoanalysis can offer in terms of psychic growth and living more fully. I would rather refer to concepts more modest than "healing," such as "Trust," "Faith,"[1] and "hope."

DOI: 10.4324/9781003203193-8

First, I would like to offer my distinction between "Faith" and "Trust," within psychoanalysis and bring forward the idea that one's Faith is an inborn quality whereas "Trust" is a capability acquired through one's relationships with a reliable caretaker. Thus, "Faith" can be thought of as a preconception of a benign potential, referring to the various possibilities that the "future" holds within it, that go beyond what is present, and can be met by the eye, at a certain moment. I perceive both "Faith" and "Trust" to be highly significant to one's ability to thrive in life and make good use of psychoanalysis (Winnicott, 1969). Faith and Trust often go hand in hand, but I believe they each hold a different function, albeit they are complementary to one another. The patient's ability to use the analyst and the analysis depends, to a large extent, on her/his ability to trust the analyst, as well as on the analyst's Faith in the method and the patient. The analyst, like a mother who can dream the baby in the future tense (as a toddler, a young child, an adolescent, etc.) holds within him/herself the potential of the patient. There is a constant dialectic tension between the patient's pain and the potential possibility for psychic growth, as well as between Faith as rooted in oneness (as an inborn quality) and Trust, rooted in twoness (acquired through mother–infant matrix).

What do faith and trust have to do with psychic growth?

From its outset, psychoanalysis has been attempting to codify its assumptions concerning the most fundamental conditions needed for one's ability to become a whole human being, one that is capable of living their life to its fullest potential. The various schools within psychoanalysis tend to differ in their focus on inborn or constitutional traits versus acquired character traits (Freud, 1940, p. 28), internal (fantasied, subjective) reality versus external (objective) reality, etc. Although these are all useful, and I, too, base my understanding of my patients' learning on the existing concepts such as drive, environment, constitution, early object relations, and culture, nevertheless, I often feel that there is something that is missing. This "something" is rather vague, but I feel that it plays a significant role in my patients' ability to use me and their analyses. In this final chapter, I would like to offer my perspective on "Faith" and "Trust" as this "something else" (Brookes, 2002) – the missing pieces – that can elucidate our further understanding of what it is that determines patients' ability to use their analyses.

Freud: putting one's faith in science

As a scientist, Freud's relationship with faith could at best be ambivalent (Zusman, Cheniaux, & Freitas, 2007). Nonetheless, it seems to me that like many others, Freud referred to "faith" as a religious concept and was shortsighted to its secular, or more spiritual dimensions, as so many of his ideas were so outstanding, it seems plausible to suggest that he too needed a lot of faith to bring them forward, as he did.

130 Faith and trust in psychoanalysis

Yet, Freud's perspective of "faith" should be viewed within a cultural context. As a European scholar Jew, he may have felt he needs to distance himself from religion, as was customary in those days within the Jewish Enlightenment movement. Britzman (2011) describes the eighteenth-century Jewish movement *"Haskala" (*education) as based on the

> methods of Jewish study of textual interpretation, in the promise of science, and in the Kantian Enlightenment dedicated to overturning superstitious thought and prejudices through secularity, cosmopolitanism, and the values of autonomy and thinking for oneself ... he [Freud] was suspicious about education and its procedures and felt that certainty and unaccountable belief tended to wreck the creative work of thinking.
>
> (p. 11)

Nonetheless, Freud's perspectives regarding faith have evolved, shifting back and forth between a "philosophical spiritual" attitude to a "scientific" one although it remained somewhat ambivalent throughout. The first references I could find, in his writings, are in two different papers published in 1890: (1) "A Case of Hysteria, Three Essays on Sexuality and Other Works*"* (1890a); and (2) In "Psychical (or Mental) Treatment" (1890b). In the latter Freud discusses one's expectations that precede the experience itself, to which he refers as one's faith:

> [a] fearful expectation is certainly not without its effect on the result. It would be important to know with certainty whether it has as great a bearing as is supposed to fall ill; for instance, whether it is true that during an epidemic, those who are afraid of contracting the illness are in the greatest danger. The contrary state of mind, in which expectation is colored by hope and faith, is an effective force with which we have to reckon, strictly speaking, in all our attempts at treatment and cure.
>
> (1890b, p. 288)

He then refers, explicitly, to faith:

> The most noticeable effects of this kind of expectation colored by *faith* are to be found in the miraculous cures which are brought about even today under our own eyes without the help of any medical skill.
>
> (p. 288, italics added)

It seems that in these texts, Freud is referring to a certain state of mind, that exists *before* one's actual encounter with the external reality. This prior state of mind, which he refers to as "expectations," is colored by various feelings and emotions, impacts the individual's encounter and coping with the actual reality, internal or external (i.e., epidemic illness). These preliminary expectations make some individuals more prone to illness than others, or to *cure*.

Faith and trust in psychoanalysis   131

But then, in what follows immediately, Freud draws the lines that he believes connect faith to religion:

> Miraculous cures properly so-called take place in the case of believers under the influence of adjuncts calculated to intensify religious feelings—that is to say, in places where a miracle-working image is worshipped, or where a holy or divine personage has revealed himself to men and has promised them relief from their sufferings in return for their worship.
>
> (p. 288)

Once again, we can see Freud's struggles to contain the dialectic tension between faith and science. Religious faith, in itself, is not enough to promote a cure, he states, and we may ask: What is it about faith that Freud perceived as a possible hinder to the psychoanalytic endeavor? And if this faith is not enough to promote cure, what else is needed?

Freud's struggle with faith continued, and in 1913 (a, b), he publishes two essays in which he articulated different views regarding faith. In his paper "On Beginning the Treatment," he seemed to diminish the contribution of faith to one's analysis:

> To the skeptic, we say that the analysis requires no faith, that he may be as critical and suspicious as he pleases and that we do not regard his attitude as the effect of his judgment at all, for he is not in a position to form a reliable judgment on these matters; his distrust is only a symptom like his other symptoms, and it will not be an interference, provided he conscientiously carries out what the rule of the treatment requires of him.
>
> (p. 126)

In another paper published in 1913(b), "Totem and Taboo," Freud, again, relates faith to religion, superstitious beliefs, and power, binding it with magical thinking and omnipotence, and contrasting it to science. In another paper published in 1920, he defines faith as unnecessary and even an unwanted feature of the analytic procedure. Still, I do find some of his ideas to be relevant to my conceptualization of Faith as an *inborn quality*. Specifically, it is possible to think of Freud's life drive and my idea of Faith as being both inner forces, implying one's potentiality. In this paper "Beyond the Pleasure Principle" (1920), Freud conceives the "life drive" as responsible for combining "organic substances into ever-larger unities" (p. 43). For him, the Eros/life drive accounts for any development or a movement forward, albeit he did feel that faith has little to do with it.

In a paper he published seven years later, "The Future of Illusion" (1927) he writes:

> In the course of a friendly reply, my colleague gave me an assurance that being a Jew was not an obstacle in the pathway to true faith and proved this

132   Faith and trust in psychoanalysis

by several instances. His letter culminated in the information that prayers were being earnestly addressed to God that he might *grant me "faith to believe."* (p. 169, italics added)

I suggest we take this seriously: It is possible that Faith precedes one's belief and that some individuals may have the faith to believe, whereas others may not. And then, finally, in 1940, in one of his latest papers to be published, "An Outline of Psycho-Analysis," he concludes this epic regarding one's faith, by suggesting that:

> Psychoanalysis lays down a fundamental postulate, the discussion of which belongs to the sphere of philosophical thought, but the justification of which lies in its results.
>
> (p. 28)

To sum Freud's perceptions of faith, it seems to me that he started with viewing the patient's faith, both in the analyst and the analysis, as not crucial for the success of the analytic process, at times even perceiving it to be an unwanted component, but then he went back to see it as an essential feature of the analytic cure. Another complication is apparent in his perception of faith as both preceding one's experience and as an acquired trait, something that seems to me to be a contradiction.

Next to Freud's scientific approach, it is insightful to look into Klein's theory, as she seems to (better) integrate the scientific with the non-scientific. This integration seems to me to be most apparent in her conceptualization of the concept of the "unconscious phantasy" and its dominance in the individual's psychic life. It is difficult to perceive the concept of "unconscious phantasy" as "scientific," but for me, Klein's expansion of psychoanalytic thinking from what is merely "scientific," is a remarkable evolution and a significant contribution.

Klein (as did Freud, albeit differently) emphasizes the interplay of mind–body, as the hub for one's unconscious phantasies. Ogden (1984) writes: "Fantasy for Klein (1952b) is the psychic representation of instinct. Instinct itself is a biological entity, and so fantasy is the mental representation of one's biology" (Ogden, 1984, p. 501).

In their conceptualization of the instinct's role and function, both Freud and Klein collaborate the drive/instinct and its biological function with the mental capacity of the psyche. Although fantasy is not biology, it is biological, and – according to Klein – it is *there, to begin with*, preceding one's encounter with the external environment. Mitchell (1981) explains this: "Klein bases her presupposition of *inherent images and the knowledge of objects separate from and prior experience* on certain more speculative passages in Freud's work, where he posits a phylogenetic inheritance containing specific memory traces and images" (p. 376, Italics added).

According to Klein (1932) the nature of one's objects (both "good" and "bad") is determined by the child's *internal setting*, out of which stems the *"belief* in the existence of kindly and helpful figures – *a belief founded upon the efficacy of his libido*" (p. 260, Italics added). Following Klein's thinking, Ogden (1984), in his discussion of Isaacs's (1952) ideas on the nature and function of the unconscious fantasy, stresses that "the idea of tearing an object to bits *is not learned*, but is part and parcel of the aim of the instinct" (p. 502, italics added). Regarding the question of how the infant's "knowledge" is formed if the child is not utilizing experience, Ogden (1984) points to the Kleinian concept of *"phylogenetic inheritance"* (Klein, 1952a), the theory's primary explanation.

Next, I would like to present some of Bion's thinking about faith. Bion did not shun his ideas about faith and its significance to the psychoanalytic process. In "Transformations," Bion (1965) quotes St. John of the Cross regarding faith:

> The road along which the soul must travel to this union – that is, Faith, which is likewise as dark as night to the understanding.
>
> (p. 159)

In this beautiful quote, Faith is the ground upon which life is carried, and psychic growth is achieved. The concept of Faith received more of Bion's attention in *Attention and Interpretation* (1970), where he relates it to a state that defers memory and desire:

> It may be wondered what state of mind is welcome if desires and memories are not. A term that would express approximately what I need to express is "faith" – A faith that there are an ultimate reality and truth – the unknown, unknowable, "formless infinite."
>
> (p. 31)

And then he adds:

> The objects of awareness are aspects of the "evolved" O[3] and are such that the sensuously derived mental functions are adequate to apprehend them. For them, Faith is not required; for O, it is. The analyst is not concerned with such sensuously apprehend them.
>
> (p. 31)

It seems that for Bion, "faith" is needed in the face of the "unknown" and the "unknowable," hence its transcendental nature; there is no need for faith when one is required to face "reality" or "real" objects. Many experience Bion's theory, at least some of it, as almost mythical, but I experience his conceptualization of "faith" as *unmythical and secular*, being "a scientific state of mind ... unstained by any element of memory or desire" (1970, p. 32). This is more explicit in the discussion of his idea of "act of faith" and O:

> The "act of faith" has no association with memory or desire or sensation. It has a relationship to thought analogous to the relationship of *a priori* knowledge to knowledge. It does not belong to the ± K system but the O system. It does

134 Faith and trust in psychoanalysis

not by itself lead to knowledge "about" something, but knowledge "about" something may be the outcome of a defense against the consequences of an "act of faith." A thought has as its realization a no-thing. An "act of faith" has as its background something that is unconscious and unknown because it has not happened.

(p. 35. Italics in original)

Bion further discuses his ideas concerning faith:

The discipline that I propose for the analyst, namely avoidance of memory and desire, in the sense in which I have used those terms, increases *his ability to exercise "acts of faith." An "act of faith" is peculiar to scientific procedure and must be distinguished from the religious meaning with which it is invested in conversational usage;* it becomes apprehensible when it can be represented in and by thought. It must "evolve" before it can be apprehended and it is apprehended when it is a thought just as the artist's O^2 is apprehensible when it has been transformed into a work of art.

(Bion, 1970, pp. 34–35, italics added)

In another place in this paper, he adds:

Receptiveness achieved by denudation of memory and desire (which is essential to the operation of "acts of faith") is essential to the operation of psycho-analysis and other scientific proceedings.

(pp. 35–36)

If religion is very much about what is *known* and *should be* thought and done, then Bion's conceptualization of "faith" is a secular one. Bion's faith is a scientific concept in the sense that he bases it on thinking that is free of the bias employed by memory (preconception) or desire and as a quest for a specific outcome. One's faith is rooted in one's openness to the "unknown" and the "unexpected"; It cannot be defined or put into a specific form; it is only one's "acts of Faith" that can be identified, or have a structure that can be perceived externally. Faith is formless and infinite and it precedes our physical life, hence, it is unstained by memory or desire and cannot and should not be comprehended based on "reality." Rather, it should be experienced as a source of internal, and perhaps eternal, state.

As in the quoting of St. John: "Faith" is the road on which one's psychic existence (the "soul") develops (travels) from "formless" nonexistence to a formed presence. In some way, it can perhaps be related to Freud's (1920) notion regarding the very beginning of life, which – in his description – is accounted for by the union of germ cells. So is Bion's "faith," as it contains the possible (future) actualization of all the potentialities that are not yet known.

These "infinite" potentialities and possibilities are to be the foundations of one's Faith. Yet, Faith is not omnipotence, magical thinking, or illusions. In fact, they contradict one another. Faith concerns the infinite potential and possibilities and it is a perception of them as "unknown" and as transcending one's immediate, and "known" present experience. Hence, it is very different than omnipotence or magical thinking by which *everything is possible* and *"known"* as a fact. Unlike these states, Faith is by no means a *disconnection from reality*, but rather, the opposite: Faith connects the individual to the immediate experience by taking into account the possibility that it holds within it some unknown potential possibilities.

Bion goes a step further than other psychoanalytic theorists by putting forward the idea that there is a supernatural element, or a process, that *precedes even the biological–physical make-up of the human existence* (i.e., the "catastrophic beta elements") from which the psyche needs to emerge. This raises the question: What is it that the individual psyche needs to make it through? What is that psychic force that precedes the biological existence that helps us pull through and out of which our existence is made possible? Given that there is such a psychic "force," or mechanism, could we label it as "Faith"?

As we have seen, different theorists have named this psychic mechanism differently. Freud has referred to it as "drives," founded upon biology, Bion argues that the emergence of the psyche, from the initial (beta) chaos, requires the transformation of experiences into thoughts and vice versa. Although their postulations sound different, they do, in my mind, hold in common the idea that there is a "platform" on which the psyche grows that is not entirely scientific; Freud refers to the philosophic aspect and Bion talks about "O."

Whatever the concept may be, all theorists have to explain what and how a psyche emerges out of the initial chaos. In writing about the genesis of the human psyche, Eigen (1985) says: "It is the psyche's basic job to transmute these initial catastrophic globs of experience into psychically soluble events. Bion calls the capacity to do this alpha function" (p. 324), and Eigen suggests that this is where faith comes in: "For Bion faith (F) is the proper primordial and developed response to catastrophe" (ibid., p. 326). Following this, I see one's Faith as an *organizing mechanism* to what, otherwise, would remain catastrophic and senseless chaos. Still, unlike Bion who positions faith as a possible *reaction* to catastrophe, I perceive it to be a *mental construct that precedes the catastrophe*. In my view, Faith is what allows and enables the individual (psyche) to emerge out of the catastrophe and proceed forward.

Winnicott and his theory of playing

Winnicott's theory was developed in the second phase of psychoanalysis, governed by theories of object relations. He has conceptualized a psychic "genesis" differently than previously. Unlike Freud and Klein, who focused on aggression and the psyche's defensive organization against anxiety,

> Winnicott perceived the evolving experience of self not so much as a defense against anxiety, or the resolution of conflict, but as an original sense of joy

136   Faith and trust in psychoanalysis

on the one hand and the rapture in the movement from transitional object to object usage, on the other.

(Bronheim, 1994, p. 682)

As I see it, such an assumption calls for the analyst to play an active role in bringing the patient's Faith to life.

Miller (1981) puts forward the importance of the patient's faith to the analytic procedure, stressing its emergence may also be the result of the analytic relationship, and its manifestations are reflected in various ways and forms. Miller refers to faith as something gained and lost throughout life, hence, representing a widely accepted notion of faith as an *acquired trait:*

Analysis rejuvenates faith in oneself and others via the experience of verbalizing rage, hatred, and anger, as well as warmth, affection, and intimacy in a non-retaliatory setting. This usually involves a review of past formative relationships with mother, father, and siblings in the nuclear family. It also can deal with mourning losses that resulted in a loss of faith; it is not until this unfinished business is settled that the patient will have the energy freed up to reinvest in more profitable and enduring interpersonal affiliations.

(p. 20)

I perceive Winnicott's (1953) conceptualization of playing as relevant to my idea regarding the patient's faith. It first calls for a brief discussion of two additional concepts of Winnicott: that of "illusion" and that of "transitional phenomena." Winnicott holds a different position than that of Freud in terms of the connection between "Faith" and "illusion," as is discussed by Eigen (1981), who wrote about Winnicott's conceptualization of "faith" concerning the infant's transitional experiencing: "the infant lives through a *faith that is before clear realization* of self and other differences" (p. 413, italics added). Winnicott positions the transitional experience at the threshold of object usage, which "takes the *life of faith in transitional experiencing forward*" (p. 413, italics added). For Winnicott, faith is a positive aspect, assisting the infant to move forward from a state in which s/he is unable to acknowledge external reality, through the phase of "transitional experiencing," to a state in which acknowledging external reality is possible, and even enriching. For Winnicott, "Faith" has a significant function, being an experience that "the infant lives out of without radically questioning its basis" (p. 414). As I understand this, Winnicott is suggesting that "Faith" precedes the infant's need – or capacity – to question one's existence. This implies that Faith exists prior to the infant's *actual relations* with the external reality/environment.

Although Winnicott does not talk about the evolution of the infant's trust in others, I am leaning on his theory. As I see it, for Winnicott, Trust is related to the infant's ability *to use the object*, resulting from the infant's realization that the object has successfully survived the infant's aggression. Eigen (1982) says that "for Winnicott, it is the subject's dawning awareness of the limitations of

Faith and trust in psychoanalysis   137

his all-out destructive attacks (which once seemed boundless), that creates the experience of externality as such" (p. 415) and I conclude that this is when Trust is needed on behalf of the subject: The infant's appreciation (and gratitude) of the object's survival necessitates that s/he acknowledges the existence of the object. From this follows that "trust" is secondary to faith, as it is founded on experience with external reality.

Next, I wish to draw the lines between my ideas regarding "trust" and Winnicott's (1969) conceptualization of "play." Both ideas emphasize the importance of the mother's reliability and the infant's ability to depend on her. It is when the infant is ready to use the object that trust becomes crucial, as "using the object" means that the infant can relate to the mother as a separate object, albeit available emotionally. Discussing the infant's ability to "wait," Winnicott (1967) coined his famous equation of x+y+z, referring to the circumstances under which the baby's trust in the mother may collapse, beyond the possibility of mending. He suggested that

> The feeling of the mother's existence lasts x minutes. If the mother is away more than x minutes, then the image fades, and along with this the baby's capacity to use the symbol of the union ceases to be a fact. The baby is distressed, but this distress is soon *mended* because the mother returns in x+y minutes. But in x+y+z minutes the baby has become *traumatized.* In x+y+z minutes the mother's return does not mend the baby's altered states.
>
> (p. 368)

The baby's ability to sustain the mother's image is based, so I believe, on both faith and trust. As I see it, the baby has to have faith, to begin with, in order to be able to develop a sense of trust in the mother's return.

Perhaps it will be helpful to think of faith as the baby's inborn belief in the mother's love, whereas trust develops out of the baby's real experiences with the mother and is, thus, founded on the mother's reliability. Still, it is the baby's inborn capacity for faith that enables him/her to wait, and survive the mother's absence (in the "y" phase). According to this formulation, the infant's Faith precedes the encounter with the external (real) object. This, I believe, is supported by Winnicott when he wrote, "It is the self that must precede the self's use of instinct" (p. 369). Winnicott, I think, is subtly suggesting that there has to be "something that precedes even instincts, or 'muscle erotism'" (Winnicott, 1963).

The environment, as a whole, and the mother, specifically, has the greatest influence on the infant's development and well-being, both based to a great extent on the child's ability to play. In his paper "The Location of Cultural Experience," Winnicott (1967) focused on "play," and I think his ideas can be applied to my perception of "Trust" and "Faith." In this paper, Winnicott suggests that the infant should be able to both draw from the cultural experience and contribute to it. The idea of the mutual interdependence between infant and environment is especially important in cases when the environment fails the infant:

The "deprived child" is notably restless and unable to play and has an impoverishment of capacity to experience in the cultural field. This observation leads to a study of the effect of deprivation at the time of the loss of what has become accepted as reliable. *Failure of dependability or loss of object means to the child damage the play area, and loss of meaningful symbol.*

(p. 371, italics added)

Winnicott theorizes the relations between the infant's capacity to *play* and the ability to *trust* the object, conceptualizing them as *interdependent*. To be able to *trust* others, the child needs to be able to *play*, and vice versa. One thing that both Trust and play have in common is that they both depend on the mother's reliability and dependability. Next, Winnicott discusses the importance of creative imagination, needed especially if and when the child is unable to "play": "In favorable circumstances, the potential space becomes filled with the products of the baby's creative imagination. In unfavorable circumstances, the creative use of objects is missing or relatively uncertain" (p. 371). I understand Winnicott to be saying that under certain circumstances (i.e., the object's failure and the infant's resultant deprivation), the infant may lose his ability to trust in a way that is beyond mending. In contrast, under good enough circumstances, the infant can use creative imagination to fill in these gaps, making up for the object's absence. I use the term "faith" to refer to this "creative imagination," meaning an inner state to which the infant can "retreat" (and re-treat, in the sense of repairing, and mending) so as to better cope with the object's failure.

Winnicott (1967) proposed that

This potential space is a highly variable factor (from individual to individual), whereas the two other locations – personal or psychic reality and the actual world – are relatively constant, one being biologically determined and the other being common property.

(p. 372)

In this, Winnicott is making a distinction between the "potential space" from "psychic" and/or "actual" reality and I would like to propose that one's "faith" lies *within this potential space*, as it is neither internal nor external; neither "biological" nor "common property."

Throughout life, faith is most crucial in times of pain, serving as a resource, and a vehicle to one's ability to cope with various struggles and hardships. Although Winnicott does not relate "play" to "faith," he does make some essential references that allow me to do so. For example, in his paper "Transitional Objects and Transitional Phenomena" (1953), he states:

it is assumed here that the task of reality-acceptance is never completed, that no human being is free from the strain of relating inner and outer reality, and that relief from this strain is provided by an intermediate area of experience which is not challenged (arts, religion, etc.).

(p. 96)

In drawing the lines between intermediate area, play, and madness, Winnicott says:

> If, however, the adult can manage to enjoy the personal intermediate area without making claims, then we can acknowledge our corresponding inter-mediate areas and are pleased to find overlapping, that is to say, common experience between members of a group in art or religion or philosophy.

(p. 96)

This differentiation is crucial as many tend to think about "faith" in relation to reli-gion and tend to relate it to obsessive rituals, or other forms of illogical thinking. Because of this popular tendency, I need to make clear that Faith is not necessarily a religious concept, but a universally human one. The most significant difference, between religion, obsessive rituals, and illogical/magical thinking and the "Faith" I am concerned with, as an inborn quality, is that the three former mechanisms often serve the subject's retreat from reality and the "Faith" I am talking about, in contrast, *serves as the opposite – it assists the subject to approach reality in a better, fuller way.*

Winnicott (1963) – in perhaps one of his most straightforward statements, regarding religion and faith and their profound differences – says the following:

> My main point is that there does exist a good alternative. The good alterna-tive has to do with the provision of those conditions for the infant and child that enable such things as *trust and belief in,* and ideas of right and wrong, to develop out of the working of *the individual child's inner processes.*

(p. 94, italics added)

So, unlike religion, magical thinking, or obsessive rituals, Faith acts as a bridge between one's internal and external world. In this sense, Faith is similar to "playing" – it is neither "created" nor "found." *It is just there.*

What does contemporary psychoanalysis have to say about faith?

In the Oxford English Dictionary (2012), faith is defined as:

1. Complete trust or confidence in someone or something;
2. Strong belief in the doctrines of religion, based on spiritual conviction rather than proof.

140   Faith and trust in psychoanalysis

Trust is defined as:

1. A firm belief in the reliability, truth, or ability of someone or something;
2. The acceptance of the truth of a statement without evidence or investigation;
3. The state of being responsible for someone or something.

It seems that faith and trust overlap in a way that does not allow for a clear distinction.

In her book titled *In the Beginning Was Love – Psychoanalysis, and Faith*, Kristeva (1987) states:

> Psychoanalysis (along with linguistics and sociology) became the last of the scientific disciplines to set itself up as a rational approach to the understanding of human behavior and its always enigmatic meaning.
>
> (p. 1).

For Kristeva (1987), psychoanalysis's primary vehicle is the "transference" through which "the person of the analyst carries me toward a focal point of power and knowledge" (p. 7). The idealized fusion with the analyst (an "other") is bound to end by the patient's (or the analyst's) realization that "I myself, at the deepest level of my wants and desires, am unsure, centerless, and divided" (p. 7). Human beings, as I see it, are forever destined and doomed to encounter that line, which divides them from the ultimate faith in narcissistic fusions.

Like narcissistically based fusions, omnipotence too is, to a great extent, a denial of separateness and differentiation. What is extremely painful for us to acknowledge is that we are each, at our core, "lone" subjects, albeit connected to others. Kristeva (ibid.) goes even further by suggesting that "What today's analyst must do, I think, is restore to illusion its full therapeutic and epistemological value" (p. 14). Much of what Kristeva focuses on has to do with faith as a religious structure; still, perhaps her most analytic suggestion lies in her reference to faith "as *what can only be called a primary identification with a loving and protective agency*" (p. 15, italics added). This analytic conceptualization refers to faith as object-related – hence, as a secondary derivative of one's relationship with a "good" object, to which I and others (i.e., Winnicott) refer to as "Trust."

In what seems to me like a good summary of the significant distinctions between Faith and Trust, Neri (2005) writes.

> Trust and faith entertain a different relationship with reason ... Trust is an emotional tension of a curative kind. *Faith*, on the other hand, presents some problems for the reason. It *transcends* reason.
>
> (p. 81, italics added)

Trust, unlike faith, "*originates from a lasting, reliable, and affectionate relationship*. We become certain of its presence when we realize that things are just the way we have been told they are" (p. 82, italics added).

Faith and trust in psychoanalysis   141

Most of the attempts to distinguish between Faith and Trust focus on the realm of object relations. Isaacs, Alexander, and Haggard (1963) suggest that trust and mistrust are a result of various components, and "it connotes an affective attitude primarily directed outward, involving a sense of comfort, confidence, and reliance that certain acts and behavior will or will not occur" (p. 462). Neri (2005) proposes – as do others – that Trust, unlike Faith, is *earned, based on experience,* and is an occurrence between two subjects:

> A sense of risk and fear often accompanies the emergence of Trust in the context of a psychoanalytic relationship. These feelings mostly derive from two factors. First, Trust inevitably introduces us to a relationship with one or more people. Once we have entered into such a relationship, we no longer have full control (or the Illusion of full control) over ourselves and what could happen to us.
>
> (p. 83)

Faith, Neri further suggests, can be more reassuring than trust "because it allows us to remain in a condition of monad-like isolation more easily" (p. 83).

I agree with the distinction Neri is making between faith and trust: He sees trust as "based on being able to count on a certain number of reliable relationships" (p. 86). One's trust is being tested, repeatedly, by encounters with disappointments. Hence, according to Neri (Ibid.), "The stabilization of trust cannot just depend upon the reliability of our relationships, but must also be based on an increase in our capacity to cope with the uncertainty of relationships, relying on our sense of security self-esteem" (p. 86). As an elaboration of Neri's ideas, I suggest that Faith is what allows this increase in one's capacity to cope, which is what one's Trust is founded upon. Although Faith is related to "acts of faith," it is not the same, and I think that it should remain an undefined "formless" concept. But perhaps Faith should not even be defined as a concept. An idea becomes a concept only after it has been realized, i.e., it encounters reality. In this sense, Faith is needed only for the "unknown," hence it should be allowed to sustain the qualities of a formless experience.

In congruence with Neri's ideas, I wish to put forward the idea Faith (as an inborn quality) leads to the feeling that the future holds within it more possibilities than the ones the individual has already encountered. Thus, Faith has to do with the individual's most inner beliefs, which I believe precede the establishment of a "self" or a "subject." Following this line of thought, I suggest that Faith assists the individual to face reality and lays the grounds for the individual's capacity to establish a feeling of trust in others. Trust, unlike Faith, is founded upon one's experiences with others and the world of external reality. I believe that we can benefit from a non-religious conceptualization of Faith, which will enable us to think about "Faith" more creatively – beyond science, biology, instincts, or religion.

To illustrate my own experience with Faith and Trust within the analytic encounter, I will describe a small part of therapy with a young woman.

Noa

Noa was forty-three when she began analysis. She was married and had two daughters. She was a successful therapist, a specialist in the field of children with special needs. She began therapy because she was feeling depressed, regardless of her feeling that she has fulfilled all she ever dreamt of. Noa grew up in a kibbutz at a time when children were separated from their parents immediately following their birth and were raised, throughout their life, in the unique method of the "communal system." Babies and children were being taken care of by multiple female members of the kibbutz and were allowed to see their parents each afternoon for three hours. Noa was the oldest daughter and had three siblings. Both her parents were also raised in a kibbutz, albeit two different ones. She described her mother as "utterly lifeless," and her father as "extremely impulsive." I am personally acquainted with the unique features of life in a kibbutz, and as an analyst, I am well experienced with treating adults who grew up there. Throughout the years, I have found many of them to share some emotional difficulties, especially in terms of their profound sense of loneliness, and extreme difficulty in trusting others. As some of my other patients who were raised in a kibbutz, Noa too had described her childhood as a mixture of both joy and extreme anxious loneliness. She described herself as a very playful and energetic young girl, very popular and "with a wild imagination." With time, I became intrigued with the way Noa was engaged with me and with the analytic relationship; on the one hand, I had experienced her as very emotionally engaged and her attachment had a desperate quality to it. Yet, the most fundamental transference issue was Noa's inability to *trust* me. She seemed to fall apart between the sessions or before my vacations. What was intriguing was that, regardless of her desperate attachment, intense emotional engagement, and her experience of "falling apart" in between the sessions, she also insisted on repeatedly declaring that she has no trust in me and no expectations from me. Although it may be easy to dismiss it as "just words," I did feel that there was something vitally important in what she was trying to tell me. And it was not just a way of "telling me a story" about her early experiences, the fact that she could not internalize my presence, regardless of her five weekly sessions, was a significant indication of her inability to form a trusting relationship with me.

It was clear to me that Noa was reenacting, in her relationship with me, many aspects of her early traumas. For months on end, she used to lie still (e.g., "lifeless") on the couch, silent for almost the whole session. I could feel her anguish but even her tears were silent. When I said I was there and asked her to try and say something about what she was experiencing, she used to say to me: "I am in hell, and there is *no one* here. I am completely alone." I would say to her: "I am here," to which she would reply "*no one* can be here. You can be there for me when I go in and maybe when I come out, and it is a lot. But down there, I am all alone." In her way, Noa was telling me that I am "no one," but not in the sense that she does not care about me, but rather, as I understood it, she was telling me that I have not (yet) become a singular mother of a singular and specific baby, hence she could not trust me to be there for her, in the way she needed me to be. Noa often related this feeling to her experience of the analysis as a "procedure": "What is happening here between us is happening in thousands of offices, between thousands of analysts and patients." Occasionally, Noa would storm out of my office in the middle of the session, only to text me a few hours later and ask for another session on that same day. I always saw her later that day. Not only did I not perceive these acts as negative "acting out," I saw it as her communication to me of how horrible her experience was, so much so that she could not stand it. I knew, intuitively, that she needed me to see her again that day, no questions asked. This was one of my ways of allowing Noa the experience of the active adaptation (Winnicott, 1953) that I believe enabled her, with time, to tolerate the frustrations inherent to the relationship with me as an external object.

With time she was able to leave the session and then return to my office after spending a few moments weeping outside and these acts of "storming out" allowed us to talk about her experiences of "firing" and "being fired" out of other people's lives. As an infant, Noa felt that she was constantly losing and re-finding her mother, only to be losing her again. She recalled how during long sleepless nights, haunted by nightmares, her mother would sit by her bed, rocking her foot: "Whenever I could finally dose off, I would open my eyes to see that she was about to walk out, and then I would cry out for her to stay with me. I know she couldn't stand it." The accuracy of these memories is not all that important. What is important is Noa's experience of holding on to her mother, desperately, exhausting her with her nightmares and her inability to let go. In her internal world, Noa felt that she had killed off her mother by exhausting her. I thought of Noa's depression as being both a result of such early and traumatic circumstances as well as a defense against her unconscious fantasy that she poses such a threat to her mother's well-being. Lying lifeless, on the analytic couch was a manifestation of both her infantile depression and that of her mother's and in either case, it was her way of protecting me from her demands (experienced by her as aggressive) and letting me know how untrustworthy I am.

Following the working through of these memories, Noa recalled that she had spent her childhood cutting babies and mothers' pictures from magazines. She spoke of how fascinated she was with those pictures of babies held in their mothers' arms and said, with profound sadness: "I cannot think of touching my mother. That gesture of tilting your back to be held by someone – I just don't have that in my body." When I said to her "you don't trust anyone to be there for you," she replied with a tone of voice that seemed surprised, "Of course not. There is no one there. It's only me."

Regardless of Noa's traumatic memories, of her "motherless childhood," as she described it, and of her nightmarish sleepless nights, she also described herself as a young girl, "bursting with energy, playful and happy." What became clear to me was that there was a significant difference between Noa's ability to trust *the object (me)* and her ability to trust *herself*. I came to think about it as two different (albeit related) kinds of "trust": One's Trust in others (the object) and one's Faith in one's strengths and options. Not that Noa was always certain (or Faithfull) about her ability to handle life; in times of severe depression, she did occasionally talk about her wish to "end it all," but she did have more Faith in herself than Trust in others. She always made clear that others are "merely guests" in her life, not to be fully trusted. She often explained to me, in a serious tone of voice that she cannot and will not ever fully trust me, as I "may walk away at any given moment," because she knows that I "do not owe anything" to her.

Noa's issues with Trust were apparent regarding many aspects of the analysis, and in fact, anything that was not "personally designed" was not to be trusted, hence the profound difficulties she had with the analytic setting (manifested in her storming out of the sessions, her constant texting in between the sessions, and her prolonged silences). Unless it was experienced as personal (and singularly "ours"), it was experienced as yet another sign of *my untrustworthiness*.

I came to understand Noa's experience of Trust as based on two major conditions: (1) that it was "personal" (designed exclusively for her), and (2) that it would be "forever" (i.e., that I would be able to promise never to leave her). She used to tell me, again and again, in a combination of utter seriousness and humor: "If you die, that's okay – not that I want you to die – but that's something I can forgive. It's people who walk out while they are still alive whom I cannot forgive."

An infant's Trust in others is conditioned on the mother's continuous presence and it seems that Noa's unique early life circumstances did not allow her to establish a stable sense of Trust, especially not as caretakers. I

Out of the innumerable moments Noa and I have shared, I have chosen two that seem especially significant to me, in terms of what helped Noa to form her Trust in me. One of them had occurred in an especially difficult time in the analysis. Noa was deeply depressed and she seemed to hang by a thread to her life (analysis). On that Friday morning, we had a painful session in which she was crying silently, throughout. When she left my office for the weekend, I was worried and asked her to be in touch with me over the weekend if she felt things were getting worse. She nodded and left my office without saying a word. That evening I received a mail from her, with a poem of Wislawa Symborska, ("cat in an empty apartment"). I was alarmed and called her immediately. She did not reply, and her phone seemed to be off the hook. I was worried and even contemplated whether I should reach out to her husband and decided not to. On Sunday, when she came into my office, I could see that something was wrong, and asked her to sit down, and not lie on the couch. I said to her: "Noa, I will not be able to bear it if you die." I had tears in my eyes. Noa looked up, and there was a look in her eyes that I had never seen before. "No one had ever said this to me," she whispered. "I will not do this again. No one has ever said to me 'Don't die.'" I felt stunned; it was so simple and so horrible, at the same time.

Another incident may seem very different than this one. For years, Noa begged me to promise her that we would stay in touch after her analysis was over. What

Faith and trust in psychoanalysis   145

she wanted me to promise her was that we would become friends. As strange as it sounded, it was not something I could not imagine to myself, and I think Noa knew that. We were of the same age and under any other circumstances, we may have become good friends. We both knew that our relationship was uniquely close, and we had shared some very personal moments. I was, of course, reluctant to promise her anything of that sort, and that had become a central issue in the sessions. For years, Noa would say to me: "If you don't want to be friends with me after the analysis is over, that's ok, but say so. I will handle it, but I have to know." For years, I insisted on interpreting it, linking it to her profound pain and separation anxiety, to her lack of experience in having a relationship with someone alive, unlike her depressed mother, etc. Then, following months of talking about it, I said to her one day, after she had challenged me again to tell her what's in the future for us: "Noa, *we will not become friends*, not even after your analysis is over"; when Noa asked me to elaborate, I added: "I will not be able to become your friend, because I will not be able to make the needed transformation in our relationship. It will not work out for me." After I said this, there was a moment of silence, but I could see Noa's face relax. She sat there quietly, but it was a calm quietness, and then she said "OK, I can understand it."

These two incidents, albeit different, lay out my thinking about the significant role the analyst has in the formation of Trust and my realization that it has a lot to do with the infant's (patient's) ability to experience the mother (analyst) as *human* and *authentic*. As an analyst, gaining the patient's trust had to do with my ability to be my*self, as truthfully as possible*. Not being a "generic analyst" and being authentic is always important but I think it is crucial when we treat patients who had experienced object-related traumas in general and those related to maternal absence in particular. In the first occurrence, I was not only Noa's analyst, but I was also a woman worried and anxious about another woman's profound pain, and in the second example, I was an individual (not only an analyst) struggling to find a way to be able to respect Noa's need for me to stay there "forever" and my honest feelings that I *will not be able* to become her friend, regardless of how much I care about her. Paradoxically, in the second instance, I needed to acknowledge, myself, that I can be only Noa's analyst and that should be enough for both of us. I think that often the mother needs to go through the same psychic-emotional processes as the infant-child does. That includes the mother's becoming sober of her omnipotence, for example in terms of protecting her child or of being the child's "everything," just as the infant/child needs to sober up from her/his fantasies concerning the mother's almighty power.

I knew, deep in my heart that I would not be able to make that change in our relationship and it had nothing to do with analytic "rules." It was not a "generic" no, it was *the most personal one*. These two different moments both had a deep effect on Noa's relationship with me. Many years afterward, when we talked about it, she said to me: "Ofrit, I never wanted to die after that day. It may sound weird to you, but never has anyone said to me: 'Please don't die,' or perhaps I was never able to hear it before that day."

Some final thoughts on: Faith, Trust and psychoanalysis

Although many relate "Faith" to religion, hence doubt its relevance to psychoanalysis, for me, it is unthinkable that Faith should be discarded from the analytic office and analyst–patient relationship. I perceive Faith to be vital to the success of the analytic process, both on behalf of the patient and the analyst. Similar to mothers who can "dream" and imagine their infants, as future toddlers, children, and adults, envisioning their potential, so is the analyst able to have Faith in the patient's potential for psychic growth and future development. In this sense, Faith both accommodates and negates Bion's notion of "no memory and no desire." Being able to "dream" the patient's future and potentiality requires both Faith and Trust of both patient and analyst and it does build, at least to some extent, on the analyst's desire and memory, as well as on the analyst's ability and willingness to put it aside. I have always found it difficult to forgo all desire and memory, but it has more to do with hope than with a concrete plan of what the patient should be when (s)he grows up (Ogden, 2019) meaning it is connected to an *experience* rather than to predicting the future.

I am thinking of the dialectical tension between "hope" and "reality" (Boris, 1976). Hope has to do with what we wish for, and not with an actual prediction, and I find it relevant to Bion's concept of the preconception. In a sense, hope is a "preconception" to which one has to accommodate her/his *actual experiences,* hence, it precedes external reality. If we understand one's Faith to precede one's *knowledge,* we can think about it as being a formless infinite internal (and eternal) *state of mind,* enabling the creation of previously unknown possibilities. It *transcends* one's immediate or previous experiences and sometimes even those imagined. An additional way to think about the analyst's hopes, dreams, or "Faith" in the patient's potential, is by Bion's (1975, 1977, 1979) and Grotstein's (1997) concept of "memories of the future," referring to future possibilities rooted in our faith and derived from possibilities that are not yet known to us. Another relevant idea is that of Safran (1999) who writes, "One has to have some hope that one has the ability to change and that the healer has the ability to help" (p. 6). Yet, Having Faith in one's ability to help someone does not exclude other feelings. Safran suggests that "In order to be able to tolerate the depths of the patient's despair, analysts must be able to tolerate whatever personal feelings of despair are evoked" (p. 7). This implies an interesting paradox as the analyst needs to have Faith in her/his ability to contain despair, both one's own and that of the patient.

Faith is related not only to the "unknowable" but also to "transformation." Starr (2008) suggests that "For Freud, who drew his analogies from the natural sciences, change was quantitative, a matter of degree" (p. 204). Nonetheless, transformation is not a matter of quantity; it is unquantifiable and it is often associated with a "leap," rather than measured by a "degree": "Individuals are said to be transformed by encounters with the divine, emerging with a sense of a reality greater than themselves, a more expansive perspective of life's possibilities, and a sharper perception of their unique purpose" (ibid., p. 204). This can also be

Faith and trust in psychoanalysis 147

connected to Winnicott's conceptualization of the "True Self" and Bion's "O," both *transcendent* and not *directly communicated*.

We are accustomed to connecting one's capacity to use an object with the ability to trust external reality (Winnicott, 1969). We are not accustomed to the differentiation of one's Trust from one's Faith or to relate Faith to one's capacity to use the object (= analysis/analyst). Using me as an object was extremely difficult for Noa – it was not part of her experience. I suggest that the perception of Trust as an acquired ability makes more sense, as it is based – to a great extent – on one's *experience*. Faith, on the other hand, can be comprehended as an *inborn potential "capacity,"* a pre-conceptualized *reservoir of feelings* underlying a sense that there are endless (and even formless) possibilities open to us. Naturally, one's Faith impacts one's ability to form Trust and one's Faith (inner beliefs in the capacity to cope) is often nourished by good enough experiences with real external objects, but these are two different qualities, both needed especially when circumstances are not favorable.

At times, circumstances of environmental failures, such as traumatic early separations, physical illness, poverty, and so on, may be so severe as to foreclose the establishment of Trust, regardless of even the most vigorous inborn Faith. Noa's Trust was extremely fragile, perhaps due to her early life circumstances, growing up in the kibbutz's communal system. Yet, *the profound sense of Faith she had in her strengths and in her ability to "find a way out,"* even when life was complicated and painful, assisted her in coping with what was most difficult for her. This was apparent not only in her childhood memories (as in recalling how she always performed the tasks required of her, being an excellent student, and of her joyful ability to play) but also in her tendency to "take care of herself." This was also apparent in our relationship – she never missed a session, was a very hard-working analysand, and exhibited imagination and playfulness. Yet, it was extremely difficult for her to trust me and acknowledge her need for me. Trusting me meant she had to be able to paradoxically hold together the possibility that I am there for her, yet not completely. Surrounding oneself to the care of someone else, not knowing whether (s)he will be there whenever and however you will need her/him, is extremely difficult for anyone who has suffered object-related traumas, and maternal absence in particular. This should be taken into consideration by therapists and psychoanalysts.

The way each of us conducts psychoanalysis may have more to do with our own "stance" than with "technique." The analyst must have Faith in the endlessly possible ways the patient may live life as a unique individual. Whatever analysts know about psychoanalysis has to do with the analyses they have already done. I have come to understand that patients, especially those who have difficulties with trust and faith, need the analyst to *re-invent psychoanalysis for them* (Ogden, 2016). It may be said that the analyst's Faith in the analytic process has to do with the future, while the ability to Trust the analytic work has to do with past experiences, both as an analyst and as an analysand. Particularly, when working with patients who lack Faith, the analyst's Faith plays a crucial role in bringing the patient back to life. For me, Faith resides within the potential space, the term Winnicott used to describe that intermediate area of experiencing that lies between fantasy and reality. Hence, both Faith and Trust require creativity, maintaining a complicated, dialectic relationship as in "a process in which two opposing concepts each creates, informs, preserves, and negates the other, each standing in a dynamic (ever-changing) relationship with the other" (Ogden, 1985, p. 130).

Perhaps it can be said that there is no such thing as a patient apart from the analyst's Faith. The analyst's capacity to have Faith in the patient's possibilities holds, within it, the dialectic tension between oneness (Faith) and twoness (Trust) and acts as an "alpha function of faith," until a Faithless patient can internalize the analyst's Faith.

Notes

1 Throughout the paper, I use Faith and Trust when I refer to my own conceptualizations and faith and trust when referring to others'.
2 Bion (1965) has denoted the sign of "O" to "a thing-in-itself and unknowable" (p. 12), "the experience" (p. 13).

References

Bion, W.R. (1965). *Transformations: Change from learning to growth.* London: Tavistock.
Bion, W.R. (1970). *Attention and interpretation* (pp. 1–130). London: Tavistock.
Bion, W.R. (1975). *A memoir of the future. Book I: The dream.* Rio De Janeiro, Brazil: Imago Press.
Bion, W.R. (1977). *A memoir of the future. Book II: The past presented.* Brazil: Imago Editora.
Bion, W.R. (1979). *A memoir of the future. Book III: The dawn of oblivion.* Perthshire: Clunie Press.
Boris, H.N. (1976). On Hope: Its Nature and Psychotherapy. *International Review of Psychoanalysis,* 65: 435–442.
Britzman, D.P. (2011). *Freud and education.* New York: Routledge.
Bronheim, H.E. (1994). Psychoanalysis and faith. *The Journal of the American Academy of Psychoanalysis and Dynamic Psychiatry,* 22(4): 681–697.
Brookes, S. (2002). "It seems to have to do with something else ..." Henry James's, what Maisie knew and Bion's theory of thinking. *The International Journal of Psychoanalysis,* 82(3): 419–443.
Eigen, M. (1981). The area of faith in Winnicott, Lacan and Bion. *The International Journal of Psycho-Analysis,* 62: 413–433.
Eigen, M. (1982). Creativity, instinctual fantasy and ideal images. *The Psychoanalytic Review,* 69(3): 317–339.
Freud, S. (1890). Psychical (or mental) treatment (1890). In *The standard edition of the complete psychological works of Sigmund Freud, Volume VII (1901–1905): A case of hysteria, three essays on sexuality and other works* (pp. 281–302). London: Hogarth.

Freud, S. (1913). Totem and taboo. In *The standard edition of the complete psychological works of Sigmund Freud, Volume XIII (1913–1914): Totem and Taboo and Other Works* (pp. vii–162). London: Hogarth.

Freud, S. (1920). Beyond the pleasure principle. In *The standard edition of the complete psychological works of Sigmund Freud, Volume XVIII (1920–1922): Beyond the pleasure principle, group psychology and other works* (pp. 1–64). London: Hogarth.

Freud, S. (1927). The future of illusion. In *The standard edition of the complete psychological works of Sigmund Freud, Volume XXI (1927/1931): The future of an illusion, civilization and its discontents, and other works* (pp. 1–56).

Freud, S. (1940). An outline of psycho-analysis. *The International Journal of Psycho-Analysis*, 21: 27–84.

Grotstein, J.S. (1997). Bion, the Pariah of "O". *The British Journal of Psychotherapy*, 14(1): 77–90.

Isaacs, S. (1952). The nature and function of phantasy. In M. Klein et al. (Eds), *Developments in psycho-Analysis* (pp. 67–121). London: Hogarth Press.

Isaacs, K.S., Alexander, J.M., & Haggard, E.A. (1963). Faith, trust and gullibility. *The International Journal of Psycho-Analysis*, 44: 461–469.

Klein, M. (1932). *The psycho-analysis of children*. London: Hogarth.

Klein, M. (1952b). Mutual influences in the development of ego and id. In *Envy and gratitude and other works, 1946-1963*. New York, NY: Delacorte Press/Seymour Lawrence, 1975, pp. 275–299.

Kristeva, J. (1987). *In the beginning was love: Psychoanalysis and faith*. New York: Columbia University Press.

Miller, C.H. (1981). The role of faith in psychoanalysis. *American Journal of Psychoanalysis*, 41(1): 15–20.

Mitchell, S. A. (1981). The origin and nature of the "object" in the theories of Klein and Fairbairn. *Contemporary Psychoanalysis*, 17: 374–398.

Neri, C. (2005). What is the function of faith and trust in psychoanalysis? *The International Journal of Psycho-Analysis*, 86: 79–97.

Ogden, T.H. (1984). Instinct, phantasy, and psychological deep structure: A reinterpretation of aspects of the work of Melanie Klein. *Contemporary Psychoanalysis*, 20: 500–525.

Ogden, T.H. (1985). On potential space. *The International Journal of Psychoanalysis*, 66: 129–141.

Ogden, T.H. (2016). Some thoughts on practicing psychoanalysis, *Fort Da*, 22: 21–36.

Ogden, T.H. (2019). Ontological psychoanalysis or "What Do You Want to Be When You Grow Up?", *The Psychoanalytic Quarterly*, 88(4): 661–684.

Safran, J.D. (1999). Faith, despair, will, and the paradox of acceptance. *Contemporary Psychoanalysis*, 35(1): 5–23.

Starr, K. E. (2008). Faith as the fulcrum of psychic change: Metaphors of transformation in Jewish mysticism and psychoanalysis. *Psychoanalytic Dialogues*, 18: 203–229.

Winnicott, D.W. (1953). Transitional object and transitional phenomena: A study of the first not-me possession. *The International Journal of Psycho-Analysis*, 34: 89–97.

Winnicott, D.W. (1967). The location of cultural experience. *The International Journal of Psycho-Analysis*, 48: 368–372.

Winnicott, D.W. (1969). The use of an object. *The International Journal of Psycho-Analysis*, 50: 711–716.

Winnicott, D.W. (1963). Communicating and not communicating leading to a study of certain opposites. In: D.W. Winnicott (Ed.) (1965), *The maturational processes and the facilitating environment: Studies in the theory of emotional development.* The International Psycho-Analytical Library, 64,1-276. London: The Hogarth Press and the Institute of Psycho-Analysis (pp. 179–192).

Zusman, J.A., Cheniaux, E., & De Freitas, S. (2007). Psychoanalysis and change: Between curiosity and faith. *The International Journal of Psycho-analysis*, 88(1): 113–126.

Index

Note: References following "n" refer footnotes.

"act of faith" 133–134, 141
'actual neuroses' concept 92
adaptation, active 5, 9, 117, 143
Ainsworth, M. 12, 15–16
Alexander, F. 93, 141
alpha-elements 97, 102
Alvarez, A. 114
analyst–patient relationship 68,
114–115, 146
analytic relationship 108, 111, 125;
analyst within 119; early mother–infant
relationship in 10; patient–analyst
relationship 68; patient's faith to
analytic procedure 136; transference and
countertransference within 124
anger 19–20, 25, 26; absent mother and 39,
82, 83; feelings of rejection and 42, 57;
pain and 40, 42; role in analytic work 86
anorexia nervosa 3, 115, 119
attachment theory 14–15
Attention and Interpretation (Bion) 133

Balint, A. 11
belonging 43, 44
beta-elements 97, 102, 135; partially
contained 91; raw 91, 101
Beyond the Pleasure Principle (Freud) 131
biological mother 17, 28n4; importance to
mother–infant relations 6–7, 27–28n2;
issues of maternal care-taking 28n4
Bion, W. R. 6, 11, 98, 103, 114, 135;
concept of preconception 146, 147;
conceptualizations of "truth" 101;
contact-barrier functioning 100;
container–contained" function 98, 102;
"dreaming" concept 97; emphasizing

vitality of mother's function 33; notion
of to-and-fro movement 97; thinking
about faith 133, 134; transformation
model of raw sense impressions
102; work on analytic function of
personality 91
body and mind *see* mind and body
body–unconscious relationship 116
Bowlby, J. 10–11, 28n3; law of
accumulated separations 15; law of
continuity 14–15

caregivers/care-givers 7, 8, 13, 34–37
caretaker as maternal figure 35
caretaker/care-taker 8, 10, 15, 17, 22, 24,
35, 46
*A Case of Hysteria, Three Essays on
Sexuality and Other Works* (Freud) 130
child(ren) 41, 43, 64; communal
arrangement 45; communal-sleeping
kibbutz 14; deprived 38; development
55; emotional needs 17; environmental
need 73; experiencing maternal
absence 2; "gifted child" 35; healthy
"bereavement" 74; home 13, 22;
in kibbutz 2–3, 14, 34; personal
environment 11; psyche 73; social role
in Israeli society 64; well-being 1, 10;
see also mother(s)
childcare 6, 12–14, 27, 28n4
child-rearing 7, 8, 12–13; arrangement
13; communal-collective method of
17; method of kibbutz 27, 31; *see also*
communal system, child-rearing system
'classic psychoneuroses' concept 92
communal sleeping arrangement 13–15

152   Index

communal system 40, 142; child-rearing system 2, 14, 31, 34–35; effects of 14; in kibbutz 14, 17, 31–32, 34, 147; pain of women's experience of 37
concrete original object (COO) 116
conscious family dynamics 69
"container–contained" function 11, 98, 102
contemporary psychoanalysis 101, 139–141
controlled intimacy 35
coping strategies 41, 44
creative imagination 138

"dead mother" 76, 86; complex 72
The Dead Mother (Green) 75
death instinct 93–94
defensive strategies 69
depersonalization 95, 124
deprivation 44, 121
"deprived child" 138
disorganization 93–94
"dreaming" concept of Bion 97–100
"drives" mechanism 135

eating disorders 3–4, 122, 125
egalitarianism 12–13
Eigen, M. 128, 135, 136
emotional experiences 3, 35, 39, 94, 97; of abandonment and neglect 107; of individuals 91; soma as core of one's true 101–103; somatic aspect of 92; unlived 96
emotional–physical experience 97
emotional–psychic experience 91
emotional shallowness evidence in children 34
employment of splitting 117
environmental provision 115, 117; deprivation 121; role in psyche–soma relationship 119
equality 16
Etchegoyan, R. H. 114
exclusion 64

Fairbairn, W. R. D. 7–8, 16–17, 73; conception of early psychic development 8; concept of tantalizing object 8–9; about loss of love object 74; tantalizing mother 16
faith 4, 128, 146–148; Bion's thinking about 133; creative imagination and 138; definition of 139; Freud's perspective of

129–135; Miller's perspective of 136; play and 138–139; and psychoanalysis 139–141; psychoanalysis relationship with concept of 128–129; religion and 139, 146; role in psychic growth 129
false localization 115
false self 43; mechanism 123–124; organization 73; personality organization 73–74
family/families 1; fatherless 54–55, 66; modern 56; mother–father 5; "normative" heterosexual 64; nuclear 43; same-gender 55
father: child's first encounter with 65; deserting 66; "otherness" 56; presence and effects on child's development 54; role in child's psychic development 53; role of analyst as 67–68; transition to external 65
"fatherless" child 3, 55, 56, 65, 68, 69
Fenichel, O. 53
Ferari's theory of the body 116
Ferenczi, S. 92–93
fibromyalgia 107
"finite" thinking 99
Fraiberg, S. 17
freedom 5, 36–38, 48
Freud, A. 17, 74
Freud, S. 4, 31, 53–55, 64, 88, 88n3, 89n5, 94; conceptualizations of coping methods 75; lost object 76; melancholic subject 72–77; perspective of "faith" 129–135; "secret" *vs.* "foreign body" discrepancy 92
frustration 33, 74, 81, 83, 92, 108, 122
Furman, Edna 74
The Future of Illusion (Freud) 131–132

Gabbard, G. O. 101
Gaddini, E. 96
Green, A. 16, 88, 88n3, 89n5, 116; conceptualizations of coping methods 75; "dead" subject 75–77; lost object 76
Green, R. 67, 72
Grossmann, K. E. 15, 16
Grotstein, J. S. 114, 146
"ground zero" 81, 85
Gubb, K. 92, 93

Haggard, E. A. 141
"*Haskala*" (education) movement 130
hate 20, 64–66, 108

Index   153

healing 128
helplessness 26, 41, 86, 87
holding environment 44, 73; mother as 97, 98, 102
Holland, J. L. 35
hope 21, 108, 128, 146
A Hunger Artist (Kafka) 3–4, 115, 118–120

illusory life 3, 74, 77, 83
impingement 98–99, 119, 121
inclusion 64
infant 32; adaptation 99; care 34; in communal-collective system 17; development in terms of "unity" and "otherness" 9–12; influencing factors in development and well-being 137; in kibbutz system 7, 8, 14, 27; perception of environment 6; psychic formation 31; well-being 5, 6; *see also* child(ren)
infant–mother relationship *see* mother–infant relationship
instinct(ual): death 93–94; gratification 53, 119; Ogden's conceptualization of 132; overcoming of 76; satisfaction 119–120
interrupted dreams 91, 94, 96
In the Beginning Was Love– Psychoanalysis, and Faith (Kristeva) 140
Isaacs, K. S. 141
Isaacs, S. 133
Israeli kibbutzim 7, 12

Jewish Enlightenment movement 130

Kagan, J. 17
Kantian Enlightenment 130
kibbutz(im) 2, 14, 31, 48n4; child-rearing method of 13, 27, 31; children 2–3, 14, 34; communal system 13–14, 17, 27, 31–32, 34, 147; infant and child 7–8; Israeli 7, 12; mothers 16; movement 13; parents in 9; rules 34; as "utopian" society 12–13
"killing of the self" 76
Kipling, R. 48
Klein, M. 33, 64–65, 73, 132–133
Kristeva, J. 140

"law of accumulated separations" 15
"law of continuity" 14–15
learning, theories of 46

Learning from Experience (Bion) 97
The Location of Cultural Experience (Winnicott) 137
Loewald, H. W. 54, 66
Lombardi, R. 96, 116, 124
loneliness 36, 41, 47; anxious 142; communal system in shades of 36; patient's experiences of 48; profound 25, 44, 48, 79; sense of 22, 24, 142
losing one's self as coping mechanism 86–87
lost love object 72; clinical illustration 77–86; losing one's self as coping mechanism 86–87; "melancholic" subject *vs.* "dead" subject 75–77; sleep–quietness or quitting 87; as trauma 73–75
love 3, 65–66

Marty, P. 93
maternal absence 2, 3, 41–44, 145
maternal care 2, 5, 6, 8, 9, 12, 16, 25, 28n4, 32, 119
maternal figure 5–6, 10, 24; caretaker as 35; substitute 12
McDougall, J. 94, 100
melancholia 74–76, 79
mental function 93; conscious and unconscious 100; overgrowth of 95, 97
metapelet 23, 28n6, 48n3
Miller, A. 43, 44
Miller, C. H. 136
mind 96; conscious 92, 97, 102; omnipotent state of 96; unconscious 91, 97, 102; undreamt dreams and 94
mind and body 116; forming functional "continuum" 96; fused or split-off relationship of 99; ill-separation of 99; shell-shocking 105
Mind and Its Relation to the Psyche–Soma (Winnicott) 115
Mitchell, S. A. 132
modern family 54, 56
mother(s) 1–2, 5–6, 16, 25, 31–32, 65; guilt 12; "near-death" experiences of 108–111; presence and absence of 2; primary maternal preoccupation 11; role 10–11
mother-figure 25
motherhood 1, 8, 12, 39, 54, 60, 61
mother–infant relationship 7, 15, 115–116, 118, 120–121, 128; possible effects

154 Index

of disruptions to 15–17; somatization in 124
mothering 10, 16, 25; biological 6–7; erratic 25
"motherless" child 56
mourning 73, 79, 87

negligence 33, 36
Neri, C. 140, 141
neurotic *vs.* non-neurotic psychological functioning 93
neutrality of analysts 114
"new human being" creation 12–13
night-guardians 48n4
night-keepers 13, 17, 28n5
"nothingness" 33–34

object loss 73, 75, 77, 81
object-relationships of adult patients 5–6; clinical illustrations 17–24; communal sleeping arrangement effects 13–15; effects of disruptions to mother-infant unit 15–17; infants' development in terms of "unity" and "otherness" 9–12; kibbutz as "utopian" society 12–13
object relations theories 32–34, 36
Oedipus complex 53; analyst as "third"/"father" 67–69; case example 61–64; changes 54; clinical material 56–64; *see also* Freud, S.
Ogden, T. H. 8, 10, 54, 65, 68, 91, 94, 101; conceptualization of instinct 132; conceptualizations of "truth" 101; differentiating "holding" from "containing" and "dreaming" 103; idea of re-minding body 100
On Beginning the Treatment (Freud) 131
otherness 9–12, 54, 56, 65
An Outline of Psycho-Analysis (Freud) 132

parents 2, 8; ability to provide personal approach with children 34; care-taking activities with children 13; hiring caretaker 12; in kibbutz system 9, 14; same-gender 54; triadic relationship with children 68; unavailability of 41, 44; unconscious fantasies 55–56; *see also* family/families; father; mother(s)
Paris School 93, 94
participation 114; artist's performance 118–119; in testing mother/analyst's capacity 119

pastoral tranquility 38
patient's coping mechanism 74
pendulum movement 37
"perfect environment" 98
"phylogenetic inheritance" concept 133
physical dream 3, 91, 99; *see also* emotional experiences; unconsciousness
physical–mental texture 33
physical sensation 97–98
"physiology of anxiety" 120
playing, theory of 135–139
Poland, W. 54
potential space 138
pre-conscious experiences 100
prenatal state 5–6
"primal phantasy" 55
primary maternal preoccupation 11, 28n2, 32, 36
primary–raw "truth" 101
primordial physical experience 99
professional self-development 32, 45
psyche–soma–mind relationship 116
psyche–soma relationship 3, 6, 96–98, 116–118; case example 121–123; dual movement of 111; experiences of maternal absence 41; "false self" mechanism 123, 124; integration of 103; mother–infant relationship and 120–121; role of environmental provision 119; somatic symptom as mediator between 108, 111; two-way transformation 124–126
psychic: apparatus 116; experiences 94; holes 72, 76; pain 119; regression 93; withdrawal 41
Psychical (or Mental) Treatment (Freud) 130
psychic–emotional conglomerate 97
psychic pressure, unresolved 97
psychoanalytic/psychoanalysis 6, 12, 96, 146–148; distinction between "faith" and "trust" within 129; and faith 139–141; Freud's perspective of "faith" in 129–135; processes 100; relationship with concept of "faith" 128; and soma 92–95; theories 35; Winnicott's theory of playing in 135–139
psychological envelope 33
Psycho-Somatic Illness in Its Positive and Negative Aspects (Winnicott) 117
psychosomatic phenomena 94

Index 155

psychosomatic symptom/illness 3, 120–121; clinical examples 103–111; "false self" mechanism in 123, 124; as foreclosure 94; handling emotional experience 91; interplay between unconscious and physical activities 95–96; as physical dreams 91, 99, 102; psycho-soma *vs.* psyche-soma 96–98; somatic symptom related with 98–101; Winnicott's perspective on 115, 117; *see also* somatic symptom/illness/ disorder
psychotherapy 35

quitting 87, 122

reality-acceptance 138–139
reality testing 78
receptiveness 134
reciprocity 32, 47
regression, psychic 93–94
religious faith 131
reparation 32, 47, 48
"responsible-caretaking adult" 46

Sacks, A. M. 74–75
Safran, J. D. 146
Sagi, A. 13–15, 34
sameness 16, 65
schizophrenia 5
self-discovery process 45
self-establishment 33
self-harm strategies 42
self-holding 35, 42, 56
self-interpretations 57
self-starvation 118–119, 121–124
separateness 42, 86; denial of 140; psychological 10
sharing and giving, values of 45, 46
skin-Ego 33
sleep–quietness 87
soma 3, 6; connection with unconscious 116; psychoanalysis and 92–95; as true emotional experience 101–103; "unlived" emotional experiences 96
somatic disturbance, positive value of 99
somatic involvement, positive value of 95
somatic symptomatology 92
somatic symptom/illness/disorder 91, 93, 98–101, 118; acting as mediator between soma and psyche 108; acts as "bridge" between psyche and soma

95; analyst's responsibility in treating 118–119; as bridge between patient's inner world and external reality 116; as bridge between unconscious and conscious aspects of mind 116; as form of regression 125–126; as intermediate zone between soma and psyche 111; psychic pain and 119; related to death instinct 93; *see also* psychosomatic symptom/illness
somatization 2, 93–96, 116; deprivation and 121; excessive use of 125; in mother–infant relationship 124; as present indicators of past failures 117
soma–unconscious relationship 116
sperm donor 54, 55, 60, 64
Spiro, M. E. 34
split-off experiences 38
Starr, K. E. 146
symptomatology 94; psychosomatic 92, 93; somatic 92
The System 26–27

tantalizing mother 9, 16
tantalizing object 8–9, 17
The Theory of Parent–Infant Relationship (Winnicott) 5
therapeutic relationship 2, 47, 48
therapist–patient relationship 31, 35, 128
to-and-fro movement 97
toddlers 28n5, 129, 146
Totem and Taboo (Freud) 131
"traditional" psychoanalysis, reluctance of 6
transference–countertransference 98, 106
Transformations (Bion) 133
transitional object 65
Transitional Objects and Transitional Phenomena (Winnicott) 138
Transitory Symptom-Constructions during Analysis (Ferenczi) 92
trauma: children's vulnerability to 74; loss of love object as 73–75; psychic 33; sexual 3–4
traumatic loss 73, 74, 77
trust 4, 25, 42, 128, 140, 146–148; case example 142–145; definition of 140; psychoanalysis relationship with concept of 128–129; role in psychic growth 129
Tustin's theory 114

156 Index

unconsciousness 35, 45, 93; conflict resolution 92; experiences 100; fantasies of 55–56, 61, 63, 65–66; interplay between with physical 95–96; mental construct 55; psychic dynamics 69; thinking 97, 99, 102, 107

"unconscious phantasy" concept 132

undreamt dreams 3, 91, 94

uniformity 13, 27, 34

unity, infants' development in terms of 9–12

unity–uniformity, absence of 34–35

verbal symbolization 125

wakes up in fear" of individual 94

Winnicott, D. W. 5–6, 9, 11, 17, 31, 36, 54, 73, 91, 95, 96, 98, 101, 123; conception of psyche-soma 99; conceptualizations of "truth" 101; defining role of environmental provision 119; defining ruthlessness of patients 118; about "perfect environment" 98; discussing "physiology of anxiety" 120; perspective on psychosomatic illness 115; psychosomatic disorders, conception of 97; about somatic symptoms 111; theory of maternal care and development of healthy baby 7; theory of mother as holding environment 97, 98, 102; theory of mother–infant relationship 115–116, 118; theory of playing 135–139; theory of psyche–soma relationship 116–118; transitional phenomena 67, 74; views about physical act of feeding 119–120; work 10

witnessing 114; in artist's performance 118–119; in testing mother/analyst's capacity 119

women 32; anorexic 122; balancing childcare and career 12; in kibbutz system 45; participation in the labor force 1; personal choice of 31; responsible for children's well-being 1; role in kibbutz community 13; socialized to prioritize motherhood 54; see also mother(s)

women therapists 35; in communal system 40; "false self" mechanism 43; object relations theories of 36; pendulum movement of 37; professional self 46; psychic withdrawal of 41; reciprocity 47; self-discovery 45; self-holding of 42; split-off experiences of 38; therapeutic role 46–47

Printed in the United States
by Baker & Taylor Publisher Services